JOSEPH SHUMAN
JOURNALISM COLLECTION

POINT PARK COLLEGE

RACISM AND THE MASS MEDIA

Racism and the Mass Media

A study of the role of the Mass Media in
the formation of white beliefs
and attitudes in Britain

PAUL HARTMANN &
CHARLES HUSBAND

ROWMAN & LITTLEFIELD
TOTOWA, NEW JERSEY

First published in the United States 1974
by Rowman and Littlefield, Totowa. N.J.

ISBN 0-87471-450-8

Printed in Great Britain

Contents

Acknowledgements

We would like to declare our indebtedness to the head-masters and staff of the schools we visited for their co-operation and efficiency. Special thanks are due to the children and adults who answered our questions with an honesty and frankness which is the basis for valid survey data. We are very aware of the trust they placed in us, and would like to reaffirm our guarantees of confidentiality. We would like to thank the staff of Social and Community Planning Research for their care and efficiency in carrying out the interviews with the adult sample. The processing of the data would have been a much more arduous activity if we had not been fortunate in receiving the specially vital, and gracious, co-operation of Mrs Judy Lay of the computer laboratories.

To all our friends and colleagues we acknowledge an unknown debt for their part in forming our approach to this research. Their willing ears have been our sounding-board as we have pressed our ideas upon them at length. The critical response which often followed, though on occasions painful, has been invaluable.

To the clerical staff at the Centre we offer our sincere thanks and record our admiration for their consistently high standards. It is not only their capacity to translate our tortured drafts into presentable text, but also their personal encouragement which has placed us deeply in their debt.

Grateful acknowledgement for the funding of the research is made to the Social Science Research Council and the Television Research Committee.

Finally we would mention two people for whom there can be no adequate expression of our indebtedness: Liz Hartmann and Liz Husband.

I

The British Response to Coloured Immigration

Since the 1950s race relations have been added to the catalogue of British social problems. Along with industrial relations, inflation, juvenile crime, and Northern Ireland, the matter has been widely discussed, pronounced upon, legislated about, and studied. Increasing attention has also been focused on the role of the mass media in society. They have been hailed as potent instruments of mass education and enlightenment, condemned as corrupters of youth and eroders of cherished values, and periodically accused of causing or exacerbating whatever social problem happens to be in the limelight. This book is part of the growing body of social science research effort that has come to be devoted to race relations on the one hand and the mass media on the other. It results from an attempt to answer the question : What part do the mass media play in the formation of white attitudes to coloured people in Britain?

Our research involved an examination of the beliefs and attitudes of sections of the white population, as well as of the way that questions of race and colour have been presented by the mass media. The work, therefore, was crucially concerned with how people conceive of the world they live in and how they orient themselves to that world. We start from the value position that racial discrimination is a social evil, and that the existence of hostile, derogatory or apprehensive attitudes among whites towards coloured people engenders a social climate conducive to racial discrimination, exploitation and injustice.

The findings from our surveys and analysis of media content relating to race in Britain and the role of the media are reported in later chapters. Here we outline briefly the history of coloured immigration to Britain.

Immigration and Legislation

Although it is only over the last twenty years that race relations within Britain have emerged as a matter of major concern, British contact with coloured people and their presence in

A*

Britain has a long history. As early as 1596 Elizabeth I complained '. . . there are of late divers blackamoores brought into these realms, of which kind there are already here to manie, considerynge how God had blessed this land with great increase of people . . .'[1] The majority of these 'blackamoores' were slaves brought to England as servants.

British colonial expansion in the seventeenth century, the settlement of the West Indies, and the expansion of the trade in slaves, gold and sugar between Africa, the colonies and Britain marked the beginning of the entry of blacks into Britain in noticeable numbers. The importation of a largely enslaved black minority continued throughout the eighteenth century, and towards the end of the century the size of the black community had become a matter of concern to the host community. Walvin cites an estimate for 1770 which set the number of Negroes in London at 15,000.[2] At this time Edward Long, a Jamaican planter, echoed Queen Elizabeth's sentiments of nearly two centuries earlier: 'We must agree with those who have declared, that the public good of this kingdom requires that some restraint should be laid on the unnatural increase of blacks imported into it.'[3] It is not clear what became of this early black community, how many of them were returned to the colonies, and how many were absorbed into the local population.

Slavery in Britain was never legalized by the passing of specific legislation; rather its legality rested upon legal precedents, and successive rulings contradicted and overruled each other. It was not until 1772 that the 'Mansfield judgement' was interpreted in such a way as to make slavery illegal in England. Not that this ended *de facto* slavery. For it was only in 1807 that the decline of the plantation economies, and the cumulative impact of the philanthropists led to the abolition of the slave trade. The institution of slavery itself in British colonies was not abolished until 1834.

The entry of coloured people to Britain continued in the nineteenth century with the settlement of small numbers of seamen from Africa and Asia in dockland areas, but significantly large numbers of coloured immigrants did not begin to arrive until the twentieth century. During the Second World War, West Indian servicemen were stationed in Britain, as were American Negro G.I.s, but both of these groups returned home after the war.

[1] Quoted in James Walvin, *The Black Presence* (Orbach & Chambers, London, 1971, p. 12).
[2] Ibid, p. 15.
[3] Ibid, p. 10.

From about 1950 relatively large numbers of coloured immigrants started to arrive in Britain for permanent settlement and we may date the emergence of the modern 'colour problem' from then. In 1952, after the United States Government passed the McCarron-Walter Act, which blocked West Indian emigration to the United States, the flow of West Indians to Britain became significant. This diminished somewhat in the mid and late 1950s as a decline in the British economy reduced the 'pull' factor in the emigration.[4] As the demand for labour increased in 1960 so did the immigration rate, accelerated by a further factor. There was at this time increasing parliamentary pressure for the introduction of restrictions on the number of coloured people entering Britain, and it was fear of controls being introduced that provoked an unprecedented increase in immigration.[5] For the eighteen months from January 1961 to June 1962, when legislation was introduced to control immigration, the net arrivals from the West Indies approximated 98,000 people. This same fear of controls being imposed caused a dramatic rise in the number of people coming from Pakistan and India, which had been considerably less than that from the West Indies throughout the 1950s. In 1961, net arrivals from India quadrupled and those from Pakistan increased ten times compared with the previous year.[6] At this time any citizen of British colonies or Commonwealth countries had the automatic right of entry and settlement in Britain.

The panic migration of 1961-62 aided the arguments of those who wished to impose restrictions on coloured immigration, and the pressure for restriction resulted in the Commonwealth Immigrants Act of 1962. This Act imposed a voucher system on entry by Commonwealth citizens for purposes of employment. That this legislation was concerned to limit *coloured* immigration and not immigration as such is clear from the absence of controls on Irish immigration which remained unrestricted, although immigrants from the Irish Republic constituted the largest ethnic minority in Britain. Nor were any changes introduced in the controls governing the entry of aliens for whom there was no fixed ceiling.

In 1965 a White Paper discontinued the issue of vouchers to

---

[4] For an analysis of West Indian emigration to Britain see: Ceri Peach, *West Indian Migration to Britain – A Social Geography* (OUP/IRR 1968).
[5] Ibid, p. 49.
[6] For a fuller discussion of this immigration see: E. J. B. Rose et al. *Colour and Citizenship* (OUP/IRR 1969, Chapters 5, 6, 7 and 8).

unskilled people without definite jobs to come to and restricted the total number of work vouchers to be issued annually to 8,500 of which 1,000 were set aside for Malta. Again no change was made in legislation governing the entry of Irish and alien migrants. The effect of this White Paper was to reduce the number of new workers entering Britain from the Commonwealth, but not to stop the flow of dependants of immigrants already here. In 1969 Rose et al described the effect of this legislation as follows : 'The balance of immigration has been shifted from the Caribbean to India and Pakistan. The balance within the labour force has been switched progressively from unskilled to skilled and professional workers, and the balance within the immigration has changed from a preponderance of wage earners to a preponderance of dependent wives and children.'[7]

There was one category of coloured immigration which was not affected by the Commonwealth Immigrants Act of 1962, nor by the White Paper of 1965. This was the immigration of Asians holding United Kingdom passports who were leaving East Africa, and Kenya in particular, because of local policies of Africanization. The British Government had given an undertaking to the Kenya Government at the time of Kenyan independence that those Kenyan residents who chose to retain British passports rather than take up Kenyan citizenship could do so. Now, under pressure from within Kenya, many of those with British passports were taking up their rights of entry into Britain. However, the vast majority were coloured, and concern was expressed in Parliament and elsewhere about their possible arrival. The government responded by passing the 1968 Commonwealth Immigrants Act which placed a ceiling on entry of 1,500 workers per annum for this type of immigrant, and also imposed further restrictions on the rights of entry of dependants of immigrants. 'A Rubicon was finally crossed in the spring of 1968. This was when the British Government decided, on grounds which were quite openly those of expediency rather than principle, that it would no longer accept responsibility for certain of its citizens because of the colour of their skins.'[8]

Finally the Immigration Act of 1971 was passed. This created two categories of Commonwealth citizen, 'patrials' and 'non-patrials'. Patrials are people who have a direct connection with the United Kingdom (such as a parent born here) and this

7 Ibid, p. 82.
8 Ibid, p. 11.

12

category consists mainly of citizens of the white Commonwealth countries, many of whom remain free from control and have the right of abode in Britain. The position of non-patrials has been brought more into line with that of aliens. They will require a work permit issued for a specific job for a limited period (normally twelve months) and will have to obtain permission to change jobs. After four years they may apply to register as UK citizens. Irish citizens, however, will not need work permits. In less than ten years successive acts of legislation have reduced the original rights of entry and abode of the majority of coloured Commonwealth citizens to a position very similar to that of aliens.

Two further Acts of Parliament enacted in the '60s had significance for British race relations. In 1965 in fulfilment of election promises the Labour government passed the Race Relations Act. This was intended to counter racial discrimination and incitement to racial hatred. Its scope was limited to discrimination in public places, and conciliation, not criminal penalties, was to be the means of countering discrimination. This Act also established the Race Relations Board to supervise the conciliation process throughout the country. In 1968 a further Race Relations Act extended the scope of the legislation to employment and housing, but did not at the same time strengthen the powers of the Race Relations Board.[9]

The Position of Immigrants, and Discrimination

The geographical distribution of coloured immigrants shows distinct areas of concentration in the country as a whole. In 1966, 70 percent of Indians, Pakistanis and West Indians, taken together, were within the six major conurbations of England and Wales (i.e. Tyneside, West Yorkshire, South-East Lancashire, Merseyside, West Midlands and Greater London), whereas only 35 percent of the total population lived in these areas.[10] Within cities also there has been a tendency toward clustering of immigrants in particular areas. For example, in the middle sixties, certain local wards in Birmingham contained up to eighteen percent coloured immigrants, and eleven relatively small areas of the city, which contained only 9.4 percent of

[9] For discussion of the legislation see: E. J. B. Rose et al; Paul Foot, *Immigration and Race in British Politics* (Penguin Special 1965), and Michael and Ann Dummett, 'The Role of Government in Britain's Racial Crisis' in Lewis Donnelly *Justice First* (Sheed and Ward, London, 1969).
[10] *Institute of Race Relations: Facts Paper on the United Kingdom 1970-71* (Institute of Race Relations, London, 1970, p. 14).

the city's population, contained over 60 percent of the coloured immigrants.[11] Local concentration of the coloured communities within cities is at least partly a reflection of their housing situation. Housing is a scarce commodity and not easily obtained by newcomers or people with low incomes, and immigrants have found themselves in competition with the indigenous population for accommodation. The central areas of cities have therefore become the main areas of immigrant settlement. One reason for this is that these areas have become relatively less desirable to the indigenous population, which has over the years tended to move outwards from the city centres. However, housing conditions for immigrants are for several reasons inferior to those of the host community. For example, houses in the older inner city areas are often large Victorian buildings which are expensive to buy and maintain, and new owners may have to sub-let in order to meet mortgage payments or the payments on money borrowed at very high interest rates because building societies are often unwilling to advance money on this kind of property. Also, because of the demand for accommodation, such premises are often bought by speculators as an economic investment and converted into flats or rooms at high rents. Pressures of demand and supply thus make accommodation, even in the inner city, expensive and scarce. For coloured immigrants there is a further restraint on their housing opportunities because of discrimination against them in letting and selling. This makes it difficult for them to leave the decaying areas of inner cities and at the same time makes them more vulnerable to financial exploitation.[12]

The housing situation of the coloured immigrants as opposed to the English may be illustrated by statistics from 1966. In the London conurbation 43.6 percent of the coloured immigrants rented furnished accommodation, with the associated absence of security of tenure, as compared with only 7.3 percent of the English. This disparity is due in part to the relatively high proportion of single men among the migrants, and to recent arrivals, but these factors are not on their own sufficient to

[11] P. N. Jones, *The Segregation of Immigrant Communities in the City of Birmingham* (University of Hull publications, 1967).
[12] For a fuller discussion of the housing problem and immigrants see: E. J. B. Rose, op. cit., pp. 120-48 and pp. 232-63. *Report of the Committee on Housing in Greater London.* (Cmnd 2605, The Milner Holland Report, HMSO London, 1965.) Elizabeth Burney, *Housing on Trial* (OUP/IRR London, 1967). J. Rex and R. S. Moore, *Race, Community and Conflict* (OUP/IRR London, 1967). W. W. Daniel, *Racial Discrimination in England* (Penguin Special, 1968).

account for the difference. The difference in housing conditions is also apparent from a comparison of the density of occupation per room. In the London conurbation the density for all coloured immigrants combined was 1.05 and for the English population 0.57 per room. One and a half persons per room is referred to as 'an indicator of severe overcrowding'.[13] Using this as a basis, the 1966 census revealed that 30.0 percent of coloured immigrants in the West Midlands conurbation and 27.7 percent in London lived in overcrowded accommodation as compared with under 3 percent of the native English.[14]

There are also differences between immigrants and the native population in the area of employment. Coloured immigrants in Britain differ from the indigenous population in their socio-economic distribution, and in their location in different industries. On the whole, they are heavily over-represented in the lower socio-economic categories of semi-skilled and unskilled manual work.

Although they are employed in a wide range of occupations, they are concentrated within certain industries. This differs from area to area, and from one immigrant group to another. For example, in the West Midlands there are very heavy concentrations of Indians and Pakistanis in the metal manufacture industry and of Pakistanis in the metal goods industry. In this area these two industries employ over half the Indians and Pakistanis in employment. Coloured people are over-represented in such industries as clothing and footwear, transport and communication, and significantly under-represented in the distributive trades.[15]

The location of immigrant groups within British industry is partly a reflection of the skills they brought with them; many have an essentially rural background. But lack of skills is not a sufficient explanation for their employment patterns. One feature of immigrant labour is that it tends to fill positions vacated by indigenous labour. Peach[16] has shown that West Indian immigrants have acted as a replacement population in those areas of Britain where labour demand was not being matched by the indigenous labour supply. Rose et al explain this by saying, 'These differences are probably more accountable in

[13] *Institute of Race Relations: Facts Paper on the United Kingdom 1970-71*, p. 26.
[14] Nicholas Deakin et al., *Colour Citizenship and British Society* (Panther Modern Society, 1969, p. 69).
[15] E. J. B. Rose et al. op. cit., pp. 167-174.
[16] Ceri Peach, *West Indian Migration to Britain – A Social Geography* (OUP/IRR 1968).

15

terms of "clean" and "dirty" jobs, employers' preferences, and local labour's reluctance to meet the demands within certain industries rather than the particular skills possessed by the immigrant.'[17]

For the future of race relations in Britain, perhaps the most significant feature of the employment characteristics of the immigrant groups is the widespread discrimination against them. The extent of discrimination, which reflects the indigenous workers' prejudice and fear of competition, is difficult to assess accurately. One reason for this is that discrimination is not always visible and the victims are not always aware that they have been treated unfairly. Even when they are, discrimination is notoriously difficult to prove. However, the PEP report[18] on racial discrimination in Britain of 1967, and the research of Jowell and Prescott-Clarke (1970)[19] and Selby-Smith (1970)[20] give a consistent picture of discrimination against coloured workers. Perhaps symptomatic of the attitude toward them is the fact that the Race Relations Act of 1968, which was designed to prevent discrimination, has a clause which allows employers to operate racial quotas, and another which excludes some kinds of employment on aircraft and ships from the provisions of the Act. There is also the apparent impotence of the Race Relations Board to achieve a reduction in discrimination. (Recently the operation of the Race Relations Board has been the object of some criticism.)[21] Employment is one of the areas of real conflict between immigrant and host in Britain. There is particular cause for concern because it appears that 'second generation immigrants', who are 'British' in all but colour, are also discriminated against.[22]

It is important to be clear that the discrimination suffered by the coloured immigrant in housing and employment is related to his colour, not only to his immigrant status. The PEP report, in

[17] E. J. B. Rose et al. op. cit., p. 172.
[18] W. W. Daniel op. cit.
[19] R. Jowell and P. Prescott-Clarke, 'Racial Discrimination and White-Collar Workers in Britain', *Race XI*, No. 4, 1970.
[20] C. Selby-Smith, 'Racial Discrimination by British Employers', *Race XII*, No. 2, 1970.
[21] See, for example, articles in *Race Today*, October 1971.
[22] For a fuller discussion of immigrants and employment see: E. J. B. Rose et al. op. cit., Chapters 13 and 19. B. Hepple, *Race, Jobs and the Law in Britain* (Penguin Books, London, 1970). K. McPherson and J. Gaitskell, *Immigrants and Employment: Two Case Studies in East London and Croydon* (IRR Special Series, London 1969). P. Wright, *The Coloured Worker in British Industry* (OUP/IRR London, 1968).

its concluding chapter, states that, 'In the sectors we studied – different aspects of employment, housing and the provision of services – there is racial discrimination varying in extent from the massive to the substantial. The experiences of white immigrants, such as Hungarians and Cypriots, compared to black or brown immigrants, such as West Indians and Asians, leave no doubt that the major component in the discrimination is colour.'[23] The author notes that West Indians suffer most in this respect because 'prejudice against Negroes is most deeprooted and widespread', and that the main reasons for discriminating against them are 'physical and racial'. Discrimination against Asians was often on cultural grounds, the report found, but nevertheless 'some people practise colour discrimination indiscriminately and view all coloured people alike'. As far as the question of colour is concerned, the findings of the PEP report match closely an Elizabethan proverb : 'Three Moores to a Portuguese, three Portuguese to an Englishman.'[24]

The research that has been done shows that the discrimination suffered by the immigrants is not solely the product of the discriminatory actions of particular hostile individuals. To a large extent it is institutionalized in the sense that the policies and practices of many British institutions operate to their disadvantage, irrespective of the goodwill and intentions of particular whites involved. Systems of council house allocation, for instance, have often functioned in such a way as to exclude coloured immigrants. The length of time on the waiting list which is normally a criterion of eligibility for council housing, or the policy of rehousing only families and not single men, or owners but not their tenants in slum clearance programmes, all tend to penalize coloured immigrants disproportionately.[25]

Similarly, the system of special educational provision for backward children has resulted in large numbers of West Indian children being allocated to schools for the educationally subnormal through the use of inappropriate intelligence tests, applied, we must assume, by people who have only the child's best interests at heart.[26] The very constitution of many British

---

[23] W. W. Daniel op. cit., p. 209.
[24] Quoted in G. K. Hunter, 'Othello and Colour Prejudice', Annual Shakespeare Lecture of the British Academy 1967. From: *The Proceedings of the British Academy*, Vol. LIII (OUP London).
[25] Elizabeth Burney, op. cit.
[26] Bernard Coard, *How the West Indian Child is made Educationally Subnormal in the British School System* (New Beacon Books, London, 1971).

institutions is such that coloured people have been likely to suffer even without there being any active hostility against them. Hostility and prejudice are, however, widespread and make the position of coloured people particularly difficult.

Prejudice

A study of white British attitudes toward coloured people was carried out by Abrams[27] between December 1966 and April 1967, using a prejudice-tolerance scale. This study reported 35 percent of the sample as 'tolerant', 38 percent 'tolerant-inclined', 17 percent 'prejudice-inclined' and 10 percent as 'prejudiced'. These findings have, however, been criticized,[28] and this global presentation of the results seriously underestimates the true extent of white hostility. Abrams reports, for instance, that in reply to the question 'Do you think the majority of coloured people in Britain are superior, equal or inferior to you?' – 53 percent of respondents regarded them as inferior. And in reply to the question 'Suppose there are two workers, one coloured and one white, who do exactly the same work. If one, and only one, had to be declared redundant, should it be the coloured or the white worker?' – 42 percent of respondent· thought the coloured worker should be dismissed. Of these, two-thirds, over 28 percent of all respondents, justified this view by saying that 'this is a white man's country' or that 'whites should always be preferred'. These responses give some indication of the prevalence of racial hostility in Britain, and suggest that Abrams' own conclusion that only 10 percent are 'prejudiced' is unduly optimistic.

Racial prejudice is reflected in other widely held attitudes, particularly in attitudes toward immigration. A table published in Rose et al shows that the percentage of the British population advocating some degree of control over immigration has shifted from 65 percent in 1958 to 95 percent in 1968. A 1968 Gallup Poll showed that 75 percent of a national sample agreed with a speech by the politician Enoch Powell. In this speech he had said, 'We must be mad, literally mad, as a nation, to be permitting the annual inflow of some 50,000 dependants, who are for the most part the material of the future growth of the immigrant-descended population. It is like watching a

[27] E. J. B. Rose et al. op. cit., Chapter 28.
[28] See correspondence in *New Society* of 14 August, 21 August and 11 September, 1969; letters from John Rowan, Daniel Lawrence and Mark Abrams, also D. Lawrence, 'How Prejudiced Are We?', *Race Today*, October 1969.

nation busily engaged in heaping up its own funeral pyre'.[29]

This brief summary should serve to highlight a number of central features of the present situation. Firstly, there is the fact that coloured groups in Britain occupy relatively disadvantaged positions in the British social structure. Secondly, it is clear that their relatively low status is due in part to active discrimination against them. There is also ample evidence of hostility towards them among the white population, opposition to their entry to the country and pressure for their repatriation. Finally, it appears that prejudice and discrimination are related to their colour, and not only to their immigrant status and ethnic origins.

Central to our study of white beliefs and attitudes is the notion of colour prejudice, and before presenting our findings it is necessary to discuss this more fully. In the two chapters which follow, therefore, we examine the nature of British colour prejudice by sketching its history and defining our own approach in relation to the main traditions within which prejudice has been studied in social science. We argue that to study prejudice simply as an individual disposition is inadequate to a true understanding of the phenomenon.

[29] Bill Smithies and Peter Fiddick, *Enoch Powell on Immigration* (Sphere Books, 1969, p. 37). See also Paul Foot, *The Rise of Enoch Powell* (Penguin Special, 1969).

2

British Images of the Black Man

*The evidence suggests that Racism had assumed an
active form in the British overseas empire right at the
beginning of Victoria's reign. The Darwinian revelation
injected scientific and sociological content; and the
Indian Mutiny and the 'mini-mutiny' in Jamaica provided the 'rivers of blood' to justify prejudices. The
last quarter of the century saw Racism reach a plateau,
being manifested in the Empire which had then attained
its widest bounds. Today, in the Imperial afterglow, we
survey our lost domains from the same plateau of Racism
in what is now our supposedly beleaguered island home.*

HUGH TINKER[1]

The main ideas about race and colour that have been current in
Britain developed as a result of colonial expansion from the late
sixteenth century onwards. Since that time the essential character
of relations between the British and the indigenous inhabitants
of other continents has been domination of the non-white by the
white, whether by military conquest, enslavement, or economic
and political ascendancy. When British people came into contact
with coloured people in the colonies, the coloured man was
typically in the subordinate role. It is hardly surprising, therefore, that European ideas about the coloured man stressed his
inferiority to the white. As the colonial period progressed, these
ideas became elaborated and more and more widely diffused,
until by the end of the nineteenth century the idea of white
superiority held a central place in British national culture. Many
authors – notably Winthrop Jordan,[2] James Walvin[3] and
Christine Bolt[4] – have analysed the history of white attitudes to
blacks between Elizabethan and Victorian times. We draw on

[1] 'Race and Neo-Victorianism', *Encounter*, April, 1972.
[2] Winthrop D. Jordan, *White Over Black* (Penguin 1969; first published by University of North Carolina Press, 1968).
[3] James Walvin, *The Black Presence* (Orbach & Chambers, London,
1971).
[4] Christine Bolt, *Victorian Attitudes to Race*, Routledge, 1971.

their writings for evidence to help us sketch the development of British thought.

Early Ideas

At the time that colonial expansion was getting under way and Negroes were first beginning to appear in Britain there was already available from medieval tradition a number of ideas and associations surrounding blackness, and images of the black man, in terms of which the English responded to coloured people. Blackness was traditionally associated with evil, and the devil was commonly represented as black. Guy Hunter,[5] for instance, refers to Bede's interpretation that the Ethiopian baptized by Philip turned white in consequence. Hunter has also pointed to a European artistic tradition in which the tormentors of Christ often included Negro figures, and has illustrated this with examples of English-made alabasters. He also notes that blacked-up figures traditionally represented the devil, wickedness and paganism in medieval morality plays and pageantry. It seems probable that these traditions owe much to the conflict between Christendom and Islam, and to early travellers' tales, interpreted within a biblical and theological framework which itself contained references to blacks, and in which blackness was the common symbol of evil.

The success of Shakespeare's *Othello*, Hunter argues, must have depended on the symbolic significance that the Elizabethan audience would automatically have attached to the appearance of a Moor on the stage. Othello, when he appears, is noble, chivalrous and a Christian. The audience, however, would have expected evil, barbarity, paganism and lasciviousness – expectations which Shakespeare does little to discourage before the entrance of the Moor himself. The opening scene portrays the distress of Desdemona's father at the news that his daughter is in the 'gross clasp of a lascivious Moor'. He is told that 'an old black ram / Is tupping your white ewe', and is convinced that she could not have married a Moor had she been in her right mind, but must have been drugged or bewitched through 'practices of cunning hell', so to 'err / Against all rules of nature'. Othello is also referred to as a 'barbary horse' and 'the devil'. The dramatic success of the play, Hunter argues, depended on the tension between the traditional expectations associated with a Moor and the character of Othello as it actually unfolds,

[5] G. K. Hunter, 'Othello and Colour Prejudice', *The Proceedings of the British Academy,* Vol. LIII (OUP London, 1967).

between physical and symbolic blackness and whiteness.

A stereotype of the black man as barbaric, libidinous, un-Christian, and associated with evil, that pre-dated the still embryonic African trade and colonial expansion, was available from medieval tradition even in Elizabethan times. As the colonial endeavour gathered momentum and contact with people of other continents increased, elements of this earlier tradition became incorporated into later ideas about coloured people. Many of the earlier ideas provided ready justifications for slavery and colonial exploitation and formed the basis on which specifically racist ideologies were elaborated.

One of the more common of earlier explanations of blackness and its significance was that it resulted from the curse laid upon Ham (Cham), the son of Noah. In 1578, George Best explained that Noah 'straitely commaunded his sonnes and their wives, that they should with reverence and feare beholde the justice and mighty power of God, and that during the time of the floud while they remained in the Arke, they should use continencie, and abstaine from carnall copulation with their wives'. Cham, however, was tempted by the devil and disobeyed 'for the which wicked and detestable fact, as an example for contempt of Almightie God, and disobedience of parents, God would a sonne should bee borne whose name was Chus, who not onely it self, but all his posteritie after him should bee blacke and lothsome, that it might remain a spectacle of disobedience to all the worlds. And of this blacke and cursed Chus came all these blacke Moores which are in Africa . . .'[6] The equation of blackness with being 'lothsome' is apparent also in the Song of Songs, where the woman encourages her lover with the thought that she is 'black but comely'.

This biblical anthropology is in line with the Christian tradition of representing one of the three Magi as black, these being the representatives of the three branches of humanity descended from Noah's sons. Best's version of the Bible story seems to have come from Hebraic texts. The Vulgate and the later King James version simply say that Ham discovered his father's nakedness. However, the sexual connotation remains, as does the tradition that Ham's posterity were condemned to be slaves, or 'servants of servants'. Christine Bolt notes that such interpretations of the significance of racial differences were 'still popular in Victorian times'.[7] Certainly one version or another

[6] James Walvin, op. cit., p. 36.
[7] Christine Bolt, op. cit., p. 211.

of the story was referred to in various writings on Negroes and slavery in the sixteenth and seventeenth centuries. As Jordan says of Best's interpretation: 'The inner themes running through this extraordinary exegesis testify eloquently to the completeness with which English perceptions could integrate sexuality with blackness, the devil, and the judgement of God, who had originally created man not only "angelike" but "white".'[8] The still-current notion of the enormous size of the Negro's penis was to be found, according to Jordan, in the illustrations of medieval cartographers and was explicitly connected with the curse of Ham by Richard Jobson in 1623. After commenting on the fact that Mandingo men were 'furnisht with such members as are after a sort burthensome unto them', Jobson explains the phenomenon as follows: 'Undoubtedly these people originally sprung from the race of *Canaan,* the sonne of *Ham,* who discovered his father *Noah*'s secrets, for which *Noah* awakening cursed Canaan as our holy Scripture testifieth the curse as by Scholeman hath been disputed, extended to his ensuing race, in laying hold upon the same place, where the original cause began, whereof these people are witnesse'.[9]

It seems probable that there is a near universal element in the association of white with good and black with evil, as an extension of the symbolism of day and night, light and darkness. It is clear, however, that the use of this imagery in the tradition we have illustrated went well beyond the merely aesthetic or allegorical and formed the basis of a quite literal ascription of different qualities to different races of men.

Slave and Subject

The themes of barbarism, heathenism and sexual promiscuity already associated with the Negro in Elizabethan times are to be found elaborated and more widely diffused in the eighteenth and nineteenth centuries when they were used to justify slavery and exploitation. In this period the idea of Negro inferiority became more explicit. The main change was that biblical and theological interpretations lost ground to scientific ones; and as industrial and commercial values became more central to British society so the negative evaluation of the black man came to be expressed in terms of these, laziness and lack of ambition being added to his list of vices. The main elements of the eighteenth century-stereotype of the Negro, that had come into full flower

[8] Jordon, op. cit., p. 41.
[9] Ibid, p. 35.

after two centuries of slavery, may be illustrated from Edward Long's *History of Jamaica*, published in 1774. He wrote: 'In general, they [Negroes] are void of genius, and seem almost incapable of making any progress in civility of science. They have no plan or system of morality among them. Their barbarity to their children debases their nature even below that of brutes. They have no moral sensations; no taste but for women; gormandizing and drinking to excess; no wish but to be idle,'[10] and, '. . . I do not think that an orang-outang husband would be any dishonour to a Hottentot female, for what are these Hottentots? They are . . . a people certainly very stupid, and very brutal.'[11]

Long refers, in support of his views to Hume, possibly the most eminent intellect to give explicit support to early scientific racism. Hume had written (1754): 'I am apt to suspect the Negroes, and in general all the other species of men . . . to be naturally inferior to the whites. There never was a civilized nation of any other complexion than white, nor even any individual eminent either in action or speculation. No ingenious manufacturers amongst them, no arts, no sciences.'[12]

Three-quarters of a century later, after the abolition of slavery, and when the sugar colonies were declining, a Victorian caricature of the Negro was presented by Carlyle in his *Discourse on the Nigger Question*. In this, idleness is an even more central vice in the nigger's make-up, commercial exploitation a more explicit objective, and the 'work ethic' a more central value. Thus he wrote: 'The West Indies, it appears are short of labour, as indeed is very conceivable in those circumstances. Where a Black man, by working about half an hour a day . . . can supply himself, by aid of sun and soil, with as much pumpkin as will suffice, he is likely to be a little stiff to raise into hard work!'[13] and '. . . with regard to the West Indies, it may be laid down as a principle . . . that no Black man who will not work according to what ability the Gods have given him for working has the smallest right to eat pumpkin, or to any fraction of land that will grow pumpkins . . . but has an indisputable and perpetual *right* to be compelled, by the real proprietors of the said land, to do competent work for a living.'[14]

For Carlyle, the Negro ('poor Quashee'), properly handled,

[10] Walvin, op. cit., p. 118.
[11] Ibid, p. 122.
[12] Jordan, op. cit., p. 253.
[13] Walvin, op. cit., p. 139.
[14] Ibid, p. 140

was : 'A swift supple fellow; a merry-hearted, grinning, dancing, singing, affectionate kind of creature, with a great deal of melody and amenability in his composition.'[15]

The Positive Element

It would be wrong to represent the development of British thought about the Negro as totally negative. From the seventeenth century in particular, other ideas were beginning to make an impact on British consciousness. These included the romantic notion of the 'noble savage' which represented the black man as an innocent child of nature; the beliefs of the anti-slavery and philanthropic movements; and the growing pressures for political democracy and universal suffrage. The noble savage concept was often applied in a paternalistic way and did not necessarily undermine the essential idea of white superiority, and could even serve to justify the need for continued white 'guardianship'. In the same way, as Christine Bolt has shown, even the abolitionists and philanthropists were not free of the common prejudices and assumptions. She notes, for instance, that at the time of the Jamaica revolt : 'the defence of the black rebels in sections of the Liberal press reveals a similar implicit sympathy for the Negro cause and indifference or aversion for the Negro.'[16]

The humanitarian and libertarian impulses relating to the black man never became as well-embedded in British culture as the more negative stereotypes and were in any case seldom expressed in a form inconsistent with the assumption of white superiority. Indeed, many of the ideas current in the nineteenth century served simultaneously to uphold emerging conceptions of social justice at home and to justify the exploitation of the black man abroad. Thus it was widely accepted, and still is today, that white men were incapable of working in hot climates; and that the freedmen of the West Indies and the American South were 'not ready for self-government' though this remained an ideal that might be envisaged in the distant future. Bolt quotes Liberal MP Sir John Kennaway, one of the 'genuine friends of the Negro' as believing in 1867 that 'all races and all classes are entitled to justice, but all are not ready for self-government'.[17] Such sentiments need to be seen in historical perspective in the light of the fact that effective universal male suffrage was not achieved in Britain until 1884, something which

[15] Ibid, p. 142.
[16] Christine Bolt, op. cit., p. 85.
[17] Ibid, p. 89.

itself is a useful reminder that present-day assumptions are inappropriate yardsticks by which to judge the thought of a different era. Our purpose here is not to judge but to sketch the origins of and illustrate continuities in British thought relating to race.

The Indian

So far we have referred exclusively to conceptions of the Negro. British ideas about the Indian are, however, also important for our purposes considering that over half the present coloured population of Britain is of Asian origin. Conceptions of the Indian were never as stereotyped or unrelievedly negative as of the Negro. There has always been a degree of admiration in Britain for Indian culture and civilization, and the Indian was never enslaved, hence there were always more positive elements in British images of the Indian. This is not to say that the Indian was not regarded as essentially inferior to the white, only that anti-Indian prejudice never had quite the intensity and viciousness that is evident in many writings about the Negro. British ideas about the Negro represented not simply a doctrine of black inferiority, but of white superiority, and through this all non-white peoples shared a relatively low evaluation. Where the Negro was despised because he was black and a slave, the Indian was looked down upon initially because he had been conquered and was not white. A passage by H. B. Evans, a surgeon with West Indian experience, written in 1855, quoted by Christine Bolt illustrates all these sentiments: 'The Indian is docile, harmless, and industrious, and when he has the opportunity, saving . . . under the guidance and protection of a European, whom he reveres, he will do almost anything; and even in the lowest castes, there is a degree of refinement about them which is surprising. They are gregarious in their habits, and unlike the Negro, do not evince that love for a savage state of life which the latter is so fond of indulging, when not under restraint. They are quick, apt, and intelligent workmen, and make capital servants; the great secret in the management of them is kindness and fair dealing, with a tolerance of their harmless prejudices.'[18] Bolt suggests that the stereotype of the 'mild Hindu' only lost ground to that of the 'cruel scheming Oriental who needed and only respected strong Government',[19] following Victorian outrage at the Indian Mutiny of 1857.

The religious and related cultural practices of the Indian

[18] Ibid, p. 178.
[19] Ibid, p. 178.

sub-continent (including suttee and child marriage) also provided an important reason for denigrating the Indian. Whereas African religion was commonly dismissed as mere fetishism, Indian religions were objected to on other grounds including their apparently greater resistance to Christianity. According to Bolt: 'an article written by the Rev. J. S. Robertson of the Church Missionary Society's Bombay and West India station was typical in its condemnation of the "abominable festival" called the Koli, the "yearly carnival of the polluted Hindoos, during which they practise abominations such as may be supposed to be acceptable to the demon of lust".'[20]

The British attitude to the Indian and other coloured peoples, was not simply a matter of ethnocentrism and scorn or revulsion at aspects of a foreign culture, but was quite definitely racial. 'As a clergyman speaking at an Ethnological Society meeting in 1863 remarked, nations which had adopted Christianity were those, like Britain, "that had been raised to the highest conditions of superiority", but it was equally clear that racial superiority was given by God "for the accomplishment of some good work upon this earth".'[21]

The racial inferiority of the Indian, furthermore, and the objectionable features of his culture, were linked to his colour. Bolt points out that the interpretation of the Indian caste system along colour lines came naturally to the Victorian British, and that 'not unexpectedly, a greater degree of barbarism was detected in the black races of Southern India, whose kin were to be found in Africa, the Malay Peninsula and elsewhere, and who were regarded as the most inferior of the Indian peoples. According to Charles Johnston ". . . it was to this black race, passionate, magnetic, of wild imaginings, we must trace every lurid and demoniac element in the beliefs of India. This is their contribution to the common sum: a contribution fitting in the kin of the African Voodoo, the Australian cannibal, the Papuan head-hunter".'[22] Aspects of the negative stereotype of the Negro tended to rub off on the Indian and other coloured peoples on grounds of colour alone. Bolt notes that 'towards the end of the (19th) century race prejudice was reinforcing the British weakness for generalizing about coloured peoples. Shortly after the Mutiny, in fact, it was common to find "Indian niggers" spoken of with a "coarse contempt and vulgar hatred".'[23]

[20] Ibid, p. 167.
[21] Ibid, p. 213.
[22] Ibid, p. 168.
[23] Ibid, p. 178.

Christine Bolt has drawn for her evidence on serious writings in documentary sources available to the educated elite of the Victorian period. Fine distinctions between different coloured groups were even less characteristic of the more popular culture of the time and for the ordinary Briton there was a much greater tendency to lump all coloured groups together. A well-known example of this blurring, dating from 1899 is the still much-loved children's story of *Little Black Sambo*.[24] The name 'Sambo' is most commonly applied to people of Negro descent and derives from the Spanish *Zambo*, used, among other things, for an American ape (though it may be mistaken to assume synonymity in these two uses of the word). Sambo is commonly portrayed in illustrations of the story as a stereotypical Negro boy with a love for flamboyant Western clothing in settings suggestive of the Caribbean. However, he is threatened by tigers, animals of Asia, not found either in Africa or the Caribbean. The tigers are finally reduced to 'a pool of molten butter (or "ghi" as it is called in India)' with which his mother makes pancakes. This random mixing of Negro and oriental detail is not uncharacteristic of popular British consciousness of coloured people. What matters is that they are coloured. To this extent at least, they are 'all the same'.

We have illustrated the long history of British colour prejudice which, despite counter-currents of thought, had by the end of the nineteenth century become an integral element of British culture. The essence of this prejudice is the taking for granted of white superiority and black inferiority. This idea became more important, more widespread, and more elaborated as Britain's colonial involvement increased, and was an accurate reflection of the typical relationship between the white British and coloured peoples; a relationship of master and servant, employer and employee, conqueror and conquered, settler and native. The balance of wealth, power, and esteem was always on the white side. But colour prejudice was more than simply an acceptance of colour as a factually accurate indicator of subordinate status – which it was, and, on average, remains. Colour prejudice – or racism – exists when colour comes to signal a lesser *entitlement* to the enjoyment of power and resources.

By the beginning of this century, colour-linked status dif-

[24] The correspondence in *The Times* during May 1972 about *Little Black Sambo* provides some interesting examples of the inability of white Britons to perceive a stereotypical presentation of the Negro as offensive to blacks.

ferentials had come to be perceived by whites not simply as facts, but as natural and even necessary. It not only came to seem normal that blacks should be subordinate to whites, but the idea that things might be otherwise seemed unnatural, ludicrous, or wrong. Whether the rightness of this state of affairs was explained as the will of God, as necessitated by the coloured man's innate depravity or childlike simplicity, or on other grounds is not crucially important; various justifications were developed over the centuries. So long as the idea of differential entitlement is preserved, the particular legitimations that surround it may change as one loses credibility and others seem more convincing. Whether you argue that Rhodesian Africans, for instance, are biologically inferior to whites, that they are not yet civilized enough to govern their own country, or something else, is relatively immaterial so long as the argument provides a convincing reason for denying them political rights. By the end of the nineteenth century the assumption of differential entitlement on grounds of colour was embodied in all aspects of British culture. The central assumption was perhaps most economically encapsulated in the oft-quoted lines of Kipling, for whom the White Man's Burden was

> *To wait in heavy harness*
> *On fluttering folk and wild –*
> *Your new-caught sullen peoples*
> *Half-devil and half-child.*

Continuities

The important point for present purposes is that racist beliefs such as we have illustrated are not just interesting relics of a dead past, but live on in the cultural repertoire of present-day Britain, and form part of the perspective through which we view contemporary events. It is true that many of the more blatant features of racist ideology – such as the belief in the biological inferiority of the black man – are no longer respectable. But this does not mean that they do not still command wide respect, or survive implicitly in many of the more 'respectable' assumptions and imagery still current today. The culture into which today's children are being socialized contains a strong legacy of slavery and imperial glories, and in a multi-racial Britain it is important to see this for what it is.

The most cursory examination of popular literature and entertainment available to both adults and young people over the past few years will confirm the survival of the symbolism of white superiority and its legitimating beliefs. We examine news and entertainment media in some detail in later chapters. Here a few examples will serve to make the point.

In a survey of books for children in print in January 1970 carried out by a working party of librarians, the editor, Janet Hill,[25] states that too many books on Africa 'embody outdated colonial concepts of the continent and its peoples' and that 'books remain in print and continue to be published which contain not only errors of fact and biased opinions but reflect built-in attitudes of superiority and condescension . . .' She also notes that many books are 'blatantly biased and prejudiced' and that 'not surprisingly this criticism applies most strongly to books about countries that have been closely connected with England, notably India, Pakistan, and the African countries.' Of the 184 books surveyed dealing with Africa, 47 (25 percent) were 'not recommended because their negative characteristics, whether bias, prejudice, inaccuracy or dullness, outweigh all other considerations'. Included in this category, for example, is the still popular W. E. Johns' *Biggles and the Black Raider,* set in Africa. The reviewer notes that the attitudes expressed in it are 'pernicious'. Biggles accepts the job 'on the understanding that there's no interference by bureaucrats. I want no bleating in the House of Commons about a poor innocent native being shot . . . Nobody says a word if fifty British Tommies are bumped off; but let one poor benighted heathen get the works and the balloon goes up. Then people wonder why things are going to pot.' The assumption of British superiority and the theme of savagery and heathenism that we noted as early as the eighteenth century are central to the value system of the hero.[26]

Even at the level of factual day-to-day news in the press, the imagery of colonialism and stereotypical views of blacks surface from time to time. This is not the main characteristic of the press coverage of race and coloured people, but its existence is indicative of an underlying perspective in British culture which provides a ready interpretative framework on matters of race

[25] Janet Hill (ed). *Books for Children: The Homelands of Immigrants in Britain* (IRR, 1971).
[26] For a discussion of ethnocentrism in British school textbooks see Felicity Bolton and Jennie Laishley, *Education for a Multiracial Britain* (Fabian Research Series 303, Fabian Society, 1972); for a report of the presentation of non-whites in children's comics see Jennie Laishley, 'Can comics join the multi-racial society?', *Times Educational Supplement,* 24 November 1972.

and colour. The prevalence of stereotypes deriving from the colonial experience may be gauged from the existence of a number of traditions of cartoon jokes. These include the missionary in the pot, the fakir on his bed of nails, the snake-charmer, and the polygamous Eastern potentate with his harem. We do not think that these examples are particularly important in themselves, except as an index of the widespread familiarity with the image of coloured people that they carry. It does, however, become disturbing to find this kind of outmoded image obtruding itself into the media handling of current events concerning real people; so that elements of the cultural legacy that are at best ethnocentric and at worst racist come to influence reactions to and interpretations of race-related events in Britain today. The tendency may most clearly be seen in headlines and in cartoon comment, where the use of a phrase or image that will evoke a similar set of associations and meanings in virtually all members of the society to which it is directed enables a complex point to be crystallized unambiguously and memorably in a few words or a single picture.

In its front page report of the discovery of forty illegal Indian immigrants in a Bradford cellar in July 1970, the *Daily Express* of 2 July used the heading 'Police find forty Indians in "black hole".' This is an instantly recognizable allusion to the 'black hole of Calcutta', which, by evoking colonial associations suggests that the appropriate attitude to adopt towards these Indians is that adopted towards the natives in the days of Empire. We are not suggesting that this is what the *Express* intended, only that this is the sort of reaction that the heading is likely to have achieved.

A similar effect was created by the cartoon in the *Sun* on 3 July in which an illegal immigrant asking the way addresses a white man as 'Sahib', and in the cartoon in the *Mirror* on 6 July which showed two lovers on a beach, one of whom was saying 'I thought you said this was a quiet beach' while the beach was being overrun by illegal immigrants in turbans, including a man riding on an elephant, a snake-charmer complete with snake, and a man carrying a bed of nails. The reiteration of this kind of image, not merely at the level of joke or fantasy, but in relation to actual events, can only perpetuate an outlook which is antithetical to good race relations and likely to influence perceptions of current events.

A cultural tradition may be at least partly self-sustaining. The image is used because it exists and is known to have wide currency and therefore enables easier communication. By virtue of being used it is kept alive and available for further use.

On 8 June 1970, the *Daily Mirror* carried a human interest picture item. The 13" × 6" picture showed an African man, dressed in bushjacket and long trousers brandishing an umbrella, assegai-like. The headline was 'Tarzan Flies in with a Brolly in Place of a Spear' and the text read : 'The man they call Tarzan began his greatest adventure yesterday . . . armed with an umbrella. Edwardo Omara didn't really need the brolly. It was just his way of showing the natives that he was friendly when he arrived at London's Heathrow Airport at the end of a journey from the African bush. Back home in his village in Uganda, Edwardo wears a leopard skin and carries a spear. But that wouldn't do for his visit to the big white chiefs in London, especially as he is going to meet the chief of them all . . . the Queen. Edwardo earned his Tarzan title when he saved a white gamekeeper from an enraged elephant. He killed the elephant with his spear and was awarded the Empire Gallantry Medal, later renamed the George Cross. Edwardo will meet the Queen at a reunion of Victoria Cross and George Cross heroes on Wednesday. Meanwhile he's praying for rain . . . so that he can try out his brolly.'

The themes of savagery, the big white chief, the faithful if simple native, so neatly invoked are straight out of the tradition of boys' adventure stories of the heydey of Empire.

The tendency to focus on colour as the crucial element and the failure to make distinctions between different coloured groups that we have noted may also be illustrated from the *Mirror* which, on 15 February 1968, carried an editorial on the Kenya Asian question. This long and dramatically-written piece accounted for all editorial matter on the first and second pages, a treatment given by the *Mirror* only to matters of major importance. The banner headline read 'MIRROR – ON IMMIGRATION'. Below and covering the left-hand side of the page was a face, the one side of which was from a photograph of a Negro and the other from a photograph of a white, the two joined together to give a composite picture. What is interesting about this is that although the text and the controversy to which it referred was about Asians, the picture used a Negro countenance. Whether the *Mirror* was aware of any discrepancy between text and picture is not important. The use of this picture illustrates how distinctions between different coloured groups are marginal in popular British thought, and how images of the Negro may be introduced into discussions of an Asian group without seeming out of place. Certainly the picture the *Mirror* used was a more effective way of symbolizing multi-racialism than a half-Asian face would have been, for the Negro is more richly evocative in British culture, representing the epitome of blackness and differentness from the white. And as the *Mirror* said, 'We are talking about colour as well as numbers. This *is* a colour question with all the human, emotional and practical problems that the colour confrontation urgently poses.'

Examples like this illustrate the vitality of the white colonial view of the world even today, a view of the world in which the entitlement of whites is seen as essentially different from that of non-whites. This makes it possible for an Ulster politician to object to the imposition of direct rule on the grounds that Ulster is not a 'coconut colony'. Treatment that is accepted as appropriate for non-white nations ('coconut colonies') is unacceptable when whites are the recipients.

American views of the black man which have become part of the cultural stock in trade of the British through American films and literature are discussed in a later chapter. Here we might mention in passing the long popular 'nigger minstrel' tradition. It would be difficult to imagine a better stylization of Carlyle's caricature of the nigger as a 'merry-hearted, grinning, dancing, singing, affectionate kind of creature, with a great deal of melody and amenability in his composition' than BBC television's 'Black and White Minstrel Show'. There are also the cowboy-and-Indian films, comics, stories, songs, games and clothing through which children learn the rudiments of imperial conquest at a very early age.

The self-perceptions of coloured groups

The importance of 'colonial' origins and racist tendencies in our cultural perspectives is not only that they structure white perceptions of the British racial situation, though it is this with which we are chiefly concerned. Such perspectives also have consequences for the images that members of the coloured communities have of themselves and their relation to the wider society. Insofar as coloured people are being socialized into the values and norms of Britain – and this in one form or another is the aim of official policy towards immigrants – they are being offered a culture in which they are implicitly defined as inferior. The damaging effects of such social definitions on both the personalities and social patterns of minority groups have been so well documented both in the United States and this country as to be beyond argument.[27] Recent work by Tajfel and his colleagues[28] has shown that even Scottish children incorporate a ' "devaluation" of their own group' from the dominant English culture at an early age. Their work is important because it shows that the values of a dominant group may influence the self-perceptions of minorities even where there are no intense intergroup tensions and in the absence of clear 'visibility' of group differences.

To the extent that 'white' definitions of the significance of skin colour become part of the perspectives of coloured groups, these groups are rendered the more exploitable and racial injustice can continue more easily. Significantly, Black Power ideologies are concerned with redefining the cultural significance of blackness so that blacks may think of themselves as 'beautiful' rather than as ugly, or inferior. Where coloured groups reject the way they are defined in a 'white' society, without there being a concurrent revision of white perspectives as well, the result can only be to increase their sense of bitterness and alienation with an accompanying heightening of racial tension.

[27] See for instance:
Fanon, F. *Black Skin, White Masks* (Paladin, Granada Publishing Ltd, 1970), and *The Wretched of the Earth* (Penguin, 1967).
Eldridge Cleaver, *Soul on Ice* (Jonathan Cape, 1969).
Grier, W. H., and Cobbs, P. M., *Black Rage* (Basic Books, New York, 1968).
Wilcox, R. G. (Ed). *The Psychological Consequences of being a Black American* (Wiley, 1971).
Hauser, Stuart T., *Black and White Identity Formation* (Wiley, 1971).
Milner, D. 'Prejudice and the Immigrant Child' (*New Society,* September, 1971, pp. 556-569).
Thomson, Susan S., 'The Development of Ethnic Concepts in Children' (Thesis in partial fulfilment of MSc., Dept of Psychology, University of Strathclyde, 1970).
Derek Humphrey & Gus John, *Because They're Black* (Penguin, 1971).
[28] Henri Tajfel; Gustav Jahoda; Charlan Nemeth; Y. Rim and N. B. Johnson, 'The devaluation by children of their own national and ethnic group: two case studies' (*British Journal of Social and Clinical Psychology,* 11, 3, pp. 235-243, September, 1972).

3

The Study of Prejudice

The point of the discussion so far has been to establish a number of simple points :

1. British relations with non-whites in all parts of the world have been characterized by white domination, so that
2. colour has become, on average, a factually accurate index of relative wealth, power and status.
3. The ideas and imagery surrounding white domination have served to legitimate the assumption that colour confers a differential *entitlement* to status and resources.
4. In spite of decolonization, the beliefs and imagery of white superiority are still common currency in Britain and represent a widespread tendency to accept the relatively disadvantaged position of blacks as natural, and even necessary.

It is important to appreciate the connection between those traditional cultural assumptions and the present-day position of non-whites, both in Britain and elsewhere. So long as such attitudes persist, even in muted and attenuated form, so long will it continue to seem normal to find blacks mainly in menial jobs at home, and under-nourished and ill-educated abroad. Conversely, so long as Third World poverty and racial injustice in Southern Africa persist and blacks remain socially disadvantaged in Britain, so long will the assumptions of white superiority and black incapacity appear to be vindicated by the very social relations of which they are the cultural correlates. Furthermore, it is difficult for a view of society in which colour is no longer a role-sign to gain ground, where this is belied by the observable social facts. Prejudice feeds upon injustice, as injustice thrives upon prejudice. Though our concern is with Britain, it should also be clear that to discuss questions of racial prejudice and discrimination solely in terms of social and political processes within this country is artificially to isolate the phenomenon from its true global dimensions.

The Nature of Colour Prejudice
Though the open expression of racial prejudice tends to be

officially frowned upon in this country, racist beliefs and assumptions remain an aspect of the dominant value system of British society. It is important to be clear what we mean by this. We do not mean that explicit racist ideology is endorsed by all white Britons; only that it is generally *recognized as normal* for whites to expect preferment over blacks. This is true even of those who actively deplore and oppose racial prejudice and discrimination. In this sense colour prejudice may be said to be normative in Britain. The situation is not altered by the fact that colour prejudice conflicts with other values. The ideals of freedom and equality, for instance, are felt by many people not to apply to coloureds in the same way as they do to whites, and the function of the various legitimations of colour prejudice – such as the belief in biological or cultural inferiority – is precisely to uphold such values while excluding blacks from their scope. Racist ideas and the officially endorsed values of freedom and democracy coexist in British culture. Racist beliefs and imagery are culturally ubiquitous and the historical implications of skin colour which are part of the cultural legacy of all Britons constitute a potential basis of perception and action. This is why it can be quite misleading to label people as prejudiced or unprejudiced as though prejudice were a purely personal characteristic, present in some people and absent in others, and largely a matter of individual morality or pathology. Prejudice resides in the culture. People differ in the degree to which prejudiced cultural assumptions rather than equalitarian assumptions enter into their perspectives on the world and underlie their actions; but the root assumptions are the familiar property of all.

One further point needs to be made. The idea of white superiority and black inferiority which is central to colour prejudice, is what distinguishes it from many other kinds of intergroup attitudes. There has been in Britain, and still remains, a great deal of anti-German prejudice, for instance. This feeling may contain elements of ridicule, contempt, resentment, fear and even hatred but it does not have as its central feature the idea of the inferiority of the German as opposed to the Briton, and it did not arise in circumstances of enslavement or colonization of the Germans. The same may be said of anti-white prejudice on the part of blacks, which, however intense, does not rest on any historically normative assumption of white inferiority. Nor have such prejudices ever served the social function of maintaining one group in a position of subordination to another. A major exception to these statements is the case of Anti-Semitism which shares many features with colour prejudice, from biblical justification to the social function of maintaining a group in a pariah role in Western societies.

The essential notion of inferiority which is the distinctive feature of white colour prejudice is something that has often been ignored by writers on the subject. Where the object in view is to understand the mental mechanisms underlying prejudice – stereotyping, over-generalization, rigidity, projection and so on – it may be legitimate to treat all inter-group attitudes as psychologically equivalent. Where the object is to understand the relationship between groups in a particular historical situation it becomes crucial to pinpoint the distinctive features of the attitudes and to see them in the light of the relative positions of the groups, past and present. A prejudice against a previously enslaved group is almost certain to be different from a prejudice against a conqueror or an imperial rival, both in the content of its legitimating beliefs and in its implications for intergroup relations.

The Psychology of Prejudice

It will be helpful at this point to comment on the inadequacies of the more common approaches to the study of racial prejudice. In the psychological literature two approaches to the understanding of prejudice have been emphasized. The one approach sees prejudice as rooted in the personality of the individual and satisfying psychological needs for those who manifest it; the other has sought to understand prejudice as a matter of conformity to social norms. It is generally recognized that the two approaches are not mutually exclusive.

The 'personality' approach to prejudice has received most attention from writers in the psycho-analytic tradition, and its best known exposition is the theory of the authoritarian personality.[1] This research arose directly out of concern over the Nazi persecution of Jews.

According to this theory, intense prejudice against outgroups is part of a broad syndrome of attitudes which represent the protective adjustment of an insecure personality. The prejudiced person is unable to accept his own shortcomings and socially unacceptable impulses. These he represses and projects onto minority groups. He then sees in them all the characteristics and tendencies that he fears in himself. In doing this he simultaneously protects his own precarious sense of personal adequacy

[1] T. W. Adorno, Else Frenkel-Brunswick, Daniel J. Levinson and R. Sanford Nevitt, *The Authoritarian Personality* (Harper, New York, 1950).

and finds a suitable outlet for his otherwise unacceptable aggression. The hostility directed towards outgroups may be seen as displaced aggression originally aroused by overstrict parents or other authority figures against whom the expression of hostility is proscribed. In view of the inhibitions and guilt surrounding sexuality in Western societies, this kind of interpretation helps to account for the persistent attribution of sexual promiscuity to coloured groups that we have already noted and which is otherwise difficult to explain. Other features of the protective armoury of the prejudiced person include mental inflexibility, intolerance of ambiguity, a rigid and conventional moralism, a high level of concern with status and success, and preference for clear and hierarchical social structures, strict discipline and strong authority. These characteristics are associated with a rigidly strict and punitive upbringing.

Although the original research on authoritarianism has come in for considerable criticism on methodological and other grounds, many studies on various aspects of the theory have now been carried out and it is difficult not to accept that there is a tendency for ethnocentrism, prejudice, authoritarian attitudes, and rigid childhood discipline to cohere into a pattern.[2] What is less clear is whether it is necessary to invoke psycho-analytic personality dynamics to explain the connection between prejudice and authoritarianism. It remains possible that they go together, not because prejudice is a function of an authoritarian personality structure but because both are independently related to particular environmental circumstances such as low socio-economic status and poor education. By this explanation prejudice and other 'authoritarian' attitudes are psychologically unrelated products of particular kinds of childhood experiences and social circumstances, and prejudice serves no greater psychological need than conformity to any other group norm. Our own preference is to accept the Berkeley researchers' theory as providing at least part of the psychological explanation of prejudice for some individuals. The extreme and apparently pathological bigotry of many people is otherwise difficult to understand.

One of the more noteworthy offshoots of the debate surrounding the work on the authoritarian personality has been the

[2] See particularly Richard Christie and Marie Jahoda (eds) *Studies in the Scope and Method of 'The Authoritarian Personality'*. (The Free Press, Glencoe, Ill., 1954); and R. Christie and Peggy Cook 'A guide to Published Literature Relative to the Authoritarian Personality through 1956' (*J. Psychol.*, 1958, 45, 171-199).

theory of Milton Rokeach.[3] He argued that it was important to distinguish between the content of beliefs and the *structure* of belief systems. The F scale,[4] a questionnaire constructed by the authors of *The Authoritarian Personality* to measure authoritarianism, Rokeach suggested, measured authoritarianism of the right, but it was equally possible to have authoritarianism of the left. The crucial feature of authoritarianism was the cognitive *style* that he called 'closed mindedness' or dogmatism, a style characterized by mental rigidity and an inability to revise old beliefs in the light of new information and an unwillingness to entertain beliefs conflicting with one's own. Rokeach constructed a scale (the Dogmatism scale) to assess dogmatism which he defined as general authoritarianism, rather than authoritarianism of the political left or right. He assessed content of political belief separately. Dogmatism was a characteristic of the personality as such, while the content of the social and political attitudes of the dogmatic person were the result of his social and political circumstances. It is important to distinguish individual personality dynamics from ideological beliefs, and to this extent his contribution is valuable.

Regarding racial prejudice, he put forward the belief congruence hypothesis.[5] According to this, the rejection of outgroups may be explained as the result of the belief that their members hold beliefs different from those of one's own group. The prejudiced person believes that their beliefs are not congruent with his own. Dogmatic (authoritarian) persons are particularly prone to reject members of outgroups because dogmatism entails a high propensity to reject beliefs conflicting with one's own, and with them persons thought to hold such beliefs. The dogmatic individual is also less capable of restructuring his belief system in the light of new information, and hence is less susceptible to attempts to reduce misinformation and prejudice against minority groups. The theory seems to be valid to the extent that prejudice is based upon ignorance and misconception and there is evidence to this effect.[6]

[3] Milton Rokeach, *The Open and Closed Mind* (Basic Books, New York, 1960).
[4] F stands for Fascism; the original intention was to assess the tendency to Fascist ideology.
[5] See also Rokeach, op. cit., *Beliefs, Attitudes and Values* (Jossey Bass, San Francisco, 1968).
[6] See e.g. C. R. Smith et al. 'Race, sex and belief as determinants of friendship acceptance' (*J. Pers. Soc. Psychol.*, 5, 127-137, 1967); D. D. Stein et al. 'Race and belief: an open and shut case' (*J. Pers. Soc. Psychol.*, 1, 281-290, 1965).

The shortcoming of Rokeach's approach with its heavy cognitive emphasis is that it does not relate the beliefs of different groups to the relative social positions of the groups. The crucial beliefs in an intergroup situation are those relating to the appropriate roles and entitlements associated with group membership, and these are not adequately catered for within Rokeach's theory. The research has tended to concentrate on other kinds of belief.[7] *Of course* the white bigot will reject the black man who disagrees with his bigotry (belief incongruence) while accepting those that he knows agree with him that they are inferior (belief congruence) and who behave in an appropriately obsequious manner![8]

In practice the F Scale and Rokeach's D Scale are typically highly correlated and both have been shown to relate to measures of racial prejudice.[9] It remains true, however, that the function of prejudice in serving the psychological needs of insecure personalities amounts to no more than a tendency which seems to be important only in a minority of individuals. Many 'authoritarians' do not show more than a 'normal' degree of prejudice, while many strongly prejudiced people do not have an authoritarian personality structure.[10]

The greater part of social prejudice needs to be explained on other grounds, and there is broad agreement among psychologists that the phenomenon of widespread prejudice against blacks and other minority groups is, from the point of view of the prejudiced individual, largely a matter of conformity to social norms.[11] The shortcoming of much of the psychological

[7] See for instance Stein et al., op. cit., and most of the studies cited in *The Open and Closed Mind* and *Beliefs, Attitudes and Values*.

[8] This is a point which has been noted but not pursued by Rokeach, see *The Open and Closed Mind,* p. 166.

[9] Dennis Howitt, 'Dogmatism and Authoritarianism – Where the Difference Lies' (CMCR, Univ. of Leicester, 1972, mimeo). Rokeach, M. and Fruchter, B. 'A factorial study of dogmatism and related concepts' (*J. Abnorm. [Soc.] Psychol.* 60, 1956). Fruchter, B. et al. 'A factorial study of dogmatism, opinionation, and related scales' (*Psychol. Rep.* 4, 1958). Warr, P. B. et al. 'A note on the factorial nature of the F and D scales' (*Br. J. Psychol.* 1969, Vol. 60).

[10] See for instance the Abrams study in E. J. B. Rose et al. *Colour and Citizenship* (OUP/IRR, London, 1969, p. 565). As many as 20 percent of those scoring very low on authoritarianism were rated as 'prejudiced' or 'prejudiced inclined'.

[11] For discussions of the acquisition of prejudiced attitudes through social learning see G. W. Allport, *The Nature of Prejudice* (Addison Wesley, 1954) and John Harding et al. 'Prejudice and Ethnic Relations' in G. Lindzey and E. Aronson (eds) *Handbook of Social Psychology,* 2nd edn, Vol. 5 (Addison-Wesley, 1969.)

work on the subject for our purposes is that the explanation seldom goes any further.

Since our object is to say something about a particular inter-racial situation and not only to understand human mental processes, we cannot simply accept a norm of prejudice as given. We have to ask how prejudice comes to be the social norm. We also need to ask about the relationship between normative attitudes and the relative social positions of different groups, and what social functions, as well as personality functions, prejudice serves. The answers given to these questions will radically influence any interpretation of the present British situation and the kind of action that might be recommended to reduce prejudice and discrimination. In short, the dynamics of intergroup relations cannot be reduced to the laws of individual psychology.

It should be apparent from what we have said that prejudice cannot be regarded simply as a matter of misinformation or wrong-headedness that might be put right by the provision of appropriate information, education and propaganda. This is because racial prejudice serves the function, among other things, of maintaining whites in an advantageous position relative to blacks. Prejudiced attitudes cannot be changed significantly, independently of the structural relationships to which they relate. An analysis of race relations situations which does not seek to relate individual attitudes and cultural norms to underlying social structures is unable to generate proposals capable of leading to real social change.

We stress this point because much of the work on racial prejudice has been content to treat prejudice as if it were something in the mind, and beliefs and attitudes as though they existed independently of the system of social relations to which they refer. Much of this work also, often under the cloak of 'value-free' objectivity, betrays an acceptance of prevailing norms about race and colour, which results in a begging of the question, and an inability to pinpoint the essential nature of racial prejudice.

An essay on prejudice by Hashmi, for instance, shows a failure to get beyond the purely psychological level of explanation and to relate social attitudes to social structures.[12] The author is therefore able to state, quoting Allport almost verbatim, 'from the point of view of social consequence, much polite prejudice is harmless enough, confined to idle chatter'. He goes on

[12] F. Hashmi, 'The Psychology of Racial Prejudice', Appendix to Derek Humphrey and Gus John – *Because They're Black* (Penguin 1971).

to warn of the danger of allowing prejudice to escalate into race riots. It may be true that the 'idle chatter' type of prejudice is harmless in its immediate effects, and may be undisturbing to the consciences of those who indulge in it. 'Harmless' prejudice does, however, help to perpetuate a social norm of looking down on blacks, and this is not harmless for it serves to sustain an essentially unjust social situation in which blacks may be looked down on because they are down, and they are down because they are looked down on. What is unacceptable about racial injustice is not only that it may lead to violence, but that it is unjust. An unjust social order does not become acceptable simply because it is not attended by violence in the streets.

Banton[13] interprets a finding of Tumin that 30-40 percent of Britons would not like West Indians as neighbours or friends as being the result of 'fear of identification' with coloured people. In other words they recognized the existence of a social norm associating colour with low status and did not wish other people to identify them with coloureds. This may explain the personal motives of Tumin's respondents but does not explain either the existence of the norm, nor its persistence, and in itself provides no basis on which policy to reduce prejudice or discrimination might be planned.

There has been a tendency among authors studying racial prejudice to take prevailing social structures and values for granted and then to analyse *variations* in measured 'prejudice' between individuals and groups, rather than to try to explain the existence and social functions of prejudice itself. Within such a perspective it becomes impossible to question whether racial prejudice might not in some way be encouraged by or even necessary to the existence of particular social orders.[14] Symptomatic of the acceptance of prevailing cultural values is the practice of describing 'unprejudiced' people as 'tolerant'. It is possible to be tolerant of someone with bad breath or other undesirable characteristics. To talk of being 'tolerant' of coloured people is to accept beforehand that there is something undesirable about them.

Another instance of the uncritical acceptance of the prevailing social structure and value system is to be found in sociological

---

[13] Michael Banton, *Race Relations* (Tavistock Publications, London, 1967, p. 390).
[14] A notable exception to this tendency is the work of Oliver Cromwell Cox – *Caste, Class and Race: A Study in Social Dynamics* (Doubleday New York, 1948).

explanations of prejudice in terms of status inconsistency.[15] This approach seeks to explain extreme and deviant social attitudes as the product of inconsistent rankings on various criteria of social status. Thus it might be predicted that a person with high racial or ethnic status (i.e. who is *white*), high education, but low income and occupational status will show a high degree of ethnic prejudice. This is because of the 'inconsistency' in his various status ranks; he is neither high on all of them nor low on all of them. A theory of this type may be able to predict variations in the intensity of prejudice, but becomes tautological as a means of explaining the existence and persistence of prejudice. Why race should continue to be a status criterion is what needs to be explained before any meaningful attempt can be made to eradicate prejudice. To explain prejudice as the result of the fact that race, among other things, is a status sign is to beg the question, because the fact that race is a status sign is the essence of prejudice.

Authoritarian Values and Social Structure

The main merit of the 'status crystallization' approach is that it sees prejudice as related to social structures and value systems, something which many psychological approaches do not take sufficiently into account. To this, the debate surrounding the authoritarian personality is no exception, most of the discussion centring on aetiology, personality mechanisms, psychometric and sampling problems. There is no need, however, to restrict interpretation of the broad findings on authoritarianism to the field of individual psychology.

Empirically authoritarianism is usually assessed by means of a version of the F Scale, and a great deal of attention has been devoted to revising and refining it. It has been described as a 'psychometric nightmare',[16] and there has been puzzlement and frustration over the fact that although on the whole it 'works', the internal consistency of its items is not particularly high and its factorial structure is complex and unstable.[17] Surprisingly little attention, however, has been given to the social origins of the common F Scale items, though their common historical

[15] See e.g. S. Joseph Fauman, 'Status Crystallization and Interracial Attitudes' (*Social Forces*, Sept., 1968, 47, No. 1). For a critique of status inconsistency see Steven Box and Julienne Ford, 'Some Questionable Assumptions in the Theory of Status Inconsistency' (*The Sociological Review*. Vol. 17, No. 2, July, 1969).
[16] R. Christie and Peggy Cook, op. cit., p. 173.
[17] R. Christie and Peggy Cook, op. cit.; Dennis Howitt, op. cit.

origin provides a convincing reason why many of them cohere in a pattern in spite of the apparent lack of logical, statistical or psychological consistency among them. A significant feature of these items is that few of them can be regarded as foreign to the dominant value systems of modern Western societies. Consider the following statements, endorsement of which contributes to an 'authoritarian' score on the F Scale :

> If people would talk less and work more, everybody would be better off.
> The businessman and the manufacturer are much more important to society than the artist and the professor.
> The wild sex life of the old Greeks and Romans was tame compared to some of the goings-on in this country . . .
> What this country needs most, more than laws or political programmes, is a few courageous, tireless, devoted leaders in whom the people can put their faith.
> Nobody ever learned anything really important except through suffering.
> What the youth needs is strict discipline, rugged determination and the will to work and fight for family and country.
> People can be divided into two distinct classes – the weak and the strong.
> No weakness or difficulty can hold us back if we have enough willpower.

These all represent what in a British context may loosely be called 'Victorian' values, stressing as they do discipline, subordination to authority, devotion to work, a Puritan and ascetic attitude to pleasure, and the capacity to succeed through grit and willpower. Though an extreme and rigid adherence to such values may signal an insecure and repressed personality, the values themselves hold considerable sway in our society. They may also be seen as historically necessary concomitants of industrialization in a society with extreme inequalities in the distribution of wealth, that has engaged in recurrent wars requiring the mass mobilization of its civilian population. Many authors, most notably Weber,[18] have drawn attention to the connection between value systems of this kind and the rise of capitalism. Repressed and authoritarian personalities may therefore be seen as a by-product of repressive and authoritarian features of the social system, and its specific values as the

[18] Max Weber, *The Protestant Ethic and the Spirit of Capitalism* (Unwin, 1930). See also R. H. Tawney, *Religion and the Rise of Capitalism* (Penguin, 1972, [first published 1926]).

legitimations of an institutional order that requires the bulk of its population to devote most of its waking life to intrinsically unsatisfying work, the product of which is unequally distributed. The continued existence of our society in its present form would seem to depend on broad respect for, if not passionate adherence to, this kind of value. The force of this argument is not diminished by claims that previous societies or current alternative social systems may be more authoritarian and repressive, militaristic or otherwise unsatisfactory. For our purposes, it is sufficient to note that it would appear to be no accident that those who rigidly and passionately endorse some of the central values and legitimations of early capitalism should also tend to racial bigotry, when the social origins of racism, that is slavery and colonialism, were integral concomitants to the emergence of industrial capitalism.

The possible connection between racial prejudice and the social structures of modern Western societies and their value systems becomes clearer when other findings growing out of the theory of the authoritarian personality are taken into account. The researchers found a clear relationship between authoritarianism and concern with status and success. Frenkel-Brunswick[19] found evidence suggesting that people with a sense of 'marginality' showed more status concern coupled with an authoritarian outlook and ethnocentrism, than those who did not feel 'marginal'. She defined marginality as a discrepancy between status aspired to and actual status, a concept similar to Merton's 'anomie'.

This is something we shall examine in more detail in a later chapter. What is important about this approach is that it allows hostility towards minority groups to be seen as the direct outgrowth of a social system in which the achievement level of large sections of the population must always fall short of the normatively sanctioned aspiration level. A minority group may then come to serve as a scapegoat, a means of 'explaining' the discrepancy between achievement and aspiration, while maintaining intact the value system, with its emphasis on striving for success through hard work, upon which the social system depends. As Rex has said, 'the indication of a scapegoat is a social mechanism whereby resentment may be expressed and the existing power structure maintained. It is the social process par

[19] Else Frenkel-Brunswick, in R. Christie and Marie Jahoda, op. cit.
[20] John Rex – 'The Concept of Race in Sociological Theory' in Zubaida, S. (ed.) *Race and Racialism* (Tavistock, London, 1970, p. 45).

excellence which literally fulfils Parson's description of one of his functional sub-systems as pattern maintenance and tension management.'[20] If hostility against an ethnic minority can also maintain that group in a disadvantaged and low status position, the majority benefit, both by a greater share of resources and through the satisfaction of not being at the bottom of the status ladder.

The above discussion is intended to outline our perspective on racism. This we see not simply as a psychological matter, but also as a cultural phenomenon historically rooted in social relationships, integral to the value systems of modern Western societies, and serving particular interests in existing social structures. This approach to the question has implications for the significance to be attached to research data regarding racial prejudice and discrimination, particularly the findings of attitude surveys. Since this kind of data is central to our own work it is necessary to discuss the concept of attitude and attitude measurement before presenting our results.

Attitudes and Behaviour

Much of the psychological interest in prejudiced attitudes over the past fifty years has been motivated by a concern to understand and to be able to predict prejudiced behaviour, an attitude being thought of as a tendency to behave in particular ways. It was soon apparent, however, that any strong direct relationship between attitudes, as commonly assessed, and behaviour, was difficult to demonstrate. People with strong prejudices do not always behave in a hostile or discriminatory way towards blacks, and relatively unprejudiced people may practise discrimination. It therefore became important to specify the conditions that determine whether or not people will behave in accordance with their prejudices. Linn,[21] for example, in a convincing situational experiment, found that although high scores on a measure of prejudice were fairly good predictors of subsequent behaviour, 'tolerant' scores were not. He interprets this finding as the result of a desire on the part of his 'tolerant' subjects to conform to the norms of important reference groups. Many similar findings both before and since have served to underline the poor predictive validity of typical attitude measures, and to direct attention towards the social context in which behaviour occurs. The situation – including the norms

[21] L. S. Linn, 'Verbal Attitudes and Overt Behaviour: A Study of Racial Discrimination' (*Social Forces*, 43, pp. 353-363, 1965).

of membership and reference groups, the expectations pertaining to different social roles, and the material and social rewards accruing from different types of behaviour – has increasingly come to be seen as a crucial factor in interracial behaviour, and there has been a steady shift of interest from attitudinal to situational determinants of behaviour.[22]

It has become apparent that the goal of accurate behavioural prediction so long pursued by psychologists is unlikely to be attained in any practically useful form, particularly where broad social attitudes such as colour prejudice are concerned. Indeed there is evidence to suggest that people may bring their attitudes into line with the behaviour required by the situation in which they find themselves, rather than vice versa.[23] Fishbein, an eminent theorist and practitioner of attitude research, has concluded that it is not possible to predict behaviour from attitudes unless the behaviour to be predicted can be exactly specified and various other things about the person are all known, including his intentions, his normative beliefs, the way he thinks others expect him to behave and his motivation to comply with their expectations.[24] Fishbein's model would appear to be useful for predicting highly specific behaviours in highly specifiable situations – such as buying a particular brand of soap powder in a supermarket. In the field of race relations, where prejudice is normally assessed as an index of propensity to discriminate, and where the possible range of behaviours and situations covered by the term discrimination are both enormous and difficult to specify, his formulation makes the assessment of prejudiced attitudes seem of little value. The relationship between prejudice and prejudiced behaviour is a crucial one, however, for any study of racial attitudes which makes any pretensions to social relevance. The key question is : what is meant by discrimination, or prejudiced behaviour, that prejudiced attitudes are supposed to predict?

What is Discrimination?

We have pointed out already that racial discrimination in Britain has to be seen as more than a series of hostile or dis-

---

[22] See John Harding et al. 'Prejudice and Ethnic Relations', op. cit., and George E. Simpson and J. Milton Yinger, *Racial and Cultural Minorities* (Harper and Row, 1965).

[23] For a discussion of the attitude-behaviour relationship see M. Fishbein, 'Attitude and the prediction of behaviour' in Kerry Thomas (ed.) *Attitudes and Behaviour* (Penguin, 1971).

[24] M. Fishbein, ibid. and I. Ajzen and M. Fishbein, 'The prediction of behavioural intentions in a choice situation' in Thomas (ed.) op. cit.

criminatory acts by individuals treating blacks less favourably than whites. There is also the institutionalized discrimination embodied in the policies and practices of national and local government and other organizations. These include the progressive limitation of citizenship rights effected by successive Immigration Acts, local authority housing allocation policies, and the practices of estate agents, employment bureaux and other bodies in dealing with coloured clients. In these cases the source of discrimination is to be located in the policies and established practices, and not necessarily in the personnel who administer them. In the typical large organization it is often not possible to attribute the adoption of policies or the establishment of practices to the actions and decisions of particular individuals. Standard practices that discriminate against blacks may emerge by default as much as through deliberate policy. Discrimination embodied in policies then shades into the situation where institutional procedures are discriminatory in practice though there exists no policy to discriminate. There may even be a deliberate effort to benefit coloured people. Such would seem to be the case in some of the instances of wrong placement of West Indian children in special schools for the educationally subnormal through the inappropriate use of intelligence testing, described by Coard.[25] What occurred here is that classification procedures devised when immigrant children did not form an important part of the school population continue to be operated in a changed situation with children to whom they are not appropriate. The discrimination here consists in the failure to recognize the tests as inappropriate and the procedures as discriminatory. (The situation, as Coard describes it, also contains elements of deliberate policy and individual hostility.)

What is important is that the effect of discrimination, considered both as the hostile actions of individuals and as embodied in institutional procedures, whether by deliberate policy or by default, is the creation and maintenance of a system of social relations in which whites typically have more access to the means of power, wealth, and esteem than blacks. The term discrimination, therefore, may be used to refer to this system of social relations as well as to the actions, policies and practices which bring it about.[26]

The danger of thinking about discrimination in oversimplified and individualistic terms is underlined by John Rex in his general

[25] Bernard Coard, op. cit.
[26] George Eaton Simpson and J. Milton Yinger, *Racial and Cultural Minorities*, 3rd edn (Harper and Row, New York, 1965, p. 13).

sociological model for race relations situations. He writes :

> Colour discrimination itself includes a variety of different situations for the coloured group and a wide variety of policies pursued towards the group. As we have seen it might mean denial of admission to the full social, political and legal rights of citizenship in an advanced country; it might mean unfair competition against a coloured group with regard to some facility; it might mean that the group is made a scapegoat; it might mean that it is assigned to a position of rightlessness and economically exploited; and it might mean that the group faces hostility in an inter-communal situation. 'Discrimination', moreover, might turn out to mean that the group is forced either to assimilate or to be segregated; it might be held in an inferior position in the society; it might seek secession and be forcibly denied the right to secede; it might be denied the right to emigrate; it might be forced to emigrate to another country or to a segregated area of the same country; it might be subject to punitive policies and it might be destined for extermination.[27]

Elements of many, though not all, of these kinds of situation and policy are features of the present British situation. Rex and Moore[28] have argued that racial tension in inner city areas and accompanying discriminatory practices may be seen as the result of competition for scarce housing combined with scapegoating of sections of the immigrant community as a means of explaining and excusing bad housing conditions. The importation of immigrants as labour in some of the less attractive and less well-paid jobs, and attempts to confine them to such occupations are also factors in Britain. The desire of many coloureds, particularly West Indians, to assimilate is resisted, by means of discrimination in housing, social clubs and so on. At the same time, coloured groups, particularly Asians, are castigated for wishing to preserve their own culture and *not* wanting to assimilate. There has also been pressure for repatriation of immigrants.

Viewing discrimination as a system of social relations achieved by a variety of means and serving a range of interests and social functions, we may return to the problem of the relationship between prejudice and discrimination. It appears that the

[27] John Rex – *Race Relations in Sociological Theory* (Weidenfeld & Nicolson, London, 1970, p. 130).
[28] John Rex and Robert Moore, *Race, Community and Conflict* (OUP/IRR, 1967).

difficulties of psychologists in predicting discrimination from measures of prejudice arises from the unduly narrow meaning usually given to 'discrimination'. The major psychological studies have conceived of discrimination or 'prejudiced behaviour' as some overt observable act. Thus Linn's subjects were required to sign a photographic release form, La Piere's hotel-keepers were required to accept or refuse a Chinese guest, and other investigators have required people to accept or reject Negro partners in some project.[29]

If this narrow concept of 'behaviour' is replaced by the broader concept of 'social action' as defined by Max Weber, the relationship between prejudice and discrimination is less of a problem. He wrote :

> In 'action' is included all human behaviour when and in so far as the acting individual attaches a subjective meaning to it. Action in this sense may be either overt or purely inward or subjective; it may consist of positive intervention in a situation, or of deliberately refraining from such intervention or passively acquiescing in the situation. Action is social in so far as, by virtue of the subjective meaning attached to it by the acting individual (or individuals), it takes account of the behaviour of others and is thereby oriented in its course.[30]

By this definition discriminatory behaviour or 'action' may, from the point of view of the individual, consist in not doing anything as much as in taking a positive decision to discriminate, or in not interfering in discrimination practised by others. Discrimination might even consist in being unaware that discrimination is taking place, in failing to define a given situation as a discriminatory one. In this case, in Weber's terms, the individual would be acquiescing in a situation (as, for example, the allocation of West Indian children to subnormal schools) to which he attached a subjective meaning of fairness, rightness or normality.

Prejudice, in its essence, is the taken-for-granted assumption about the lesser entitlement or capacity of blacks, which structures the subjective meanings which people attach to their world in a way which leads to racial discrimination. It is the state of mind in which people are not surprised to find blacks

[29] L. S. Linn, op. cit., R. T. La Piere, 'Attitudes vs Actions' (*Social Forces*, 13, 1934) and see e.g. Milton Rokeach, 'Race and Shared Belief as Factors in Social Choice' in *Beliefs, Attitudes and Values*, op. cit.

[30] Max Weber, *The Theory of Social and Economic Organization* (Free Press, New York, 1964, p. 88).

working as bus conductors, labourers, or station porters, but feel there is something improper about black policemen, foremen or managing directors. Prejudice in Britain is the state of mind in which people, while adhering proudly to the British ideals of justice and fair play, can at the same time discuss proposals for the compulsory repatriation of coloured immigrants, and find the rightlessness of Rhodesian and South African blacks acceptable and even desirable. It is probable that this kind of 'latent' prejudice only becomes active hostility when blacks seek to change the social order by aspiring to equality with whites. Defining discrimination as 'social action' in this sense, rather than as 'behaviour' in the narrower sense, the relationship between prejudice and behaviour is no longer problematic. Prejudice in individuals and groups can then be seen as predictive of discrimination at the level of individual action (in supportive situational contexts), at the level of inaction or non-perception, and at the level of the social norms to which individuals may be expected to conform.

The Measurement of Prejudice

It remains to say something about the assessment of prejudice in social science. Prejudice is normally assessed by one of a number of standard psychological methods of attitude measurement. These most commonly consist of a series of statements about the attitude object with which people are asked to indicate their agreement or disagreement. In our own work we have used statements such as 'Everyone in this country should be treated equally regardless of their colour' and 'Coloured immigrants should only be given jobs that the English don't want'. The two most common approaches are those devised by Thurstone[31] and by Likert,[32] which have been shown to be capable of yielding essentially similar results.[33] The social distance scale pioneered by Bogardus[34] is a variant of the Thurstone approach. In social distance scales people are asked to indicate the acceptability to them of outgroup members in

---

[31] L. L. Thurstone and E. J. Chave, *The Measurement of Attitude* (Univ. Chicago Press, 1929).

[32] R. Likert, 'A technique for the measurement of attitudes' (*Arch. Psychol.*, 1932, No. 140); G. Murphy and R. Likert, *Public Opinion and the Individual* (Harper, New York, 1937).

[33] Edwards, A. L. and Kenney, Katherine C. 'A comparison of the Thurstone and Likert techniques of attitude scale construction' (*J. Appl. Psychology*, 1946, 30, pp. 72-83).

[34] E. S. Bogardus, 'Measuring Social Distances' (*Journal of Appl. Sociology*, 1925, pp. 299-308), reprinted in Thomas (ed.) op. cit.

a graded range of relationships such as 'I would admit him to citizenship of my country', 'I would work together with him', and 'I would admit him to near kinship by marriage'. The procedures employed in making attitude measures are the same in essentials as those used in the construction of intelligence tests.[35]

The advantage of the standard psychological methodology is that it enables the user to know whether it is meaningful to talk of *an attitude* to coloured people, for instance, or whether it is necessary to consider, say, two or three independent attitudes. The methodology also has the advantage of providing information on the reliability and likely level of accuracy of the scores he obtained. For these reasons scales that are properly constructed according to psychometric principles are to be preferred to the *ad hoc* questions that have been so common in British work on colour prejudice. The difference between using a properly standardized measure and more intuitive approaches may be compared to the difference between gauging the temperature of water with a properly calibrated thermometer and by hand. If you are concerned to test the baby's bath water, an elbow will do; if you are conducting a scientific experiment, exact temperature may be crucial. In a similar way a community worker in a racially mixed area may be able to gauge the interracial temperature in his area from his day to day experience. A researcher coming in briefly from outside, and whose purposes are different from the community worker's, is much less likely to be able to do this reliably, and even if he could, his work could not be acceptably replicated by other research workers. Our research methods, described in the next chapter, included a standardized measure of attitude to coloured people. It is necessary to say something, in the light of the foregoing discussion, about what a scale of this kind measures.

In 1935, G. W. Allport defined an attitude as 'a mental and neutral state of readiness, organized through experience, exerting a directive or dynamic influence upon the individual's response to all objects and situations with which it is related.'[36] Allport's definition is often taken as the starting point of discussions of attitude. The definition stresses the idea of attitude as tending to influence behaviour.

[35] For an account of attitude measurement techniques see A. L. Edwards, *Techniques of Attitude Scale Construction* (Appleton-Century-Crofts, New York, 1957).

[36] G. W. Allport, 'Attitudes in the History of Social Psychology' in G. Lindzey (ed.) *Handbook of Social Psychology* (Addison-Wesley, 1954, Vol. 1), excerpt reprinted in Marie Jahoda and Neil Warren (eds) *Attitudes* (Penguin, 1966, pp. 15-21).

Attitudes have frequently been treated as having three components – cognitive, affective and conative (action tendency). Different definitions of the concept have reflected the theoretical preferences and operational requirements of their proponents. Some definitions have stressed the affective element of attitude. Thurstone, whose work was an early milestone in the methodology of attitude assessment, defined attitude as 'the degree of positive or negative affect associated with some psychological object',[37] an emphasis that is echoed in many subsequent definitions. Sarnoff,[38] for instance, defined attitude as 'a disposition to react favourably or unfavourably to a class of objects'. Some approaches have emphasized behaviour and behavioural intention, as in social distance scales.[39] Others have stressed the cognitive component. According to Rokeach, for instance, 'an attitude is an organization of several beliefs focused on a specific object . . . or situation, predisposing one to respond in some preferential manner.'[40] This definition derives from the cognitive emphasis of Rokeach's theory in which the 'belief' is taken as the basic element of cognitive structure. It also has convenient operational implications for people relying heavily on questionnaire methodology. The study of 'stereotyping' of one group by another may also be counted among the research traditions having a primarily cognitive emphasis.[41]

Although there are differences in the way that different workers have conceptualized attitude, research has shown that the scores derived from the various types of attitude measure commonly in use represent a predominantly affective component. In other words, the standard attitude scale, though it may sample significant beliefs on the one hand, and though its items may tap explicit behavioural intentions on the other, is first and foremost measuring an affective/evaluative dimension of attitude. This has been convincingly demonstrated by Fishbein,[42] who showed that a measure of attitude towards Negroes yielded

[37] L. L. Thurstone, Comment (*Amer. J. Sociol.*, 52, 1946, pp. 39-50).
[38] J. Sarnoff, excerpt from *Personality Dynamics and Development*, (Wiley, 1962) in Marie Jahoda and Neil Warren (eds) op. cit., p. 279.
[39] e.g. E. S. Bogardus, op. cit.
[40] Rokeach, M. 'A theory of organization and change within value-attitude systems', (*J. Soc. Issues*, XXIV, 1, 1968).
[41] See e.g. Henri Tajfel, 'Stereotypes' (*Race*, Vol. V, 2, 1963) and Nelson R. Cauthen et al., 'Stereotypes: A Review of the Literature 1926-1968' (*The Journal of Social Psychology*, 1971, 84).
[42] M. Fishbein, A consideration of beliefs, attitudes, and their relationships, in I. D. Steiner and M. Fishbein, *Current Studies in Social Psychology* (Holt, New York, 1965, 107-120).

results essentially the same as those obtained by asking people to place the concept 'Negro' along a good-bad dimension. Similar results have been reported by others.[43] The advantages of the standard type of attitude scale over simple ratings of liking or favourable evaluation include the probable greater reliability, invisibility and public acceptability of scales as opposed to simply asking people 'Do you like or dislike coloured people?'. There is also the fact that the content of scale items yields additional cognitive information not obtainable by simple ratings. Thus the definitions of Thurstone or of Sarnoff remain the best simple statement of what an attitude scale measures: 'the degree of positive or negative affect associated with some psychological object' or 'a disposition to react favourably or unfavourably to a class of objects'. Attitude as commonly measured is a uni-dimensional affective characteristic.

One implication of this is that what is measured by an attitude scale is something much narrower than 'attitude' as employed in ordinary discourse or, as conceptualized by many attitude theorists. This fact must be borne in mind when we refer to attitudes to coloured people as assessed by our own attitude scale in later chapters.

How then does 'attitude to coloured people' as measured by such a scale fit into our earlier discussion of the nature of British colour prejudice? We pointed out that the essence of prejudice was the belief or assumption, conscious or unconscious, that coloured people have less entitlement to resources than whites, that they are somehow less important, worthwhile or desirable than whites. Prejudice is the psychological correlate of a culturally normative system of social allocation of roles and rewards based ascriptively on colour, or on ethnicity where colour is taken as a typically valid indicator of ethnicity. In a particular individual, racial prejudice may be a latent and marginal aspect of his view of the world, or it may manifest itself in a desire to avoid coloured people, or even spill over into active hostility toward them. Prejudice in the sense in which we have defined it is not confined to an attitude of overt hostility or dislike, and it need not preclude goodwill towards coloured people either individually or as a group.

It is the hostility or dislike 'the degree of positive or negative affect', that may arise out of prejudice that is measured by the typical 'prejudice' scale, and not the existence of prejudice

[43] See, e.g. Charles E. Osgood, George J. Suci and Percy H. Tannenbaum, *The Measurement of Meaning* (University of Illinois Press, Urbana, 1957, Chapter 5).

itself. We may take a 'high' score on such a measure as indicating hostility or dislike, and a lower score as indicating relatively less negative affect. A low score, however, does not necessarily indicate an absence of prejudice, for it may represent, for instance, a feeling of patronizing goodwill towards an inferior race. A score on a prejudice scale is therefore no more than an index of a generalized evaluative tendency. Being evaluative it is indicative of the saliency of particular social *values*. The attitude scores which we shall report later are not identical with prejudice or racism. Racism is endemic. A score on an attitude scale indicates the saliency of racist values as opposed to other kinds of values in an individual's perspective on the world. It tells us how far he reacts to his world in terms of racist assumptions rather than other assumptions. In a particular individual, a hostile or derogatory attitude towards coloured people may be rooted in an authoritarian personality, it may be largely a matter of passive or active conformity to social norms, it may be related to the particular experience the person has had with coloured people, or it may reflect his perceived interests; and it is empirically difficult to disentangle the different contributions that these factors may be making to a score on an attitude scale. We shall be more concerned to explain why different circumstances should give rise to different levels of hostility or dislike, why latent racism should be activated in some circumstances rather than others, and to assess the effect of this hostility on the ways in which people understand their world.

Stereotypes

Another important tradition in the study of prejudice is research into stereotyping. This is an essentially cognitive approach to intergroup attitudes though, in line with attitude studies in general, the evaluative implications of group stereotypes have not been ignored, as the definitions of Allport and Duijker and Frijda show.

ALLPORT :
A stereotype is not identical with a category; it is rather a fixed idea that accompanies the category. For example, the category 'Negro' can be held in mind simply as a neutral, factual, non-evaluative concept, pertaining merely to a racial stock. Stereotype enters when, and if, the initial category is freighted with 'pictures' and judgements of the Negro as musical, lazy, superstitious, or what not.

A stereotype, then, is not a category, but often exists as a fixed mark upon the category. If I say, 'All lawyers are crooked,' I am expressing a stereotyped generalization about a category. The stereotype is not in itself the core of the concept. It operates, however, in such a way as to prevent differentiated thinking about the concept.[44]

DUIJKER AND FRIJDA:
A stereotype we shall define as a relatively stable opinion of a generalizing and evaluative nature. A stereotype refers to a category of people (a national population, a race, a professional group, etc.) and suggests that they are all alike in a certain respect. It is therefore an undifferentiated judgement. Furthermore, it contains, implicitly or explicitly, an evaluation.[45]

Stereotyping arises out of a fundamental characteristic of normal thinking, namely, categorization. By developing categories, people are able to impose a structure and meaning upon events and objects.

Categories allow us to introduce order and simplicity into a reality which is infinitely varied and highly unpredictable, and aid the interpretation of experience. They enable us to draw upon past experience to assist us in current activity. In using a finite number of categories to interpret an almost infinite variation in objects and situations, we *must* simplify the world. To quote Allport again: 'Open-mindedness is considered to be a virtue. But strictly speaking it cannot occur. A new experience must be redacted into old categories. We cannot handle each event freshly in its own right. If we did so, of what use would past experience be? Bertrand Russell, the philosopher, has summed up the matter in a phrase, "a mind perpetually open will be a mind perpetually vacant".'[46]

Categorization involves the identification and labelling of different objects, situations and experiences, and in so doing focuses attention on some characteristics of objects rather than others. What is focused on are the specific defining characteristics of the category. It we define a liquid as a medicine, for instance, our attention becomes focused on its curative properties rather than on its taste, appearance or texture. If, on the other hand, it is called a beverage, then its health-giving characteristics

---

[44] G. W. Allport, op. cit., p. 187.
[45] H. C. J. Duijker and N. H. Fridja, *National Character and National Stereotypes* (North-Holland Publishing Co., Amsterdam, 1960, p. 115).
[46] G. W. Allport, op. cit., p. 19.

become largely irrelevant (as with beer or coffee), while its taste, appearance and texture assume major importance.

The mere process of labelling something structures our perceptions of it – makes them *biased*, if you like. More than this, however, labelling tends to result in an exaggeration of the similarity of objects within the same category, and of the differences between objects in different categories. This exaggeration is not random but occurs only for those characteristics put into focus by the labelling process. Thus people tend to exaggerate the extent to which beverages are palatable, and to exaggerate the difference in palatability between beverages as a class and medicines as a class. This of course is a distortion, for many medicines, in fact, taste better than many beverages.

These processes of exaggerating differences between categories and similarities within categories have been neatly demonstrated in an experiment by Tajfel and Wilkes.[47] They asked three groups of subjects to estimate the length of eight lines. For the first group the four shorter lines were labelled A, and the longer ones B. For the second group the lines were labelled A or B, but randomly. For the third they were unlabelled. Even though they were not asked to categorize the lines, but to estimate their length, and even though the order of presentation was randomized so as to obscure the relation between labels and length, subjects in the first group did respond to the task on the basis of the potential categories A and B. Compared with the other two groups they exaggerated both the differences in length between lines marked A and lines marked B, and the similarity between lines within each category. In other words they *stereotyped* the lines on the basis of the latent system of categorization contained in the labelling. As Tajfel has said elsewhere,[48] 'stereotyping can, therefore, be considered as an inescapable adjunct to the human activity of categorizing.'

If stereotyping occurs so readily with such simple and neutral judgements as the length of lines, it is not surprising to find that it is a major factor in the complex and value-laden area of the perception of social groups and situations. When the objects of perception are more complex, more complex stereotypes tend to be invoked. In the case of ethnic stereotyping whole clusters of characteristics tend to become associated with the ethnic label, but the same process occurs as in the case of the lines.

[47] H. Tajfel and A. L. Wilkes, 'Classification and Quantitative Judgement' (*Brit. J. Psychol.*, 1963, 54, pp. 101-114).
[48] H. Tajfel, 'Stereotypes', *Race*, 1963, Vol. 2.

Secord, Bevan and Katz[49] showed that when shown photographs of Negroes, subjects attributed dirtiness, dishonesty and laziness to those they perceived as Negro but not to those they misperceived as white. Tajfel, Sheikh and Gardner[50] established the stereotypes commonly associated with Indians and Canadians. They then had students rate four people, two Indians and two Canadians, on the basis of their performance in interviews. The Indians he found were rated more similarly on those characteristics – being spiritualistic, for instance – that were part of the stereotype of Indians than they were on traits that were not part of the stereotype. The Canadians were seen as being most alike on those traits that were in the prevailing stereotype of Canadians.

Various studies have also shown that children assimilate national and ethnic stereotypes – particularly their evaluative aspects – at a surprisingly early age. By the age of seven, for instance, British children have absorbed a negative evaluation of Russia, even before they have acquired such factual information as the relative size of Russia and Britain. Similarly, children become aware of the negative connotations of dark skin and form stereotypes on this basis by the age of five or six, and this is the emotional base upon which fuller and more elaborate stereotypes are subsequently erected.[51]

[49] P. F. Secord, W. Bevan and B. Katz, 'The Negro Stereotype and Perceptual Accentuation' (*J. Abnorm. Soc. Psychol.*, 1956, 53, pp. 78-83).
[50] H. Tajfel, A. A. Sheikh and R. C. Gardner, 'Content of Stereotypes and the Inference of Similarity Between Members of Stereotyped Groups' (*Acta Psychologica*, 22, 1964, pp. 191-201).
[51] H. Tajfel and G. Jahoda, 'Development in Children of Concepts and Attitudes About Their Own and Other Nations: A Cross-National Study' (*Proceedings of XVIII International Congress of Psychology, Moscow, 1966, Symposium 36*, pp. 17-31).
H. Tajfel and G. Jahoda, 'The Development in Children of Ideas About Their Own and Other Countries' (*The New Era*, Vol. 48, No. 5, 1967). See also: Margaret R. Middleton, H. Tajfel and N. B. Johnson, 'Cognitive and Affective Aspects of Children's National Attitudes' (*The Brit. J. of Soc. Clin. Psychol.*, Vol. 9, part 2, June, 1970) and N. B. Johnson, Margaret R. Middleton and H. Tajfel, 'The Relationship Betweeen Children's Preferences for and Knowledge About Other Nations' (*The Brit. J. of Soc. Clin. Psychol.*, Vol, 9, part 3, Sept., 1970). Mary Ellen Goodman, *Race Awareness in Young Children* (Collier Books, New York, 1966).
Geoffrey Brown and Susan P. Johnson, 'The Attribution of Behavioural Connotation to Shaded and White Figures by Caucasian Children' (*The Brit. J. of Soc. Clin. Psychol.*, Vol. 10, part 4, December, 1971).
Susan S. Thomson, *The Development of Ethnic Concepts in Children*, Department of Psychology, University of Strathclyde, Glasgow. In part fulfilment of M.Sc. degree.

Our normal process of thinking then tends to make us see all members of a group to whom the same label is applied as more alike than they really are; that is it inhibits differentiated thinking about them. This is the feature of stereotyping that is stressed in the definitions of both Allport, and Duijker and Frijda quoted above. The ideas that make up the stereotype become so firmly identified with the category that to use the category inevitably invokes the stereotype. To this extent, no judgements can be unbiased, and all perception is selective perception. As we have said before, our perceptions are structured by the categories we use to make sense of the world. This is a psychological point about the nature of cognitive functioning in general. It has direct implications for the media treatment and public perceptions of ethnic minorities. The process of stereotyping also has a parallel that we shall develop later, in the way that mass communications are shaped by the defining attributes associated with such categories as 'news', 'good television' and so on, in media organizations.

Because there is a natural tendency to think in stereotypes there is a danger, where race relations are concerned, that people will see what should be there (according to the stereotype) rather than what is; that they will make people and events fit into existing categories rather than make categories fit the people and events.

4

The Design of the Study

We set out with the objective of assessing the contribution of the mass media to people's conceptions of the racial situation in Britain. Finding out what people's beliefs and attitudes are is not particularly difficult; discovering how they acquired them is more problematic. The very ubiquity of many notions relating to race, colour and immigration make it difficult to isolate the specific contribution of the media since the media for a large part simply reiterate beliefs that are already common currency.

Sources of Knowledge

Analytically, there are two kinds of source that are relevant for present purposes, from which people might derive their ideas. Firstly, there are *situational sources*. In this case something is known or believed because of the first-hand experience of the individual himself, or of others known to the individual, or at the very least because in the circles where he moves it is 'common knowledge' grounded in individual experiences and diffused through person-to-person contact. In the second case there are *media sources* through which people may come to know or believe things because of the accounts and images relayed by the mass media. The individual himself need not have learned it directly from the media but at second or third hand. What is 'known' or 'believed' need not be identical with what actually happened or was 'experienced' or with what was carried by the media. It is sufficient that either the media or first-hand experience should in the first place have *given rise* to whatever is known or believed. We may then speak of two ideal types of knowledge (or of *cultures* where this knowledge is 'common knowledge' within a group), *situationally based* knowledge and *media relayed* knowledge.

The empirical work described in this section was aimed at exploring the characteristics of these two types of culture in order to see (a) whether the mass media appeared to be making a contribution of any importance to prevailing conceptions of coloured people and race in Britain, and (b) whether the mass media appeared to be making a *distinctive* contribution, or merely to be reiterating or reinforcing ideas that were otherwise current. A *distinctive* contribution could include the changing of attitudes, the spreading of information, images, or beliefs not available elsewhere, or the providing of perspectives in terms of which the situation is understood and interpreted.

Situationally based and media relayed kinds of knowledge are of course ideal types, limiting cases, useful analytically, but they are not easy to distinguish from each other in the real world, even if it could be argued that they actually exist in pure form. One reason for this is the inevitable interaction between the kinds of knowledge that might otherwise be thought to be purely situational or purely media relayed. Such interaction includes the following. Beliefs and common knowledge that were situational in origin tend to be picked up and reiterated or reinterpreted by the mass media. Local situations and events come to be experienced and interpreted in terms of images, concepts and perspectives derived from the mass media. In a similar way media relayed images may be interpreted and reacted to in terms of situationally generated understandings and perspectives.

The best that can be done empirically is to seek circumstances that approximate to the ideal types and to study these. The closer this approximation, the more convincing are the results of the investigation likely to be. By studying white beliefs and attitudes regarding race in populations containing a relatively high proportion of coloured people, we sought to identify the important features of situationally generated cultures. At the same time by studying situations in which there was little opportunity for first-hand experience of coloured people or race relations we aimed to discover the main characteristics of media-relayed knowledge. This sampling strategy was supplemented by asking people to tell us where they thought they had derived their ideas from, with some built-in checks on the validity of their answers. This also helped to take account of some of the interactions between situationally derived and media derived ideas.

Media Definitions

We see the media as capable of providing frames of reference or perspectives within which people become able to make sense of events and of their own experience. The media's role as 'interpreters' of the world may be thought of as analagous to

61

the role of the experienced drug user, described by Becker[1] and by Young,[2] in interpreting drug experience to the novice. For the uninitiated a first dose of marijuana may produce no noticeable effect or may simply make him feel ill. Becker describes how the novice comes to *learn* how he should feel, what sensations to attend to, which to value, and which to ignore, through the advice and comments of more experienced friends. Young describes this process as one of 'teasing out' from all the possible sensations and subjective meanings of drug-induced states those regarded as *relevant* within the culture of the group. Experiences and meanings surrounding the same drug may thus vary from culture to culture.

In an analagous way, people have to *learn* how to interpret and evaluate various aspects of their society. They have to learn what categories to apply to phenomena, what is important about them, and so on. The media provide one among many possible sources from which they may learn. The news media may be thought of as 'teasing out' from the plethora of available facts and daily events some elements for special attention, while treating others as of minor importance and ignoring some completely. In so doing they give meaning to what they portray and at the same time provide the concepts and imagery through which related events and phenomena may be understood. The meanings that events and situations are given are likely to be consistent with the cultural values with which the media are most closely identified.

Sampling

The main focus of the study was on the beliefs and attitudes of adolescents. There were a number of reasons for this. In the first place they are an important group because the attitudes developed by today's young people will have an influence on the race relations of the future. Secondly, young people still at school are a particularly suitable group for estimating media effects, because being young their experience is limited, and being still at school it is relatively standardized. There is therefore reason to expect the effects of media to be more readily evident among youngsters than in adults in whom they are much more likely to be overlaid by a wealth of varied experience. However, it proved possible to interview an adult sample as well – the

[1] Howard S. Becker, 'Becoming a Marijuana User' (*Amer. J. Sociol.*, LIX, 235-245, 1953). Reprinted in J. G. Manis and B. N. Meltzer, *Symbolic Interaction* (Allyn & Bacon, Boston, 1967).
[2] Jock Young, *The Drugtakers* (McGibbon & Kee, 1971).

parents of some of the youngsters – and this provided a means of checking some of our conclusions and of assessing the influence of parents on the youngsters' attitudes. The adults sample was also used for testing the hypothesis of a relationship between a media-induced sense of relative deprivation and hostility to coloured people.

Our initial intention was to identify a group of people who could be expected *a priori* to have learnt something about immigration and coloured people in Britain at first hand, and another group who because of their situation would be largely dependent on the mass media either at first or second hand for their information on the subject. In seeking the former type of group there are two kinds of first-hand experience or 'contact' that needed to be taken into account. There is equal-status contact in which whites may come to know coloured people on a personal basis, and there is the kind of 'contact' through which whites may come to know *about* coloured people without necessarily getting to know any coloureds personally. Situations of the latter type range from interacting with coloured people in formal roles – as bus conductors or nurses for instance – to simply seeing them about the streets without having any interaction at all. At the outset of the study we felt intuitively that it was important not to neglect the latter kind of 'contact' which occurs wherever there is a relatively high proportion of coloured people living in an area and which contributes to the 'atmosphere' surrounding race that may be sensed among whites in 'immigrant' areas but which is largely absent in places like Scotland or the north-east of England. This 'atmosphere' shows itself in a greater awareness of racial matters, a wider prevalence of racial jokes, and a consciousness generally of a coloured 'presence' in the area. It exists even among whites who seldom or never interact with any coloured people at all.

We therefore took as the major basis of our sampling the proportion of coloured people living in an area as a whole. We took part of the sample from areas where the overall level of coloured immigration was high, and part from areas where it was low. These are referred to as the High and Low areas respectively. The High area sample was taken from Warley 9.5 percent), West Bromwich (5.2 percent) and Dewsbury (5.4 percent) (figures in brackets are 1969 percentages of immigrant children in secondary schools).[3] These boroughs not only have higher than average proportions of their populations coloured

[3] These are *not* the same as the proportion of coloured people in the local population, being probably about three times as large as that, but

63

but are located in the West Midlands and West Yorkshire conurbations which are the highest areas of immigrant settlement
outside London.[4] Low area boroughs, by contrast, had lower
than average coloured populations and were drawn from conurbations or areas which, considered as a whole, had low
levels of coloured immigrant settlement. The Low sample was
drawn from Glasgow (under 2 percent), Teesside (under 2 percent), Sheffield (2.1 percent) and Southampton (2.1 percent).[5]

The difference between High and Low areas was essentially
a matter of whether the area as a whole was an 'immigrant'
area or not, and hence the degree of opportunity it provided for
first hand experience of coloured people and race relations.

It was, however, important to be able to discover whether
any differences in attitude and belief between kinds of area were
related simply to the fact of differing levels of immigrant
settlement or to differences in the degree to which members of
the two samples had been able to 'get to know' coloured people
at a personal level. The sampling was therefore designed to
equalize as far as possible between areas the opportunities for
personal contact of an equal status kind. This was achieved in
the following way.

Secondary schools were chosen in pairs from each borough so
that one contained an appreciable number of coloured pupils
(this ranged from 10.4 percent to 41.6 percent) and the other
few or none (0 percent to 3.8 percent). Apart from this the
schools were selected so as to be as similar as possible to each
other in all other respects; a secondary modern school was
always paired with a secondary modern school, and a comprehensive with a comprehensive. There were no grammar
schools in the sample because in those boroughs that still had
grammar schools there were none with an appreciable number
of coloured pupils. We thus had a pattern of High and Low
schools within the High and Low areas. While the difference
between High and Low areas was a difference in the level of
coloured population in the area as a whole, the difference
between High and Low schools was a difference in opportunity
for personal contact with coloured school peers. It also happened
to coincide with local concentrations of coloured people in the

---

are probably the most reliable available figures for the sake of making
comparisons between boroughs.
Source: *Facts Paper on the United Kingdom 1970-71* (IRR, London,
1970).
[4] Ibid.
[5] See footnote 3.

immediate neighbourhood. This sampling design allowed us to treat the factors of personal contact with coloured peers at school and the scale of coloured settlement in an area as separate factors in the analysis. Comparisons between areas should show up the effect of living in an 'immigrant' area on beliefs and attitudes, with the effects of personal contact with coloured people held constant. Comparisons between schools, on the other hand, should show up the effect of personal contact – with the area factor held constant.

There were four schools in High areas with a high proportion of coloured pupils (Hihis), four in High areas with few coloured pupils (Hilos), four Lohis, and four Lolos. Twenty-six children were randomly selected from class lists in each school, thirteen of them in the 11/12 age group and thirteen from the 14/15 age group, and evenly divided as far as possible between boys and girls. This gave a total altogether of 104 children in Hihi situations, 103 in Hilo situations (one child was 'lost' from the sample), 104 Lohis and 104 Lolos. (This terminology [Hilo etc.] will be used from time to time for the sake of convenience. The first syllable, with a capital, always refers to the level of coloured settlement in the *area,* and the second to the school.) These 415 children are referred to collectively as the *Main Sample.*

There are two departures from the intentions of the original sampling design that need to be mentioned. The pattern of co-educational and single-sex schools in one of the High area boroughs resulted in over-sampling of boys in High areas and schools, and differences in educational systems meant that in the two Glasgow schools and the two Southampton schools the younger age group in the sample was aged 12/13 rather than 11/12. This was partially compensated for, for purposes of area comparisons, by subsequently including six 12/13 year olds instead of 11/12 year olds in the sample from a Hilo school. It is not thought that these deviations from the intended pattern make any substantial difference to the conclusions we shall want to draw from the data, but they should be kept in mind.

One further comment on the selection of the main sample seems necessary. This concerns the use of small numbers of children from many schools rather than larger numbers from fewer schools. This was done partly to avoid promoting discussion among the children and thereby affecting the beliefs and attitudes that we had set out to study. By interviewing only 26 children in any school (and only 13 in any one year group) we were able to complete our work in a school within two days with the very minimum of interruption of the normal school routine. We were also anxious that our results should reflect the characteristics of 'immigrant areas' or non-immigrant areas *in general,* rather than those of one particular area, neighbourhood or school. There was also the practical consideration of how far it was possible or desirable to prevail on the time, patience and goodwill of head teachers and school staffs who might already be working under difficult conditions.

The pattern of the main sample that we have described meant that we had to choose Low areas in which, although the proportion of coloured people was below average, there was as least one secondary school with an appreciable number of coloured pupils. This meant that even the Low areas were areas in which there were at least some coloured people, and these areas were not as 'Low' as they might have been. All sections of the main sample, except possibly the Lolo group, had the opportunity of some first hand experience of coloured people of one kind or another. For the sake of testing inferences derived from the main sample about the relative contributions of mass media and local experience on beliefs and attitudes about coloured people, we therefore drew a further sample called the No sample. This consisted of 148 11/12 and 14/15 year old boys and girls from two schools, one in County Durham and the other in South Yorkshire. The coloured populations of these places were virtually nil and what contact the children there had had with coloured people had occurred almost entirely on visits to large towns or holiday resorts. The members of this sample were almost completely dependent on the mass media for their information, and their beliefs and attitudes on race in Britain probably come as close as it is possible to get to a 'pure' media-relayed culture. The distribution of the children's sample by age, sex and area is shown in Table 4.1.

It also proved possible to interview 317 of the parents of the children in the main sample (154 fathers and 163 mothers). Only one parent of any one child was interviewed, and choice of father or mother was random and unrelated to the sex of the child. This we refer to as the parents' or adult sample. The age distribution of the parents is shown in Table 4.2 and class distribution of both parents and children are shown in Tables 4.3 and 4.4. The figures in Table 4.4 must be regarded as less reliable as those in Table 4.3 because they are based on the children's descriptions of their parents' occupations and these were often very vague. Both tables make it clear, however, that the samples were predominantly working class. Whether the results we report would have been any different had they contained a higher proportion of middle class subjects we do not know.

The Interview Schedule and Questionnaire

The interviewing of the children was carried out by the two authors, subjects being randomly allocated to each. The interviewing of the parents was carried out by Social and Community Planning Research, using trained and experienced interviewers whose briefing for the assignment was supervised by one of the authors.

In the previous chapter we argued that the measurement of attitudes, a standard approach in much work in the race relations field, typically gets at the evaluative element in white people's conceptions of coloured people, for the typical attitude measure distils out the affective and evaluative. This is an important feature of one group's consciousness of another group and it is arguably the most valuable single piece of information that the researcher into race relations might seek. In our view, however, the measurement of attitudes on their own is not sufficient, particularly in a study concerned with mass media. It is important to take account also of the broader understandings, the definitions of the situation, within which and about which attitudes are held. This is one reason why we found it necessary to make some assessment of major beliefs about coloured people and the situation in general beyond the strictly evaluative, and why we made use of a relatively large number of open-ended questions in the interviews. We took care to avoid as far as possible the danger which is present in all survey research, of 'putting ideas into people's heads', or words into their mouths, and so we started with the most open-ended and unstructured questions and became more focused and directional in our questioning as the interview proceeded. We were especially careful to ensure that the subjects did not know beforehand that the interview was to be about race or about the mass media.

The full text of the children's interview schedule with explanatory notes is given in Appendix 1. The main open-ended question is Question 5 : 'Can you tell me what you know about coloured people living in Britain today?' The next three questions were also open-ended but more directional – Question 6 : 'Do you think there are any problems connected with coloured people living in this country?'; Question 7 : 'How does the fact that coloured people have been coming to live in Britain affect you now?' and Question 8 : 'How do you think that the presence

67

of coloured people in this country might affect your life in the future?'

Subjects could say as much as they liked in answer to these questions and were encouraged to do so. After they had answered each question, the interviewer went back over each statement they had made and asked 'How do you know about that?', 'Where did you find out about that?' or a similar question, and recorded the answers given. Once again, the subject could give as many sources of his belief or opinion as he liked. Great care was taken not to prompt or suggest sources, especially media sources, to the subject. The object of these source probes was to see whether different kinds of belief or opinion were differentially associated in our subjects' minds with different kinds of source. Specifically we wanted to see whether any particular kind of statement was typically associated with mass media sources. Other questions regarding coloured people and race are evident from the questionnaire and will be explained as necessary when the results are reported.

In addition, during the interview the attitude scale (Q. 29) was administered (see also Appendix IV), and each child's rating of his own attitude, that of his school peers, his parents and 'most people who live near you' were obtained on the rating scale (Q. 11). Information was also gathered on credibility of news and television drama material (Questions 30 and 40-42), news consumption (Questions 31-39), and contact with coloured people (Questions 15-21). The data on news consumption and contact with coloured people were used to derive the index of news consumption, and the contact indices, respectively, which are described in Appendix IV.

The children also completed the written questionnaire shown in Appendix II. The most important information obtained from this was an estimate of the number of hours spent watching television each week (Item 7) and an index of documentary viewing and documentary liking. The latter measures were obtained by scoring the responses to the four documentary programmes in Item 6 of the written questionnaire and summing them. The programmes were 'Panorama', 'World in Action', 'Tuesday Documentary' and 'This Week'. Frequency of viewing responses were scored from 0 to 3, and amount of liking from 0 to 4, with higher scores for more viewing and greater liking respectively. The Television Preference Scale (Item 9) and the Children's Dogmatism Scale (Item 10) are explained in Appendix IV, along with the attitude scale.

The Parents' Questionnaire

The parents' questionnaire which is shown as Appendix III
was the same in essentials as that given to the children with some
appropriate modification of items, and the addition of items to
measure localism (Qs 1, 2, 3 and 5), relative deprivation (Q 48),
media-induced relative deprivation (Qs 37 and 38).

MEDIA EXPOSURE
AND INTERRACIAL CONTACT

Television and Leisure Activities

The first question on the written questionnaire was designed to
show the relative importance of different media activities in each
child's leisure life. Children were asked to rank ten leisure
activities in order of preference. For the children's sample as a
whole, listening to records, playing sport, being with friends,
and watching television, in that order, were the ones most
frequently allocated to the first three ranks. These four remained
the top favourites, with minor variations in their order, for
boys, girls, and first years, considered separately; for fourth
years, television was pushed into fifth place by youth clubs or
similar activities. In general, sport was most important for boys
and first years, and records for girls and fourth years. Television
was relatively more important for first year boys than for the
rest, and less important for fourth year girls, though still ranked
among their favourite activities. There were no important
differences in this pattern of preferences in different areas or
types of school.

Our data agrees with the findings of Elizabeth Eyre-Brook[6] in
placing the three peer-oriented activities, records, sport and
friends in the first three places. Television came only seventh
in her data, however, but fourth in ours. This is almost certainly
because about half of her sample was middle class while ours
were predominantly working class; hers was also older and contained a large rural contingent. It would appear that television
occupies a relatively more important place in the lives of
younger, urban, or working class adolescents, than of those who
are older, rural or middle class. A class and age difference is also

[6] Elizabeth Eyre-Brook et al., *Television and Young People* (Inter-
nationales Zentralinstitut für das Jugend- und Bildungsfernsehen,
Munich, 1972).

69

reflected in the greater importance of books for her group which ranked them sixth out of ten,[7] while for ours they came eighth. These results should therefore not be generalized to the youth of Britain as a whole without due caution.

The finding that television viewing is among the best liked leisure activities of our sample is important because television proved to be one of their main sources of news and current affairs information. However, the main attraction of television for most of the young people was its entertainment rather than its informational content.

The significance of television in these children's lives is shown by their answers to the next two questions on the written questionnaire. Firstly, they were asked to say which of the same ten activities they would feel most like doing if they were 'in a good mood'. Here once again sport, records, and friends were the most frequently chosen, but television dropped to seventh place. The pattern was similar for boys, girls, first years and fourth years. They were then asked to choose which activity they would feel most like doing if they were 'feeling unhappy'. In response to this television rose to first place, followed by records and books. This suggests that television viewing, though occupying a considerable portion of young people's leisure time, is not so much something that is sought after as a source of active enjoyment – like sport, records and friends – but rather something that is turned to when there is nothing more interesting or enjoyable to do, as a way of passing the time or as a distraction from boredom or anxiety. This interpretation is supported by our finding in pilot work that asking the children to choose an activity from the same list that they would feel like doing when 'bored', 'angry' or 'in a bad mood' yielded very similar results to those obtained for 'feeling unhappy'.

Media Exposure – Children

The mean media figures for the different sections of the adolescent sample are shown in the top part of Table 4.5. The distributions of these measures were tested by chi-square for difference by area, school, age, sex, ability and class. The results of these tests are summarized in the lower part of the table.

The difficulties of assessing accurately the amount of time spent viewing television are notorious and our figure of 26.3 hours per week should be regarded as a rough estimate only. This is, however, very similar to one of the estimates made by Halloran

[7] Personal communication.

et al. on similar groups of young people.[8] It is clear from the table that only a relatively small proportion of the time spent watching television was devoted to viewing news and document- ary programmes. Nevertheless, the average member of our sample saw at least one main news broadcast per day (news summaries were not counted) and probably one documentary programme per fortnight (though actual documentary program- mes viewed are difficult to estimate from our figures which are indices intended for comparative purposes only). The average member of the sample also claimed at least to look at about one newspaper per day.

All in all, weekly exposure to news and documentary material was not inconsiderable, and was probably equivalent in hours to an afternoon's lessons on a normal school day. The lower part of Table 4.5 shows that on the whole boys consumed more news material than girls and older and more able children more than younger and less bright children. These differences were statistically significant and needed to be taken into account when relating news consumption to other variables, but the differences were not very big.

Media Exposure – Adults

Mass media exposure figures for the parents' sample were as follows: mean television viewing hours – 18.0 per week; tele- vision news broadcasts – 4.9 per week; documentary viewing index – 4.0; newspapers seen per week – 11.5; main radio news broadcasts – 0.24 per day. Total television viewing hours and the number of television news broadcasts seen would appear to be lower among the parents than among the children but the parents' and children's data were collected by different means and are therefore not strictly comparable. The figures for documentary viewing and newspaper reading were, however, derived from similar data and show that the parents viewed slightly more documentary material than their children and read over a third more newspapers.

Orientations to News

The attitudes towards news and current affairs media material typical of the adolescents were apparent from their answers to a number of questions. The four documentary programmes that they were asked to rate for frequency of viewing and for liking

[8] J. D. Halloran, R. L. Brown and D. Chaney, *Television and Delin- quency*, (Leicester University Press, 1970).

were embedded in a longer list of programmes. The best-liked and most-viewed programme among fourth years was 'Top of the Pops' which achieved a viewing index of 2.30 and a liking index of 3.38, while their best-liked and most viewed documentary was 'World in Action' which achieved a viewing index of only 1.46 and a liking index of 1.98. Overall, for all children, the mean viewing and liking indices of the non-documentary programmes on the list were 2.03 and 2.99 respectively, while for the four documentary programmes they were only 0.96 and 1.49. Quite clearly documentary programmes had a very subsidiary place in the viewing behaviour of these youngsters.

In Question 39 of the interview the adolescents were asked to say how much attention they devoted to the news pages when looking at a newspaper as opposed to things like sport, the women's page, jokes, and material relating to entertainments. The results showed that for most of our sample newspapers were read mainly for things other than news as such. 36 percent of the whole sample claimed to spend hardly any of the time reading news when looking at a newspaper, while only 15 percent said they spent most of the time on news rather than other things. News attention increased with age and ability, but did not vary by sex, class or kind of school. We did find higher news attention in our Low area as opposed to the High, but the No area did not differ significantly from the High and Low combined. Even in the higher ability group and in the fourth year, however, the proportion attending mainly to news was not high. The typical pattern of newspaper reading appeared to be that the paper was consulted for the sake of the sport (particularly by boys), the cartoons, fashions, or to see what was on television, and that in the course of this headlines were scanned and anything that looked interesting read. We do not have similar data for attention to television news but it seemed clear from the interviews that very many children were exposed to television news simply because the set happened to be on when the news was broadcast, rather than because they deliberately sought it out. This relatively low news orientation of the sample as a whole is important because it suggests that much of the information derived from the news media was picked up incidentally by most children rather than as a result of a deliberate effort to keep themselves informed.

On the other hand, with newspapers, children's attention to the news pages rather than other content was higher for those children who read more papers. This means that the most news-oriented of the newspaper readers were to be found among those that read most newspapers. There was also a strong correlation (.805) between documentary viewing and documentary liking, but no correlation between documentary viewing and total hours of television viewed (.015), showing that attention to documentaries also was not wholly a matter of incidental exposure, but that some children actively sought them out and liked them. (These correlations stood up within age and sex groupings, showing that they were not merely artifacts of age and sex differences.) Liking for one documentary in our list also tended to go with liking for the others (mean correlation .404) and viewing of one with viewing of the others (mean correlation .316). And there was a statistically significant trend for documentary viewing and liking to increase with consumption of television news, and a significant correlation of .237 between television news viewing and newspaper reading. Newspaper readership was, however, unrelated to documentary viewing and liking. Although for the *typical* member of our adolescent sample news consumption seemed to have a largely incidental character and to be very subsidiary to other media behaviour, there did seem to be a subgroup that was more news-oriented in the sense of actively seeking after news, and these are most likely to be found among those scoring high on the news consumption index. Applying chi-square tests to the News Consumption Index, boys were found to consume more news than girls and older children than younger ones. There were no significant differences by class, ability, area, or kind of school.

The parents showed much more interest in the news itself as opposed to the other content of newspapers than we found for the children. There was also a significant tendency among the parents for exposure to television documentaries to go together with exposure to television news and newspaper reading though this was not as strong as among the children.

The newspapers read among our samples were predominantly the mass circulation 'popular' papers and local evening papers. 46 percent of the parents said they read the *Daily Mirror* (or the *Daily Record* in Scotland), 20 percent the *Sun*, and 15 percent the *Daily Express*, while less than 1 percent claimed to read either the *Daily Telegraph, The Times* or the *Guardian*. Among Sunday newspapers, the *News of the World* (45 percent), the *People* (39 percent) and the *Sunday Mirror* (32 percent) were well ahead of the other papers. 73 percent of adults also claimed to read a local evening paper. The figures for children were very similar.

The children's news credibility scores derived from Question 40 of the interview did not vary by age, sex, class or ability and were unrelated to the drama credibility score from Question 30. The drama credibility score was also unrelated to other variables. News credibility among the adults (Questions 42-44), however, was related to their drama credibility score (Question 36) – correlations between .12 and .24 with the news credibility items. The most interesting finding on media credibility was the difference between newspapers and television. The response distribution for these is shown below.

NEWS CAN BE BELIEVED :	CHILDREN PARENTS NEWSPAPERS		CHILDREN PARENTS TELEVISION	
Always	35	20	201	111
Nearly always	223	134	249	136
Quite often	172	69	84	42
Sometimes	121	80	27	20
No answer	12	14	2	8

The figures show that while there was considerable scepticism about newspapers, television was almost universally regarded as a trustworthy source of information. The distribution of responses for radio news was very similar to that for newspapers among the children, but intermediate between newspapers and television for the parents.

Information Sources – Children

On many of the open-ended questions subjects were asked for the source of each item of information or opinion that they gave, in order to see whether different kinds of belief would be attributed to different kinds of source. The number of children's references to different sources for Question 5, the main open-ended question, are shown in Table 4.6 broken down by school and area. From the total figures it may be seen that 'personal experience' was the most frequently given source; after that mass media references were important, with non-specific references to television as the most common media category, followed by TV news and newspapers. From the nature of the non-specific television references it was apparent that respondents usually had news programmes in mind. Television documentaries were referred to but were not a major source. This is not surprising considering their relatively low exposure to documentary material. Radio and other media were referred to only nine times, reflecting our finding that radio was not an important news source. By comparison with personal experience and media sources, other people were referred to relatively infrequently.

It can be seen from the table that attributing information to 'personal experience' declined dramatically from High to Low to No situations, while media attributions showed a systematic increase. This is in line with the expectations upon which the sampling plan was based, that use of media as a source of information about race and coloured people would increase as the number of coloured people in the environment declined, reaching its maximum in No situations where the media would perforce become the major source of information. The differences between High and Low areas and High and Low schools were statistically significant for television documentaries and personal experience. In addition 'adults' and 'own opinion' were significantly more often referred to in Low schools than in High schools. Comparing the No area with the rest the differences between non-specific television references, television news, peers, and personal experience were all significant. By summing references to media sources the media reference 'scores' shown in the bottom line of Table 4.6 were obtained. Here the trends are the same as before, with the No area differing significantly from all other situations, and the difference between High and Low areas approaching significance. Patterns of media references for the other main open-ended questions were similar to those shown for Question 5.

Information Sources – Adults
Table 4.7 shows the pattern of source references given by the parents in answer to the same question. In comparison with the children they referred much more often to 'personal experience' as the source of their information and much less often to the mass media. Frequency of reference to personal experience did not differ significantly between areas, but television and newspapers were significantly more often given in Low areas, and the Low area sample also had a significantly higher media reference score than the Highs. The intentions of the sampling plan, regarding differential use of media sources in different areas were fulfilled in the case of the parents as well.

Validity of Source References
The conclusion that we wish to draw is that the mass media were a course of some of the beliefs and ideas expressed by our samples in answer to the open-ended questions, and that their

75

importance as information sources increased from High to Low to No situations. A possible objection to this is that the patterns of source reference that we have shown are no more than artifactual in the sense that subjects were simply giving sources that seemed plausible for their situation. 'Personal experience' is certainly a plausible source in High situations and the mass media are plausible sources anywhere. It is therefore useful to be able to show that reference to mass media as sources was related to actual media exposure, and that personal experience references were related to actual contact with coloured people.

Table 4.8 shows mean media reference scores for children with different levels of exposure to the main types of media material. The trends are all as expected in the case of news and documentary material and are statistically significant in the case of documentaries, television news and total news consumption, those with higher media exposure tending to refer more to media. That for newspapers did not reach significance. When tested within sex groupings, the pattern for total news consumption remained significant for both boys and girls considered separately; for the other measures the trends remained but did not reach significance mainly because of the small number of cases in many cells. We regard these results as providing good grounds for accepting that children's references to media sources were not just plausible answers but had validity in the sense of being related to news media exposure. Similar patterns were found in the parents' data though the tendencies were not as strong as for the children. Those who read more than the average number of newspapers per week, for instance, had a mean media reference score of 0.41, while those who read fewer papers had a score of 0.22. None of these relationships in the parents' data achieved statistical significance but they were none-the less indicative that parents' references to media sources also had some validity.

Table 4.9 and 4.10 show how children's references to personal experience as a source of information varied with different levels of personal contact with coloured people. The gross contact index and the friendship contact index described in Appendix IV were used in drawing up these tables. The data is given for the No area, and the Low and High schools separately, because both references to personal experience, and the contact indices were higher in High schools than Low schools, and lower in the No area than the rest of the sample. In all cases the trends are as might be expected if references to personal experience were in fact related to actual contact with coloured people. The trend for gross contact was significant in the No area and Low schools, but it failed to reach significance in the High schools mainly, it would appear, because the overall level of contact there was so high that the index did not differentiate adequately within the sample. Differences by friendship contact were only significant in the No area.

In Table 4.11 comparable data is shown for the parents, based on the answers to Questions 15, 21(a) and 22, in which they were asked about the residential proximity of coloured people to them in the area where they lived, about how many coloured people they had spoken to recently, and whether there were any coloured people that they would call their friends. In all cases, the more contact the adults had with coloured people the more often they gave personal experience as a source of their information or ideas about coloured people. All these trends were statistically significant. For both children and parents, then, we have good evidence of the validity of their references to personal experience as the source of information.

Differences in Contact between Areas and Schools

It remains to show how well the intentions of our method of sampling were fulfilled in respect of contact with coloured people. By taking half the children's sample from schools with a high percentage of coloured pupils and half from schools with few coloured pupils in areas of high immigration, and repeating this pattern in areas of low immigration, it was intended that those in High and Low *areas* would have a similar amount of *personal* contact with coloured people and that the difference between High and Low areas would represent only a difference in the level of coloured immigrant settlement. The difference between High and Low schools, on the other hand, was intended to entail a real difference in amount of personal contact with coloured people with the area factor held constant. The No area sample was intended to have very little contact of any kind with coloured people. In the case of the parents, to whom the school factor as such did not apply, it was hoped that, because the choice of high schools had tended to coincide with local neighbourhood concentrations of coloured people, personal contact with coloured people would also be equalized between High and Low areas, and the area factor would have the same significance as for the children.

With children we assessed contact by means of two sets of questions : Questions 15 to 20, in which they were asked how many coloured people of various kinds they knew 'to talk to' and from which the Gross Contact Index described in Appendix IV was derived, and Question 21, about friendship, from which the Friendship Contact Index was derived.

These contact measures were tested for differences between age, sex, class and ability groupings. Older children claimed more contact with adults and had a higher overall contact index than younger children. This would seem to result from the greater range of movement and experience than older adolescents have. There was also significantly less contact with coloured adults among the children of white-collar workers than among blue-collar workers' children, presumably reflecting better housing conditions in the higher socioeconomic grades, for coloured immigrants tend to be concentrated in the least desirable housing. None of the 'friendship' questions nor the Friendship Index varied by age, sex, class or ability. In Questions 19 and 20 (b) children were asked where they met coloured friends who did not go to the same school, and who the adults they had spoken to were. Their answers indicated that most of such contacts were relatively casual. In both High and Low areas non-school peer contacts tended to be casual – 'I sometimes see her when I'm out shopping', – or occurred in informal play situations – 'at the park . . . or recreation ground'. 43 percent of these contacts were of this kind. Contacts with adults were also mainly casual – 'he stopped me and asked me the way' – or relatively impersonal – 'bus conductors' – and included a number of people who lived nearby but were seldom well-known to the respondent. Such responses accounted for 62 percent of all contacts with adults reported. The parents of friends were more often mentioned in High schools in Low areas (19 percent of responses) but otherwise there was little difference in kinds of contact either by area or school.

The distribution of responses to the 'gross contact' questions by area and school and the significance of differences are shown in Table 4.12. The intentions of the sampling plan in respect of the No areas are completely borne out by the data. There was significantly less contact in the No areas than in the rest of the sample on all measures. The expectation that there would be more contact in High schools than Low schools was borne out in the case of school peers at school, school peers seen out of school and for the Gross Contact Index, but not in the case of non-school peers and coloured adults. There were no significant differences in contact between High and Low areas, except in the case of school peers. An examination of the table shows that this significant difference results less from a difference in aggregate amount of contact in the two areas than from a difference in the *spread* of responses. More of those in Low areas reported no contact with coloured children at school, and more of them also reported knowing 'more than ten' coloured school-fellows. It seems safe to conclude that if there was more personal contact with coloured school-fellows in High areas than Low – related perhaps to the actual greater number of coloured children in the High area schools that is shown in the top line of the table – the difference was not very great, and nothing like as large as the differences between High and Low schools.

Frequency distributions for answers to the 'friendship' questions and for the Friendship Contact Index are shown in Table 4.13. It can be seen that all the expectations underlying the sampling were borne out; the No areas differed markedly from the rest on all measures, the High schools differed from the Low, but there were no differences between High and Low areas.

Taking all the data together, we can see that the objectives of our method of sampling were substantially achieved. There may have been slightly greater contact with coloured school-fellows among our High area children than in the Low areas, but if so this was very small and even in this respect the two samples were approximately equated. The area difference represented mainly a difference between living in an immigrant area or not, and not to any important extent a difference in personal contact. The difference between High and Low schools, on the other hand, did represent a big difference in amount of contact with coloured people. On all measures there was also far less contact of any kind in the No areas than in the rest of the sample.

Comparable results for the parents are shown in Table 4.14 where the data from Questions 18(b), 21(a), 15(a) and 22 are compared by area. In these questions they were asked whether they came into contact with coloured people at work, how many coloured people they had spoken to recently, about the residential proximity of coloured people living nearby, and whether they had coloured friends. There were no significant differences between areas and our intentions were completely fulfilled for the adults.

5

Attitudes and the Mass Media

The researcher who is interested in the way people experience and understand their world is dependent on what they are able or prepared to tell him, and he can never be sure how good a reflection this is of what they actually have 'in their heads'. The best he can do is try to reduce as far as possible the sources and margins of error in his data. Furthermore, he should never mistake his data for the reality of people's consciousness; it is at best some kind of index of this reality. The better his data the more reliance that can be placed on his results, and if he finds a number of consistent results all pointing in the same direction he can be more confident in stating what he has found and in offering interpretations of his findings. It is with this in mind that we present our survey results. No single result is conclusive, but cumulatively they give a very clear picture of the attitudes and conceptions of our samples and of the contribution of the mass media to their understanding of race in Britain.

Differentiation

Throughout the interview we used the phrase 'coloured people' rather than specific ethnic names because this is a generally understandable term, while pilot work had shown that many people did not distinguish clearly between different coloured groups.

It is as well to report at the outset the data bearing on the adequacy of this terminology and on the meaning the phrase had for our subjects. As a check on the extent to which children distinguished between different coloured groups we counted the number of spontaneous mentions of specific ethnic names in their answers to the four main open-ended questions (Nos 5, 6, 7 and 8). We found 21 in the High areas, 7 in the Low, and 4 in the No areas; 18 in High schools, and 10 in Low schools. But even these children readily accepted the phrase 'coloured people' as meaningful and talked quite happily about 'them'. The degree of spontaneous differentiation was therefore low.

As a further check (Q. 12) children were asked whether they had any particular group in mind when they talked about coloured people, or whether they were just thinking about coloured people generally. A majority answered that they were thinking about coloured people in general – 66 percent in the High areas, 73 percent in the Low, and 90 percent in the No; and 64 percent in High schools and 75 percent in the Low schools. 13 percent mentioned Pakistanis, 11 percent Indians, and 3 percent West Indians – with some children, particularly in high areas and schools, mentioning two or three groups. Even when the children were asked whether they differentiated among different groups of coloured people, the degree of differentiation was not high. Distinctions were most often made in the high areas and schools, and then it was Asians that were primarily thought of as being 'coloured people'. This concentration on Asians rather than West Indians may be in part a reflection of the fact that local coloured populations were predominantly Asian, and Asian children accounted for nearly three-quarters of the coloured children in the schools we visited.

This relative lack of differentiation and the singling out of Asians when distinctions were made, emerged in a slightly different form when children were asked whether they would prefer any one coloured group over the others as neighbours (Q. 13) The most common response was that there was no reason to prefer one over the others – 42 percent in the High area, 70 percent in the Low, and 84 percent in the No; and 46 percent in High schools and 67 percent in Low schools. When a preference was expressed, West Indians were almost always the group preferred, an Asian group being preferred in only 5 percent of all cases. The most common reason given for preferring West Indians was that they were 'better' than Asians. Other reasons given were that they were 'cleaner', easy to get on with, or were culturally similar to the British.

This tends to confirm the idea that when distinctions are made it is Asians that come mainly to mind when coloured people are mentioned, particularly perhaps when hostility or aversion is expressed.

A further indication of how the situation was understood came from the responses to Question 4 in which children were asked to give some of the countries from which immigrants to Britain had come. This was asked before colour had been mentioned by the interviewer, though it might have been spontaneously introduced in the child's own answer to the first question. Immigration was defined for the child as 'people coming to live here from other countries'. The most frequently mentioned countries were India (mentioned by 66 percent of all children) and Pakistan (55 percent). The West Indies were mentioned by only 30 percent of respondents and had the fourth highest frequency. Again, we note that there was more awareness of Asians than of West Indians. The ability to name these three groups increased from No through Low to High situations. The third most common source given, however, (except in High areas and schools, where it was fourth), were African countries, mentioned by 36 percent of all children, more than twice as many as mentioned European countries (including Ireland) which together were only referred to by 16 percent of children. This illustrates how immigration has come to be defined as mainly a matter of *coloured* immigration. Some of the mentions of African countries were specific references to the East African Asians, and it is probable that the publicity over the Kenya Asians had helped to inflate the importance of African immigration in the minds of our sample. Very often, however, the answers were just general references to 'Africa' and their frequency seemed to be partly due to the fact that Africa was known to be inhabited by blacks and immigration was known to relate to colour. This interpretation is supported by the fact that references to Africa *increased* from High (25 percent) to Low (38 percent) to No (49 percent) areas – whereas the trend for the major coloured immigrant groups was in the opposite direction.

Attitudes

We may now examine the attitudes among our samples towards coloured people as assessed by the H scale described in Appendix IV. H scores did not vary by sex in either adults or children, nor by ability in children, but our older adolescents had scores about two points lower than the younger ones (that is the older ones showed less hostility) and the parents scored about two points higher than the adolescents as a group. Scores did not vary significantly by class; but it should be remembered that our samples were mainly working class. These are shown in Table 5.1. Tables 5.2 and 5.3 show mean scores by area, and in the case of children, by type of school. Significantly higher scores were obtained in High areas than in Low for both parents and children, and No area children scored significantly lower than the rest. Those in High schools also scored higher than those in Low schools. The general pattern, then, is the more coloured people in the environment, the more hostility.

As we showed earlier the difference between High and Low *areas* represents a difference in the size of the coloured population in the area. There is little if any difference between areas in opportunity for personal contact and actual claimed contact with coloured people, for which the two samples are roughly equated. The difference between High and Low schools, on the other hand, does represent a big difference in opportunity for contact and actual personal contact, with the area factor held constant. From Table 5.2 it is apparent that hostility to coloured people is more closely related to the area factor than to the school factor, the area difference (3.10) being larger than the school difference (1.83). It would seem that hostility to coloured people is more closely related to living in an 'immigrant area' than to the number of coloured people present in the immediate environment, and actual contact with them.

This finding is consistent with the existence of area-wide norms of hostility to coloured people in immigrant areas. It must be remembered that in immigrant areas there is more inter-racial contact of all kinds among the population at large. 'High areas' as such are areas of higher contact. We drew our samples in such a way as artificially to equate the amount of *personal* contact between our High and Low area samples, however. The difference of 3.10 points on the H scale cannot therefore be explained as the result of differences in amount of personal experience in our samples but must be taken to reflect the influence of area norms. The difference of 1.83 points between High and Low schools could be taken as indicating the contribution of direct personal experience with coloured people on attitudes, though it more probably represents a local neighbour-hood norm arising in the immediate locality of concentrations of coloured immigrants, in the same way as area-wide norms appear to arise in areas where the overall level of immigrant settlement is high. Either way, the area factor is clearly more important than the school factor.

As we have shown elsewhere,[1] however, in situations where there is opportunity for contact – that is among the High area sample, and in High schools – those who claim to have coloured friends show significantly *less* hostility than those without coloured friends. This relationship is even more apparent in the case of the parents, those with coloured friends also being less hostile. These data are shown in Tables 5.4 and 5.5. There is also a trend, significant within High and Low types of school, for children with less hostile attitudes to report more contact of other kinds, as measured by our gross contact index. These

[1] Paul Hartmann and Charles Husband, 'A British scale for measuring white attitudes to coloured people' (*Race*, XIV, 2, pp. 195-204, 1972).

findings seem to run counter to the finding that the bigger the local coloured population (as indexed by the area factor), and the greater the opportunity for contact and concomitant actual contact (as indexed by the school factor) the *more* hostile attitudes.

Overall, it would seem, the more coloured people in the environment the *more* hostility towards them. Within situations where there are coloured people around, however, contact – either on a friendship or other basis – goes with *less* hostility. This latter finding on its own would be consistent with the interpretation that having coloured people around and the opportunity to get to know them or to get to know about them at first hand results in less hostile attitudes. But this conflicts with our earlier finding that the greater experience of coloured people among the population at large in immigrant areas gives rise to a norm of greater hostility.

What are we to conclude? Does greater contact make for more hostility or less? It might be suggested that area (and perhaps neighbourhood) norms are disproportionately influenced by the reactions of the more racist members of communities where coloured people settle – hence the most hostile norms in 'coloured' areas – but that in spite of this, given the opportunity to get to know coloured people or to learn about them at first hand, children's attitudes become less hostile. If this were the case we would expect children in 'High' schools to have less hostile attitudes than children in 'Low' schools, for there is much more friendship and contact of other kinds in High schools than in Low schools. But this is not what we find; children in High schools are significantly *more* hostile than children in Low schools in spite of their greater contact. It may be that friendship and other contact make for less hostility but if this is so the effect is obviously fairly small and is outweighed by the effect of local norms. A more convincing explanation would seem to be that in a given situation it is those who are less hostile who make friends and have more contact in general with coloured people, while the more hostile avoid such contacts. There is more friendship and other contact in 'High' situations simply because there are more coloured people available to make friends with. Either way, we are left with the fact that social norms – particularly area norms – are a major influence on attitudes and that any greater 'tolerance' that may be engendered by getting to know coloured people at first hand is heavily overshadowed by the influence of hostile norms in immigrant areas. It is worth noting from Tables 5.4 and 5.5 that even those who claim to have coloured friends in High areas show more hostility than those with coloured friends in Low areas.

To summarize, the most important thing to emerge from these data on attitudes is the suggestion that there are strong area norms which have a marked influence on individual attitudes even among those who would normally be described as accepting of coloured people or 'tolerant'. It also appears that the influence of normatively more hostile attitudes in immigrant areas is independent of whether an individual is personally involved in situations of contact with coloured people or not. The norm of greater hostility affects alike the attitudes of those with minimal involvement with coloured people on a personal basis (for instance the Hilo children) and those with friendly personal relations with particular coloured individuals such as those with coloured friends in High areas. Other workers have also shown the importance of area norms though in different situations.[2]

Further indications of the importance of local norms in influencing people's attitudes may be seen in Table 5.6. This shows the correlations among the children's H score and their ratings of the attitudes of their parents, school peers, neighbours, and themselves on the rating scale (Q. 11). All correlations are positive and show a consistency between the child's H scores and the attitudes he attributes to others. Not only does he see his own attitudes as being similar to those of other people – particularly his parents and peers who must be regarded as being important to him – but he perceives the generality of other people as being similar among themselves in their attitudes. This pattern also is consistent with the existence of a social norm, to which the children's attitudes tend to correspond. This apparent conformity to membership and reference group norms would seem to be an accurate reflection of the situation, but it probably does not account entirely for the results obtained. For it would seem that a degree of selective perception was operating, with the child's own attitudes influencing the way he saw his social situation and causing him to perceive others' attitudes as being more like his own than they really were. This is shown by the fact that the correlation between children's attitude and parents' attitude, as assessed independently by the H scale, was only .174 – much lower than the figures of .4 to .5 between a child's H score or self-rating and perceived attitudes of parents shown in the table. A similar selective perception probably also

[2] See for instance the results and discussion of T. Kawwa, 'A study of ethnic attitudes of some British secondary school pupils' (*Brit. J. Soc. Clin. Psychol.*, 7, 3, pp. 161-168, 1968), and G. W. Allport, op. cit.

accounts in part for the children's perceptions of the attitudes of their peers and neighbours.

Authoritarianism

The contribution of an authoritarian outlook, as opposed to conformity to group norms, in the genesis of hostile attitudes may be gauged from the correlation of .13 that we found for the children, and .15 for the adults, between H scores and our measures of authoritarianism. It is necessary to have some reservations about both the concept of the authoritarian personality and our measure of it where the children are concerned. (See Appendix IV.) In the case of the adults, however, ours is probably a fairly good short measure of authoritarianism. The correlations are in both cases low and show that though there is a relationship, not much hostility can be explained as resulting from an authoritarian personality structure alone. We need to invoke additional explanations to account for the hostility we found.

The data, suggestive of the importance of group norms, that we have already presented is persuasive. Even the correlation of .174 between children's and parents' H scores, that might be taken as an index of the contribution of parental norms on children's attitudes is higher than the .13 between their attitudes and the authoritarian measure.

Our data does enable us to estimate in correlational terms the influence of area norms as such on attitudes. By dichotomizing H score distributions and tabulating frequencies of getting high or low H scores in High and Low areas we may calculate phi coefficients as an index of the importance of the area factor in determining hostility. This gives a phi of .20 for the children, and .19 for the parents, both higher than the obtained correlations between hostility and authoritariansm. Phi coefficients, however, typically give lower figures than product moment coefficients calculated for the same data; so we are not comparing like with like. Edwards[3] provides a method of estimating the equivalent product moment coefficient from the phi coefficient. This gives figures very close to what would be obtained by calculating tetrachoric r. (Doing this involves making the assumption that the High/Low area dichotomy may be treated as a continuum.) The correlations between area and hostility estimated in this way were .31 for the children and .30 for the parents, well above the authoritarianism/hostility correlations

[3] A. L. Edwards, *Statistical Analysis* (Rinehart, New York, p. 120, 1954).

that we found. From this, and the data previously reported, we feel justified in concluding that area norms are far more important determinants of attitude to coloured people than authoritarianism.[4]

The Influence of Attitudes on Perceptions of the Situation

Another feature of the children's perceptions of others' attitudes is that on the whole they see others as having somewhat more hostile attitudes than themselves. Whereas the mean self-rating (Q. 11) was 5.89, the mean for mothers was 6.77, for fathers 7.48, peers 7.45, and neighbours 8.23. A similar finding was reported by Abrams. This suggests that self-reported attitudes were being influenced by the ideological norm of 'tolerance' and disapproval of prejudice as well as by a norm of hostility. There is some tendency for the attribution of 'worse' attitudes to others to become more pronounced as the 'others' become socially more distant.

There are further consistencies between attitude as measured by the H scale and other perceptions of the situation. There is a small but significant tendency for higher H scores among the children to go with perception of a higher proportion of coloured people in the population (Q. 10). Among the parents this same tendency was very marked; the 76 who thought that coloured people make up half a percent of the general population had a mean score of 22.00, while the 14 who said the population was 20 percent coloured had a mean of 29.43.

Attitudes were also found to be related to the kind of answers given by the children to the main open-ended questions. Since both H scores and some of the responses to these questions varied between areas and kinds of school and with age, some of these relationships had to be tested within appropriate subgroups of the sample. Where a relationship was only significant within a subgrouping this is indicated in brackets in what follows. Where a relationship was significant for the combined sample and testing within subgroups was not necessary, no qualification is given.

In reply to Question 5; 'Can you tell me what you know about coloured people living in Britain today?' there was a greater tendency for the less hostile children to mention the prejudice and discrimination suffered by coloured people (in No areas and Low schools but not within the High schools), to make

---

[4] Even when the correlations between the various measures are corrected for attenuation the pattern of relationships that we have reported remains the same.

equalitarian statements (in the Low areas only), and to make anti-stereotype statements like 'some are good, some are bad', (within the main sample as a whole, but not in the No areas). For all the children combined the attribution of unfavourable characteristics to coloured people was more frequent among the more hostile, but this relationship did not stand up within the appropriate subgroups of the sample. The mention of unfavourable characteristics by the children does not therefore seem to be mainly a function of attitude independently of area, though this result must be seen as at least partly due to the relatively small number of subjects for whom this relationship could be tested.

On Question 6; 'Do you think there are any problems connected with coloured people living in this country?', the more hostile children more frequently mentioned the large size of the immigrant population and associated coloured people with riots and trouble. The less hostile children more often mentioned discrimination and prejudice against coloureds (No areas only), and referred to the disadvantaged position of coloured people (High areas only). The more hostile more often said that they exacerbated the housing shortage (High areas only). These relationships in High areas between H scores and references to the disadvantaged position of coloured people and their effect on the housing shortage did not show up as significant in the combined sample.

Finally, in answer to Question 8; 'How do you think that the presence of coloured people in this country might affect your life in the future?' the more hostile respondents more frequently saw coloureds as potential competitors for jobs. (This was significant for older children only, presumably reflecting the greater saliency of employment prospects for them.) It might be noted that even for the non-significant relationships discussed in this and the previous two paragraphs the trends were all in a consistent direction; many of the relationships tested failed to reach statistical significance largely because numbers were small.

The answers to these open-ended questions are discussed in the following chapter. What is important for the present is that perceptions of the interracial situation in Britain reflected in the answers to these questions are related to attitudes to coloured people as measured by the H scale, and that to some extent the influence of attitudes is independent of the area factor which we have seen is itself an important influence on attitudes. (At the same time we should not lose sight of the fact, which we discuss in the following chapter, that many important and widely held beliefs about the situation were *not* found to be related to attitudes.)

Similar relationships between parents' answers to the open-ended questions and their H scores were found, but the influence of attitudes on their perceptions of the situation was less than in the case of the children.

The pattern of the data that we have reported so far shows firstly that individual attitudes tend to be influenced by social pressures towards hostility against coloured people characteristic of immigrant areas, and secondly that there is a degree of correspondence between attitudes and the way the interracial situation in Britain is perceived.

Attitudes in Detail

If we examine responses to the H scale in terms of item content we may gain a better idea of what our subjects' attitudes to coloured people entailed. Table 5.7 lists the H scale items and the proportions of subjects giving a hostile response (that is one getting a score of 3 or 4) to each. For the children the table shows fairly broad acceptance of the norm of equal rights (Item 1), little support for the idea of coloured intellectual inferiority (Item 3), and rather more guarded defence of the idea of equal access to council housing (Item 7). On the other hand there was widespread acceptance of the idea that coloureds may not make good neighbours (Item 2), opposition to coloureds being placed in positions of authority over whites (Item 6), and belief that coloured immigrants are somehow bad for the country (Item 8). In all cases the amount of hostility expressed was greatest in the High areas; but even in the No areas at least 40 percent of the children gave hostile replies on the latter three items.

In comparison with the main sample children, the parents were less accepting of the ideal of equal rights (Item 1), more disposed to regard coloured people as intellectually inferior (Item 3), and more opposed to coloured immigration (Item 10). They were also more sensitive on the questions of having coloured neighbours (Item 2) and council housing (Item 7). On the other hand they were less inclined to accept the stereotype of coloured people as trouble-makers (Item 4), and less opposed, though still substantially so, to coloured people being in positions of authority over whites (Item 6). There is no item on which less than 20 percent of adults were hostile.

One of the more revealing of these items is Number 6, 'Coloured people should not be put in positions of authority over white people'. Half of all the children and 39 percent of the parents agreed with this, and here the true extent of British colour prejudice becomes evident. This item comes closest to expressing what we earlier described as the essence of colour prejudice, the idea that the black should always be subordinate to the white. Even many of those who uphold the British ideal of equal rights baulk at the suggestion of a coloured man being placed above a white man. People are by and large prepared to agree with the idea of equality when it is expressed in abstract ideological terms (though even the 12 percent of children and 20 percent of adults disagreeing with this ideal in Item 1 is not inconsiderable), but when this is couched in terms of authority relationships it appears that the idea of black-white equality becomes difficult for many white Britons to accept.

The idea that blacks are somehow bad for the country (Item 8), endorsed by 48 percent of all children and 50 percent of adults is also worthy of note. This is an aspect of the situation that we shall find reflected elsewhere in the data. It is accepted by many otherwise 'tolerant' people who accept the norm of equal rights, defend the rights of entry and access to housing and employment and are in general opposed to discrimination.

Hostility and Prejudice

We have shown that individual hostility to coloured people as measured by the H scale is influenced by group norms, and that these are more closely related to the level of immigration into an area as a whole than by very localized neighbourhood concentrations of coloured people. Thus, by way of an example, the mean H score of children from a school in a deprived part of Glasgow containing 28 percent of pupils from India and Pakistan was 20.35. The overall level of coloured settlement in Glasgow as a whole has been proportionately very low; it just happened that immigrants were concentrated in this particular neighbourhood. In the West Midlands, on the other hand, where immigrant settlement in the conurbation as a whole is the highest in the country outside London, in a very similar school where there were very few coloured people living in the immediate neighbourhood, and where they made up only 1.4 percent of the pupils in the school, the mean H score was 22.81, nearly two and a half points above the Glasgow school with the high coloured concentration. Neighbourhood concentrations as such did seem to give rise to local norms of greater hostility – as shown by the higher scores in our High schools compared to the Low schools – but the difference made by this was overshadowed by whether the city or conurbation as a whole, as opposed to the immediate neighbourhood, was an immigrant area or not.

It is important not to conclude from these findings that large numbers of coloured people cause prejudice or racism; that blacks create prejudice against themselves. Certainly coloured people in numbers give rise to white hostility. This happens because prejudice or racism is there to start with. We earlier defined prejudice as a set of expectations and assumptions about blacks and black/white relations that are carried in the general culture, particularly the assumption that it is normal for the black man to be subordinate to the white. This 'latent racism' gives rise to widespread and sometimes active hostility, in spite of countervailing norms of equality and fair play, when blacks enter a community and compete with the whites in sufficiently large numbers to challenge prevailing white assumptions about the black man's place. A few blacks may make little difference, for exceptions can always be made (and are made, even among the generally hostile, as we found in our interviews) at an individual level. But large numbers challenge the cultural assumptions at a structural level and this leads to hostility.

This is not to say that in some circumstances it may not be reasonable for a settled population to resent the entry of newcomers and the competition for housing and jobs that this may entail. Such resentment in itself is not racism. The report of Rex and Moore[5] is particularly important in this context for its demonstration of a realistic basis for hostility in the competition for scarce resources within the urban situation. However, the visibility of the coloured immigrants makes them easy targets for expressions of resentment where newcomers are competing with established residents for housing or other social resources. This competition, taking place as it often does in areas of deteriorating social provision is exacerbated by the fact that the immigrants are coloured and therefore perceived as having less entitlement to such scarce resources as housing. The very intensity of the reaction we have seen in Britain, the political importance that coloured immigration has assumed, the refusal to accept 'second generation' immigrants, the propensity to see a threat where none exists, can only be explained as the product of the underlying racism in British culture. To see the situation in perspective it is only necessary to ask why there is not the same intensity of social resentment and hostility against

[5] John Rex and Robert Moore, *Race Community and Conflict* (OUP/IRR, 1967).

the immigrant Irish and other (white) immigrant groups.

Dispersal of coloured people may well help to reduce hostility and tensions at the local level, but it will not of itself reduce prejudice. Prejudice will only disappear through a profound cultural change in which the language and imagery of white superiority and black inferiority fall into disuse and the fact of being white ceases to be a source of pride, and blackness ceases to be the stigma it is today, arousing variously contempt, hostility, pity or sympathy in the white breast. It is difficult to see how this kind of *respect* for coloured people, as opposed to tolerance, will come about on a large scale until coloured people are enabled to achieve actual equality in this society rather than the notional equality and actual and systematic discrimination that characterises their present position.

We can explain variations in individual white hostility as closely linked to regional norms, but the existence of more hostile norms in 'immigrant areas' has to be explained as the response of the members of a prejudiced culture to the influx of significant numbers of coloured people. The prejudice comes first, the hostility is a response which is amplified by the underlying prejudice. None of the results we have reported so far (or the results of similar studies done by others) explain the existence of colour prejudice or racism as such. Racism is endemic, and we have no reason to think that it is worse in our High areas than in our Low or No areas. It becomes more salient where blacks move in, however, and is a major contributory factor to the white hostility that then arises.

Attitudes and Mass Media Use

We may now examine the attitudes of our samples in relation to their mass media behaviour and orientations. Table 5.8 shows the mean H scores of the children broken down by amounts of exposure on our main media exposure measures. There are no significant differences. The slight trends apparent on some of the measures are accounted for by differences in both media consumption and H score between age groups, and between the No area children and the rest.

There are other media-related measures to which the H scale does relate, however. There is a small but significant correlation of .18 between Children's H scores and scores on the Television Preference Scale, and this remains when age groups are considered separately and is therefore not merely an artifact of age differences. This shows a tendency for preference of predictable and stereotyped television to go together with more hostile attitudes to coloured people. We are not entitled to conclude that consumption of this type of material *leads* to more hostile attitudes, though this could be part of a possible explanation. The relationship needs to be looked at in the light of the fact that the children's authoritarianism/dogmatism measure correlates both with the H scale (.13) and with the Television Preference Scale (.26). It would seem that the tendency to stereotyped and rigid thinking assessed by the dogmatism scale leads simultaneously to a preference for predictable and stereotyped television, and, though only to a small extent, to a greater tendency to feel hostility towards blacks. In making this interpretation we are taking the children's dogmatism scale at face value, as a measure of rigid and stereotyped thinking. How closely this approximates the kind of personality traits that other researchers on authoritarianism and dogmatism were concerned with is difficult to say, particularly in view of the fact that the children's and adults' authoritarianism scores proved to be uncorrelated (.08). This may be due simply to the unsatisfactory nature of the measures.

The link between dogmatism and attitudes to television is consistent with the findings of both Bailyn[6] and Lovibond.[7] (See Appendix IV.) It is important to emphasize that the relationships we have found are small, and that there is little reason to assume a direct link between television viewing and attitudes towards coloured people. Nevertheless, here we have our first indication of a relationship between orientations to media on the one hand and to coloured people on the other.

Another such relationship appears in the answers to Questions 27 and 28, when children were asked whether they thought newspaper and television coverage of coloured people was fair or not. Table 5.9 shows mean H scores by children's answers to these questions. There is an unmistakable tendency for the more hostile children to see the media as too favourably disposed towards blacks and for the less hostile to see them as unfavourably handled. This is what might have been expected but it does illustrate the important point that people's reactions to mass media material are consistent with their attitudes and we cannot assume a uniformity of response or effect when different kinds of people are exposed to the same material. (An incidental point worth noting from Table 5.9 is that a majority of respondents

[6] L. Bailyn, 'Mass media and children. A study of exposure habits and cognitive effects' (*Psychol. Monographs*, LXXI, 1959).
[7] S. H. Lovibond, 'The effect of media stressing crime and violence on children's attitudes' (*Social Problems*, 15, 1967).

regarded television as fair, while a majority said newspapers were too unfavourable. This reflects the greater credibility and respect for television as a medium in comparison with newspapers among our sample that we noted in the previous chapter.)

In Question 23 children were asked to say what they could remember reading about coloured people in newspapers. Many of them recalled reports of coloured people as the victims of prejudice and discrimination. Taking all children together this was mentioned by 12 percent of those with lower H scores, but only by 7 percent of those with higher H scores, and this difference proved statistically significant. Similarly, when asked what kind of parts they could recall seeing coloured people playing in films, those with low H scores more often recalled the roles of slaves (16 percent as against 9 percent), farm-hands or similar menial occupations (9 percent as against 3 percent), and coloured people playing 'good parts' (9 percent against 4 percent) than those with high H scores. These were all statistically significant for the sample as a whole. In a similar way the more hostile parents were more likely to recall reading in newspapers about coloured people involved in crime, associated with riots and trouble, or about illegal immigration; while the less hostile more often recalled reading about prejudice against coloured people and their disadvantaged position.

We have here another instance of a relationship between attitudes and media use that is suggestive of selective perception or recall. While we have found no evidence of media consumption influencing attitudes in a direct way, we have good reason to believe that people's attitudes, which are to a large extent a function of whether they live in an 'immigrant area' or not, affect the way they *interpret* media material.

It is hardly surprising to find that the mere fact of exposure to mass media is not directly related to attitude to coloured people considering that the kinds of attitudes reflected in the media and the information they disseminate is not all of one kind. The indications are that people tend to notice and recall information that is consistent with their existing attitudes. Thus the less hostile appear more likely to learn from the media about the discrimination and disadvantages suffered by the coloured population while the more hostile are more aware of their association with crime and rioting. Thus the information recalled is of a kind likely to confirm existing attitudes, and to this extent our findings are consistent with the classic view of the media as reinforcing rather than shaping or changing attitudes.

It remains possible, however, that beyond this the media provide people with a picture of the world which makes the development of one kind of attitude more likely than another. In order to examine this we need to move beyond questions of attitude as narrowly defined to consider broader definitions of the situation that people may derive from the media. This we do in the following chapter.

6

Definitions of the Situation

The open-ended questions in the interviews were included not primarily to assess attitudes but to gauge how our samples understood the racial situation in Britain, to see in what terms they defined it and what they considered as its most important feature. Responses to these questions were classified into the twenty categories listed and explained in Appendix V. Relatively fine categorization was used in an effort not to lose the sense of the data by too gross classification. Respondents could give more than one response (the mean for Question 5[1] was 1.4 per child and 2.0 per adult) but two responses falling into the same category were only counted once for any one respondent. Subjects' responses were coded from completed interview schedules with an inter-coder reliability of .81, using Scott's formula for nominal scale coding,[2] and not including 'don't know' and 'no answer' responses in the reliability check. For the sake of brevity we shall normally refer to a particular type of response by the category label given in the Appendix, and the reader may find it useful to refer to this in order to be sure that he understands what kinds of response were included in each category.

General Perceptions – Children

Table 6.1 shows the children's responses to Question 5 broken down by category and area. The figures are the number of children who gave a particular response when asked 'Can you tell me what you know about coloured people living in Britain today?' Taking all subjects together the most frequently given responses were: Objects of Prejudice, Cultural Differences, Equalitarian, Anti-stereotype, Unfavourable, Poor Housing and Disadvantaged, in that order. These we may take is indicating the kind of things that most readily came to mind when the

[1] Where the children and adults were asked the same question, the question number from the *children*'s interview schedule is used in this chapter as a shorthand way of referring to the question.
[2] W. A. Scott, 'Reliability of Content Analysis: The Case of Nominal Scale Coding' (*Public Opinion Quarterly*, Fall, 1955, pp. 321-325).

children were asked to think about coloured people in Britain, and together they accounted for 56 percent of responses given. Response patterns for the different areas were similar, with high frequency responses in one area tending also to be high frequency responses in another. There were, however, differences between areas, some of which may be seen from the listing below of response categories given by 10 percent or more of the children in each area.

'Can you tell me what you know about coloured people living in Britain today?'

RESPONSES GIVEN BY 10 PERCENT OR MORE OF THE SAMPLE
(DESCENDING ORDER) – CHILDREN

	NO AREA	LOW AREA	HIGH AREA
	Objects of prejudice	Objects of prejudice	Cultural differences
	Cultural differences	Equalitarian	Unfavourable
	Equalitarian	Cultural differences	Anti-stereotype
	Poor housing	Anti-stereotype	Objects of prejudice
		Resentment	Culture clash
		Unfavourable	Trouble
% of all answers given :	47.0%	47.4%	48.2%
No answer :	23.1%	19.2%	21.2%

Chi-square tests were used to compare frequencies of different responses between High and Low areas, High and Low schools, and between the No area sample and the rest. Differences found to be significant were as follows :

More frequent in High *areas* than Low : Culture clash
More frequent in Low *areas* than High : Resentment, Equalitarian
More frequent in Low *schools* than High : Objects of prejudice

D

More frequent in No *areas* than elsewhere : Objects of
                                                prejudice

More frequent in the main sample   Culture clash
    than in No areas :   Unfavourable
                                              Anti-stereotype

If these responses can be taken as indicative of the dominant
features of white adolescents' consciousness of coloured people
in Britain, we might ask what kind of things were most central
to their conceptions of the situation. Reference to Cultural
Differences, common among youngsters in all kinds of areas,
represented for the most part relatively superficial observation
of differences in dress, eating habits and so on – 'they wear
turbans', 'they eat curry', 'they speak a different language',
'they don't eat meat'. Responses classified as 'Objects of Prejudice'
were also very frequently given. These were on the whole
sympathetic to coloured people – 'people discriminate against
them', 'lots of white people don't like them just because they're
coloured; I think that's awful' – though a small number of
answers so classified showed a sympathy towards the hostility
described – 'they're not liked around here, and with good reason'.
'Disadvantaged' responses – 'they get all the worst jobs' – were
also largely sympathetic in tone. References to the bad housing
conditions of the immigrants, on the other hand often, but not
always, conveyed a sense of 'what else can you expect of blacks?',
'they live ten to a room/sleep four to a bed'. Together with
Equalitarian responses – 'they should be treated the same as
anyone else' – the frequency of responses classified as Objects of
Prejudice and Disadvantaged, and some of the Poor Housing
responses may be taken as a manifestation of the prevalence of
the social values of equality and fair play and in this respect the
results are encouraging. This type of sympathetic response was,
however, more frequent in situations where the coloured population was small, that is where such values were of least practical
relevance, while in 'contact situations, Unfavourable comment –
'they bring diseases', 'they smell' etc. – were more to the fore,
and the simple description of Cultural Differences was beginning
to give way to negative evaluation of these differences ('Culture
Clash' responses) – 'they won't speak English and won't mix',
'their food smells terrible'. There was a tendency, then, to react
against coloured people in 'immigrant' situations that was not
so apparent elsewhere. At the same time immigrant situations
seemed to produce a greater reluctance to make across-the-
board generalizations about coloured people as is shown by the

relative frequency of responses classified as Anti-stereotype – e.g. 'there's good and bad among them'.

Two of the differences between High and Low areas – namely the greater frequency of general expressions of Resentment and lower frequency of Unfavourable comment in Low areas – are not as clear-cut as they might appear, but result from an inter-action between the area and school factors. The area difference in Resentment responses is accounted for entirely by differences within High schools (but not Low schools). 'Resentment' responses such as 'they hold back the whites at school', or 'they cause price rises' were made by children in 'immigrant' schools in *Low* areas far more frequently than anywhere else. Living usually in one of the few neighbourhoods with a noticeable immigrant population in an otherwise 'white' town these 'Lohi' children seemed to resent the immigrants more in some respects than children in similar situations in High areas where immi-grant localities were less unusual, and to blame them more for local problems and deprivations. The area difference in frequency of Unfavourable comment was a difference within Low schools only.

We saw in the previous chapter that Equalitarian, Objects of Prejudice, and Anti-stereotype responses were related to attitude as measured by the H scale. It is therefore important to ask whether the significant differences in these kinds of response between different situations shown above were a result of differences in *attitude* or whether the variation was independent of attitudes. To check this, H score distributions were dichoto-mized and chi-square tests carried out on the low hostility and high hostility groups separately. When this was done the greater frequency of Equalitarian responses in Low areas as compared to High did not stand up and this kind of response must be seen as largely a product of attitudes. The area and school differences in Objects of Prejudice responses remained significant for the low hostility group but not for the high hostility group and must be seen as partly the result of attitude, but also apparently varying by area and school independently of attitude. In the case of Anti-stereotype responses the area effect was operating counter to what would be predicted from known area differences in attitude and further testing was not necessary. Anti-stereotype responses and the other significant differences listed must therefore be regarded as the product of different circumstances in different situations and not as reflections of different attitude norms.

This last finding is important because it shows that the

99

measurement of attitudes on their own is not sufficient to account for differences in consciousness between High, Low and No areas and schools. Our data makes it clear that there are important features of people's consciousness that are not tapped by the standard type of attitude measure (such as the H scale) and that other methods of assessment are required. This is a convenient place to point out that the kind of information yielded by the common single-score attitude measure, though useful, is always a gross over-simplification of people's consciousness, representing at best a kind of blurred average of general evaluative tendencies. In practice we found that though there was a broad correspondence between people's attitude scores and the other things that they said during the interviews, the contradictions in what they had to say were often more enlightening than the consistencies. Making unfavourable comments about coloured people did not preclude expressions of friendliness or admiration, and frankly racist opinions co-existed with the staunch defence of liberal ideals. Children were capable of expressing an elaborate negative stereotype about 'the wogs' and getting an appropriately hostile attitude score, and then going on to describe their close friendship with particular coloured individuals to whom their general denigration of the coloured population did not apply. Simple measures of attitude cannot on their own hope to do justice to mental processes that are in fact very complex.

We have shown that there are differences in what springs most readily to mind when white children in different situations are asked to think about coloured people. It also seems that, as we found with attitudes, the *area* factor makes more difference than the school factor. There were three significant differences between High and Low areas and only one between High and Low schools. In what follows, therefore, we shall concentrate on area differences by means of High/Low area comparisons among the children. This also has the advantage of allowing the parents' data to be handled in a similar way to the children's, for the school factor as such does not apply to the adults.

General Conceptions – Parents

Response frequencies by area to the same question for the parents are shown in Table 6.2. Responses given by 10 percent or more of the sample were as follows:

	LOW AREA	HIGH AREA
	Favourable	
	Unfavourable	Unfavourable
	Equalitarian	Favourable
	Resentment	Resentment
	Numbers	Culture clash
	Culture clash	Anti-stereotype
	Cultural diffs	Equalitarian
	Poor housing	Poor housing
% of all answers :	70%	70%
No answer	9%	9%

Compared with the main sample children's responses a number of things are immediately noticeable. There is a fair degree of overlap between what the children said and what the parents said – Favourable, Unfavourable, Equalitarian and Resentment responses are common to both lists of most frequently given responses. Poor Housing, Resentment, Culture Clash, Favourable and Unfavourable comment and Numbers ('there are too many of them here') appear to be more prominent in the adults' consciousness of the situation, while Objects of Prejudice and Cultural Differences are more characteristic of the children. Broadly the parents showed less awareness of or concern over the discrimination and other disadvantages suffered by the immigrants, and were more inclined to express resentment against them and anxiety about immigrant numbers, and generally to regard them unfavourably. At the same time they also more often made favourable comments than the children. Among the adults, Numbers, Objects of Prejudice, and Favourable characteristics were signficantly more often mentioned in Low areas than in High. None of these three that differed by area were significantly related to H score and must therefore be seen as the product of the area factor as such and not of differences in attitude between areas. As with the children we find that different situations appear to give rise to differences in local cultures relating to race and colour that cannot be reduced to simple attitude differences. It is worth noting that concern over immigrant numbers was more commonly expressed in areas where there were relatively few immigrants anyway. Three types of response were significantly related to H score – mentions of Cultural Differences and Equalitarian statements (both more

101

common among the less hostile) and expressions of Personal Dislike (more frequent among the more hostile) – but none of these varied significantly by area.

Source Attributions

Among both adults and children, then, a very wide range of answers was elicited by our question. They varied from simple descriptive statements of cultural differences – 'they wear turbans' – to statements, sympathetic or otherwise, about the prejudice against coloured people – 'they have a hard time because people are prejudiced', 'they're not popular around here'; from favourable comment – 'they work hard' – to unfavourable comment – 'they are lazy, dirty and stupid'; from an awareness or condemnation of their housing situation – 'they live in overcrowded houses', 'they create slums' – to the conviction that the country is being over-run – 'there'll be more Pakis than whites here soon'. The pattern of responses is interesting in itself but our main object was to assess the possible contribution of the mass media to the way matters of race and colour were thought about and understood.

For each statement made in answer to the open-ended questions the subject was asked, 'How do you know that that is the case?', 'Where did you get that idea *from*?' or an equivalent question. He was allowed to give as many sources as he liked for each statement. The source attributions obtained were classified into the categories described in Chapter 4. Media references decreased and 'personal experience' attributions increased from No, through Low, to High situations. We have seen that these source attributions were not just plausible answers but that they were significantly related to media use on the one hand and personal contact with coloured people on the other, and as such they have validity. It would probably be mistaken to attach an absolute validity to them in the sense of being able to say, for instance, that 40 percent of what people said was derived from the media. We may, however, accord a *relative* validity to this kind of data in the sense of being able to say that one group referred more frequently to media sources than another, or that one kind of information was more often attributed to media sources than another.

We need to ask how far the response differences between areas can be accounted for by differences in the use of different information sources, particularly the mass media. We also need to ask how far the similarities in response between areas (and these were more marked than the differences) resulted from the use of similar sources. Before examining the data further it may be helpful to set down systematically the main reasons why people in different situations may have different ideas, and the reasons why they may have similar ideas.

Ideas may differ between situations because of:

(a) Objective differences between situations and associated differences in the sources of information available.
(b) Different interpretations of generally available information, resulting from differences in the perspectives characteristic of different situations.

Ideas may be similar from situation to situation because of:
(a) Objective similarities between situations and associated similarities in the sources of information available.
(b) Similarities in the information yielded by different available sources.
(c) Selective interpretations within a shared perspective of different available information.

If we ignore 'no answers', the responses to the open-ended questions and their attribution to sources may be set out in a 19 x 12 table with response categories across the top and sources down the side. The resulting 228 cell table is difficult to work with because many cells are blank and others have very low frequencies. If, however, we combine media sources by collapsing rows, and 'people' sources[3] in the same way we obtain tables like Tables 6.3-6.5. The entries in these are not cases, because of the collapsing of categories and because, even before collapsing, more than one source may have been given for the same response. They represent the number of times a particular response was attributed to different kinds of source. The size of the cell frequencies (the upper figure in each cell) gives some idea of the extent to which different kinds of belief or ideas were associated with different kinds of source. A shortcoming of this data is that for a particular response/media cell we do not know whether the frequency obtained represents many people giving a single media attribution, or whether fewer people gave several different media attributions each. Either way it seems reasonable to accept a large frequency as indicating a stronger link in people's minds between a particular idea and the mass media than a small frequency.

[3] In the case of the children these included sources originally coded as peers, family, adults and other.

In the bottom part of each cell, the frequency is shown as a percentage of all source attributions given for that category. This has not been done for categories with less than ten attributions altogether, because such numbers are too low for meaningful percentages and in any case such responses are comparatively rare and unimportant. If we take any percentage greater than 33 percent as indicating a response-source link sufficiently strong to be worth taking account of, the main links in the different sections of the children's sample are as summarized below.

	NO AREA	LOW AREA	HIGH AREA
MEDIA	Disadvantaged 94% Poor housing 82% *Objects of †Prejudice 76% Taking jobs 60%	Numbers 56% Poor housing 55% Disadvantaged 50% *Objects of †prejudice 44% Taking houses 43% Trouble 38%	*Objects of †prejudice 56% Disadvantaged 44% Trouble 38%
PEOPLE		*Objects of †prejudice 36%	
PERSONAL EXPERIENCE	Cultural differences 52%	*Anti-†stereotype 92% Favourable 87% †Unfavourable 67% Cultural differences 65% †Resentment 48% *†Equalitarian 42%	Favourable 83% Cultural differences 81% *Anti-†stereotype 81% †Culture clash 76% †Unfavourable 74% Poor housing 63% Numbers 59% *†Equalitarian 55% Trouble 46% †Resentment 45%

† Differing significantly between areas
* Significantly related to H score

This list needs to be interpreted with an eye on the raw figures, though in most cases, because we have omitted very low frequency responses it is a fairly reliable guide to the main source attributions of categories of any importance.

The first thing that emerges is the expected heavy reliance on media and the very low reliance on personal experience in the

No areas, reflecting the lack of available experience there, and the corresponding lesser reliance on media and heavy reliance on experience in the High areas. We may also note the relative unimportance of 'people' as major sources. In what follows we shall be mainly concerned with assessing the relative contributions of media and personal experience.

Differences and Similarities Between Areas

The significance of the data we are dealing with derives from the fact that although the media experience of all children was very similar (since they were predominantly exposed to national media), the 'personal' experience available to them (either at first or second hand) differed from area to area.

Cultural differences was attributed mainly to experience in all three areas, reflecting the fact that the kind of distant and fleeting experience required to know about simple cultural differences was available to all our subjects. All the experience attributions in the Low area list appear also in the High area list, but not in the No area list, reflecting the comparable opportunities for experience in the High and Low areas and the lack of it in the No areas. Culture Clash responses occur in the High area list of experience attributions but not in the Low. This may be a case of differing interpretations of similar experiences in different situations.

If we turn now to the media attributions we find that Objects of Prejudice and Disadvantaged responses appear in all three areas, and this would seem to be the result of people in different situations taking the same kind of thing from the media. Information about Trouble is attributed to the media in both High and Low areas but not in the No areas. This would seem to be a case of selective media use; those in situations where there are coloured people around (the Highs and Lows) being sensitive to this aspect of media content which is not so much noticed in the No areas. The Trouble category in fact looms larger in the High area media attributions than in the Low. It is more important in the High areas because there are twice as many raw attributions as in the Low, even though the percentage figures are the same, and this too is suggestive of selective interpretation of media material. A similar process would seem to be operating in the case of Taking Jobs, Numbers, and Taking Houses responses. Taking Jobs appears in the No area list only, and Numbers and Taking Houses are in the Low areas list but not elsewhere. Given the broad similarity of mass media material available in the different areas these data are suggestive of

D*

selective use of the media by people in different situations. It seems that people's different situations may sensitize them to different aspects of media content.

Information about Poor Housing is attributed to media in the Low and No areas, but in the High areas it is attributed to experience. Numbers and Trouble are also attributed to experience in the High areas, but to the media in the Low areas. These would all seem to be instances of people in different situations taking the same kind of information from different sources. Those in High areas, for instance, do not need the media to learn about the poor housing conditions of coloured immigrants, for this information is there on their doorstep – they can learn it from experience.

It is worth noting at this point that with the exception of references to coloured people as Objects of Prejudice, all those responses which differed significantly between areas, and all those which proved to be significantly related to attitude (these are marked on the list) were attributed to experience rather than to mass media.

Parents' Source Attributions

A difference between adults and children that we noticed in Chapter 4 was the relatively infrequent reference by the adults to the media as a source of information. 16 percent, 7 percent and 12 percent of parents' source references were to the media in the Low areas, High areas, and total sample respectively, while the comparable figures for the main sample children were 29 percent, 20 percent and 24 percent. The adults on the other hand referred far more to personal experience than the children, but both samples referred equally often to other people as sources of information or opinions (15 percent of all references in each case). It may be that the demand to present beliefs and ideas as based on personal experience is stronger for adults than for children. On the other hand it seems likely that children do in fact rely more heavily on the mass media for their conceptions of the world, simply because their range of experience is restricted. It is this that makes children better subjects for estimating the contribution of media than adults.

Frequencies of source attributions by the adults for different response categories are shown in Tables 6.6 and 6.7 and the main response-source linkages in terms of percentage attributions for the major categories are summarized below. The same criteria were used in drawing up this list as for the comparable list for the children's data.

The list reflects the relatively low reliance of the adults on mass media, particularly in High areas, for the kind of ideas they expressed in answer to our question. As with the children, however, the media were a more important source of information in Low areas than in High. Like the Low area children, their parents attributed information about Numbers (and Anti-immigration statements, which are prescriptions for dealing with the numbers question) to the media. This is an interesting case of selective media use, for it was in Low areas where the proportion of coloured people was small that most references to

	LOW AREA		HIGH AREA	
MEDIA	Anti-immigration	56%	–	
	†Numbers	43%		
PEOPLE	Objects of		–	
	†prejudice	44%		
PERSONAL EXPERIENCE	*Cultural diffs	89%	Anti-stereotype	77%
	†Favourable	84%	Culture clash	77%
	Anti-stereotype	78%	†Favourable	75%
	*Equalitarian	71%	Poor housing	75%
	Culture clash	62%	Unfavourable	67%
	Poor housing	55%	*Equalitarian	63%
	†Numbers	50%	*Cultural diffs	56%
	Unfavourable	44%	*Personal dislike	56%
	Resentment	42%	Resentment	51%
	*Personal dislike	38%		

* Significantly related to H score
† Differing significantly between areas

numbers were made (the difference was significant) and this idea was partly media-derived. The Low area adults (but not the Highs) also attributed it to experience and this is perhaps another instance of selective interpretation of the situation. Apart from Numbers, the experience attributions in the Low and High area lists are identical. All the responses (marked on the list) that were significantly related to H score were attributed mainly to experience, a tendency we noticed with the children as well. The association of the kind of response that differed significantly between areas (marked on the list) with experience rather than media is not so clear-cut as with the children.

Media versus Experience

We have produced indications that the mass media do make a contribution to white people's ideas about coloured people and the racial situation in Britain. In this respect the children's data is much stronger than the parents' because they did refer much more to the media than the parents. It would appear that there is a tendency, for the children at least, to take similar things from the mass media wherever they live – the association of objects of Prejudice and Disadvantaged responses with media sources in all areas shows this. There are also suggestions from the data that people in different situations make selective use of the media – for instance, the association of Numbers with media sources in Low areas but not in High among both children and parents. Where personal experience is concerned, however, the data suggests that people derive similar things from experience insofar as their opportunities for experience are similar. Hence the similarity of experience-attributed responses between Low and High areas for both children and parents, and the almost total lack of such associations among the No area children. It will be remembered that the samples were drawn so as to equate opportunities for experience of coloured people between High and Low areas, but that there was very little such experience available in the No areas.

A convenient way of elucidating these patterns of source usage among the children is shown in the table below. The first column shows the degree of overall similarity between the response patterns of the different areas to Question 5. This was obtained by ranking response categories in order of frequency for the different areas and inter-correlating them. The next three rows were obtained by ranking and correlating the rows of Table 6.3-6.5 across areas. The figures are an index of the degree of similarity of media-attributed, people-attributed and experience-attributed responses in different areas.

The first thing to notice is that in all cases the similarity of media-attributed responses is greater than any other similarities. Similarity of people-attributed responses is consistently moderate, for as we have seen there are no particularly strong associations between types of response and 'people' as a source. The similarity of experience-attributed responses varies directly with the similarity of available experience in different areas. It is highest between High and Low areas where there were similar opportunities for experience of coloured people, and lowest between High and No areas where opportunities were least similar.

SIMILARITY OF RESPONSE PATTERNS — CHILDREN
UNCORRECTED RANK CORRELATIONS, BY AREA

	ALL RESPONSES	MEDIA-ATTRIBUTED	PEOPLE-ATTRIBUTED	EXPERIENCE-ATTRIBUTED
High vs Low	.568	.792	.488	.726
High vs No	.480	.704	.564	.400
Low vs No	.804	.811	.482	.661
Mean Rho	.617	.769	.511	.596

The pattern of relationships suggests that similarities of conception between areas are closely related to media-derived ideas on the one hand, and to similarities in available experience where these exist, on the other. In spite of indications of selective media use that we have noted it would seem that, among the children at least, the media make an important contribution to the very similar ways in which the situation is understood in different areas of the country. Some differences between areas would seem to result from differential interpretation of or attention to aspects of mass media content (the very high frequency of reference to Objects of Prejudice in No areas would seem to be an instance of this), but the main differences between areas seem to be related to situational differences. The fact that most of the children's responses that differed significantly between areas were attributed mainly to experience supports this interpretation, though this is not nearly so striking a feature of the parents' data.

The Media Contribution
We might now ask, on the basis of the evidence presented so far, what the distinctive contribution of the mass media to public consciousness on the question of race seems to be. We have seen that heavy consumption of mass media does not in itself lead to greater or less hostility towards coloured people. Hostility seems to be much more a situationally generated characteristic, and it appears that hostility is likely to lead to selective interpretation of media material, but we have no reason to think that those who depend heavily on the media for their information are any more or less hostile on that account than those with different information sources. What then is the nature of the media contribution? We might approach this by comparing the type of response most closely associated with the media with the

type of response most commonly associated with personal experience.

The most common media-linked responses that we found were classified as:

Objects of Prejudice, Disadvantaged, Poor Housing, Trouble, Numbers, Taking Job, Taking Houses and Anti-immigration.

These response categories are exemplified by statements like:

People are prejudiced against them, people discriminate against them, they are poor, they can't find jobs, they live in slums, they sleep ten to a room, they cause riots, there are too many of them coming in, there'll soon be more blacks than whites in this country, they take white people's jobs, they cause a housing shortage.

A few of these were also linked with personal experience in High areas for reasons we have discussed. Otherwise, the responses most characteristically derived from personal experience were:

Cultural Differences, Anti-stereotype, Favourable, Unfavourable, Equalitarian, Resentment, Culture Clash and Personal dislike.

Examples are:

Some are good, some are bad, just like whites; they are dirty; they are hardworking; they are clean; they should have the same rights as anyone else; their cooking stinks; they won't work but live on National Assistance; I can't stand them.

What the media-derived ideas have in common is that they are on the whole references to the general *state of affairs*, to what the situation in general is. Apart from Objects of Prejudice, none of the main media-linked responses is significantly related to attitude. The experience-derived responses on the other hand are almost all of an *affective/evaluative* nature, and we have seen that Anti-stereotype and Equalitarian responses were closely related to H score among the children and Personal Dislike among the adults. The only exception to this is Cultural Differences which represented for the most part simple observation of differences in dress and so on. And even Cultural Differences was related to H score among the parents. In these experience-linked statements the expression of approval or disapproval, liking or disliking, outweighed any reference to the general state of affairs; the evaluative element was central.

Also consistent with this general pattern of results is that there is a much heavier evaluative emphasis in the parents' responses compared to the children's, together with the parents' much greater reference to personal experience as the source of their ideas. This may be seen by comparing the two lists of most frequently given responses on page 97 and page 101.

These results fit in well with the earlier findings that attitudes as measured by the H scale were closely related to situational factors, while the media did not seem to have any direct influence on attitudes as such. It would appear that the media serve to define for people what the dimensions of the situation are. How they feel about the situation, thus defined, would seem to depend on other factors, particularly on where they live.

Other Indications

If our interpretation of these results is correct then we might expect to find corroboration from other ways of looking at the data. In particular we would expect to find differences in response to Question 5 between groups with greater and less personal contact with coloured people, and between high news consumers and low news consumers, consistent with the pattern of source attributions.

Using the gross contact index, children with more contact more often gave Anti-stereotype (within main sample only), Equalitarian, and Favourable responses, and more often mentioned Taking Jobs. Using the friendship contact index, those with more friendship contact more often gave an answer to the question, made Equalitarian statements, or mentioned Cultural Differences. All these relationships were significant when checked within appropriate subgroupings of the sample, as indicated. Apart from Taking Jobs, which is a 'state of affairs' response, most often attributed to media, these are all the kind of responses commonly associated with experience, and give a measure of confirmation to our interpretation that it is primarily the affective/evaluative or factual/observational type of belief or opinion that results from personal experience.

When responses were examined by amount of news consumption as measured by the news consumption index, the high news consumers more often gave an answer (significant for older children only), and more often made Equalitarian remarks – which we earlier found to be more strongly associated with experience than with media. Objects of Prejudice and Disadvantaged, the media-attributed responses *par excellence*, were also more often mentioned by the high news consumers. However, when sex was held constant for Objects of Prejudice, and age for Disadvantages responses, the relationships failed to reach statistical significance though the trends remained. The findings on news exposure, then, are no more than suggestive and not as convincing as the findings for contact. Nevertheless, the indications are broadly consistent with the interpretation that we offered earlier of the role of the mass media in influencing the children's conceptions of the world.

The Media Definition

If, as it appears, the media provide images of the 'state of affairs' regarding race in Britain, we might ask what the main features of this media-relayed picture are, at least insofar as they are reflected in our respondents' answers, as a first step in appraising the media's performance in this respect. The beliefs and ideas apparently derived from the media among our samples were not all of one type but tended to be broadly of two kinds. On the one hand people seem to have been made aware by the media of the discrimination and deprivations suffered by the immigrant population. Clearly in this respect the media can be said to have performed a valuable function in not allowing undoubted injustices and hardship to remain invisible to the society at large. This aspect of people's understanding of the situation is represented by responses falling under the headings of Objects of Prejudice and Disadvantaged (and some of those classified as Poor Housing), which we have seen were more characteristic of the children's ideas than the adults', of those outside immigrant areas and of the less hostile rather than the more hostile. The tendency to selective perception that we have noted probably means that some people take reports of discrimination, for instance, as evidence of the normality of discrimination and are encouraged in their own tendencies to discriminate. But selective use of media material is not something for which the media can reasonably be held responsible. The other aspect of the state of affairs as perceived by our respondents which appears to be attributable to the media is something about which it is far less easy to be sanguine. This is the perception of the immigrant population as, in one way or another, a threat and a problem as reflected in responses classified as Trouble, Numbers, Taking Jobs, Taking Houses, Anti-immigration, and in many cases of the Poor Housing responses (of the 'they create slums' variety). Insofar as the media have helped disseminate this kind of idea it is reasonable to suggest that they may have helped create a conception of the situation among the public far more conducive to hostility towards coloured people than acceptance of them. How far the expression of such ideas among our samples reflects the general drift of newspaper coverage we shall see in the following chapter. Firstly we shall summarize the results from other interview questions.

Problems

In Question 6 subjects were asked : 'Do you think there are any problems connected with coloured people living in this country?' This is a focused question in which people are encouraged to answer in terms of problems, and it is important to show that the connection between 'colour' and 'problems' is not just something imposed on them by the form of the question. Before examining the responses to Question 6, therefore, we shall look briefly at the very first question of the interview where subjects were asked : 'Could you tell me what you think are some of the problems in Britain today?' To this as many as 21 percent of children and 24 percent of adults spontaneously mentioned race, colour or immigration. Among the children it was the leading problem in No and High areas and was beaten only by the cost of living as a problem in Low areas. For Low area parents, it was the third most commonly mentioned problem, after strikes and the cost of living. Among High area parents it was second to strikes. This should be sufficient to show that for our kind of sample, at least, race ranks high as a national problem, and that Question 6 was, in fact, a meaningful question to ask the subjects. The children who mentioned race, colour or immigration in reply to Question 1 were asked how they knew this to be a problem. 57 percent gave the mass media as the source of this idea, 25 percent other people, and only 18 percent personal experience. The role of the mass media in defining the general state of affairs is again evident.

Responses to Question 6 were classified into the same twenty categories that were used for Question 5. The response patterns for children and adults are given in Tables 6.8 and 6.9. Responses given by more than 10 percent of the children's sample were in order of frequency as follows :

NO AREA	LOW AREA	HIGH AREA
Objects of prejudice	Objects of prejudice	Objects of prejudice
Numbers	Trouble	Resentment
Trouble	Numbers	Numbers
Taking jobs	Resentment	

Objects of Prejudice occurred significantly more often and Resentment significantly less often in the No area than in the main sample, and equalitarian statements were more frequent in Low areas than in High areas. Apart from these there were no other significant differences either by area or school. What is striking is the close similarity in response patterns between areas, and the fact that all the major response categories listed above, except Resentment, are ones which emerged as closely linked to media sources in our analysis of the Question 5 data, and are of the 'state of affairs' type reflecting an awareness of white hostility towards coloured people on the one hand, and the perception of them as a threat on the other.

Responses given by 10 percent or more of parents in order of frequency were:

LOW AREA	HIGH AREA
Resentment	Resentment
Numbers	Unfavourable
Taking jobs	Culture clash
Culture clash	Numbers
Unfavourable	Poor housing
Objects of prejudice	Taking houses
Trouble	Taking jobs
Poor housing	Objects of prejudice

The parents' responses show the characteristic greater emphasis of parents on evaluative and attitudinal reactions that we noted in Question 5. But we may note also that when asked about problems there was a distinct shift to giving a 'state of affairs' type of response in comparison to their heavily attitudinal response to Question 5. There is also close similarity between the High and Low area lists. The only significant differences between areas were that Cultural Differences, Equalitarian and Anti-immigration statements – all low frequency responses on this question – were more often mentioned in Low areas.

There was also a higher frequency of reference to media as a source of ideas among both children and parents than there was on Question 5 (40 percent as against 32 percent for the children, and 23 percent as against 12 percent for the adults). The closer association between media and conceptions of problems connected with coloured people than with the responses elicited by the earlier more general question, is reflected also in the response-media links found when media references are taken as a percentage of all source references for each category. These are shown below using the same criteria for inclusion as were used for data on Question 5.

The main response-media links among the children were:

NO AREA	LOW AREA	HIGH AREA
Numbers	Taking houses	Objects of prejudice
Objects of prejudice	Objects of prejudice	Trouble
Trouble	Trouble	Numbers
Taking jobs	Taking jobs	Disadvantaged

The very large overlap between these media linked categories and those most commonly associated with media in the Question 5 data should be noted. The main media linkages among the parents were:

LOW AREA	HIGH AREA
Anti-immigration	Disadvantaged
Trouble	Trouble
Numbers	
Poor housing	
Disadvantaged	

The greater contribution of the media in the answers to Question 6 compared to Question 5 is particularly striking for the parents. As for Question 5, the media appear as more important sources of information in Low areas than in High, but it is significant that for Question 6 there were two response categories strongly linked to media sources for the High area sample, while for Question 5 there were none. This suggests that the media play a particularly important part in defining the problem aspects of situations. It should be noted that all the media-linked answers to this question, for both adults and children, are of the 'state of affairs' type, and there are no affective/evaluative answers closely associated with media sources.

All in all, the pattern of response to Question 6 provides further support for our earlier suggestion that the main role of the mass media is to define for people what the situation is. We also have indications that the media may be particularly important in delineating the *problem* aspects of the situation, since the media appear to have played a larger part in influencing the answers to Questions 1 and 6 than to Question 5. Also, however, the role of the media in maintaining the social visibility of injustices and antagonism endured by coloured people (Objects of Prejudice and Disadvantaged responses) is again evident.

We have evidence that suggests strongly that the mass media, by making available particular kinds of information, and by the range of perspectives they present, by what they emphasize and what they play down, may help to influence public conscious-ness in the sense of influencing what is widely known and what is not, and what is thought important, and we have shown what the main features of this media-derived picture are.

However, the media do not of themselves determine people's reactions to the picture of the world that they present. On Question 6 people's attitudes had a strong influence on their answers. Among the children, the following media-linked responses were found to be significantly related to H score : those with lower H scores more frequently gave Objects of Prejudice (in the No area) and Disadvantaged (in the High area) responses, while those with higher H scores were more inclined to say that the problems were Numbers and Trouble (these both in Low areas and Low schools), and that coloured people were Taking Houses (in High areas). What this amounts to is that the more hostile respondents tended to see the whites as having problems caused or occasioned by coloured people, while the less hostile were more aware of the problems faced by coloured people themselves. We mentioned these relationships earlier as an example of attitudes influencing people's interpretation of their world. In the light of the very close links between these five response categories and the mass media, revealed in our analysis of Question 6, we can now see that this is a case of selective interpretation of media-relayed information. What is important, however, is that though the more hostile and less hostile differed in how they conceived of the racial situation as a problem, in that they apparently selected differently from what was made available through the media, the media would still appear to occupy a central place in the process because for both they define the situation as a problem and supply the range of problem definitions from which to select.

The role of the media in defining *problems* is highlighted by comparing the adults' response to Question 6, where they were asked about problems, with their response to another question where they were asked : 'Do you think there are any good things that result from coloured people living in this country?' 87 per-cent of the sample were able to give an answer to the question about problems, and 23 percent of the sources given for these answers were media sources. Only 56 percent of people were able to think of good things resulting from coloured immigration, and only 10 percent of the sources given for these were media sources. In the High areas only 5 percent were media sources, as against 18 percent media sources for the question about problems. Not only did our subjects find it more difficult to think of good things about multi-racial Britain than to think of problems, but the mass media were of more help to them in thinking about problems than in calling good things to mind. 'Good things' most commonly mentioned were coloured people working as medical staff, doing jobs that otherwise wouldn't get done, their contribution to keeping public transport going, and simply that they were 'nice people', in that order. None of these was closely associated with media sources.

Further indications of the mass media contribution to people's understanding of their world come from the children's answers to the next two open-ended questions. In Question 7 they were asked; 'How does the fact that coloured people have been coming to live in Britain affect you now?' The most noteworthy thing about their answers was the high frequency of 'it doesn't', 'don't know' and no answer responses. (See Table 6.10.) These accounted for 71 percent of all responses, and 58 percent even in the High areas. Where an answer was given it was most frequently an Equalitarian statement – which was not really an answer to the question. After that came references to Numbers, Resentment, Unfavourable Characteristics, and Taking Jobs. The most commonly-given source of these beliefs and opinions was 'personal experience' (38 percent of all sources), while media made up only 10 percent of all source attributions. Clearly there was not a very great sense that coloured immigration had impinged on their lives. When asked in the next question (Question 8); 'how do you think that the presence of coloured people in this country might affect your life in the future?', however, the children were more forthcoming. (See Table 6.11.) Though the overall response level was low, it was higher than for the previous question. Overall, 49 percent gave no answer or said that it would not affect them. The most frequent responses were coded as Taking Jobs (19 percent), Numbers (15 percent), Taking Over (8 percent), and Trouble (5 percent). Of these, 34 percent of the source attributions for Numbers, and 45 percent of the source attributions for Trouble responses were media references. It would seem that not only do the mass media play a part in shaping people's conceptions of the world, but they also help to shape anticipations of the future. It is worth noting that if responses to Question 8 are rated as positive, negative, or 'other' anticipations, the negative ones heavily outweigh the others – 71 percent, 73 percent and 84 percent of anticipations were negative in No, Low and High areas respectively, as opposed to only 3 percent, 2 percent and 2 percent of positive anticipations. Anticipations of the future effects of coloured immigration, when they were expressed, were overwhelmingly pessimistic, with the mass media making a significant contribution to these anticipations.

In the case of the parents, only one question was asked instead of the two asked to the children, namely : 'Does or will coloured immigration into Britain affect you personally?' Most strikingly, as with the children, the majority, 64 percent (57 percent in High areas) said No or gave no answer. Where answers were given, Taking Jobs (13 percent of sample), Resentment (11 percent), and Numbers (9 percent) were the most common. The majority of source attributions were to personal experience (33 percent) but 16 percent were to the mass media, which is higher than the percentage for the general open-ended question (Q. 5).

Findings consistent with those we have reported came from the answers to two other questions. Subjects were asked; 'Do you think anything should be done about coloured immigration to Britain?' (Q. 9 children, and Q. 13 adults). 23 percent of children and 10 percent of adults said nothing should be done or gave no answer, 6 percent of children and 1 percent of adults suggested some positive measure such as combating discrimination or providing better housing for immigrants, and 6 percent and 5 percent of children and adults respectively gave unclassifable answers. The rest, that is 66 percent of children (85 percent of adults), said that immigration should be limited (35 percent and 37 percent respectively), stopped (19 percent and 33 percent), or recommended repatriation (11 percent and 14 percent). Among the children those in High areas did not differ from those in Low areas, but those in No areas were significantly less likely to want action, or strong action, than either of the other groups. Among the parents, those in High areas more often suggested strong restrictive action than those in Low areas. The most frequently given source for the opinions given here was 'own opinion', with 'people' also an important source for the children, mass media made up 22 percent and 28 percent of all source references for children and adults respectively. The kind of contribution made by the mass media is evident from the fact that they were hardly ever given as the source of the few positive measures recommended. The media were never given by the parents as sources of the positive measures suggested, and made up only 5 percent of all such source references among the children.

In Question 14 the children were asked : 'Do you know what any of the politicians – members of parliament for instance –

have said about coloured immigration into Britain?' 53 percent gave no answer, with boys giving more answers than girls and older children more than younger children. There was no significant difference in frequency of giving an answer between High and Low areas but the children in No areas were less often able to answer than the rest. Powell was the most frequently mentioned politician, and 161 of the children altogether named him, whereas only 31 were able to name any other politician. 126 gave policies which they attributed to politicians without being able to name the politicians in question. Media sources predominated massively as the origin given for this kind of information, making up 89 percent of all source references given. This predominance did not vary greatly whatever politician was mentioned or whatever policy was described. Repatriation was the policy most often attributed to Powell, followed in frequency by statements that he advocated that immigration should be stopped, and that he disliked coloured people. Where another politician was named or where no name could be recalled (and this latter happened most often in No and Low areas), the most frequently given policy was that immigration should be stopped, followed by statements about the negative consequences of immigration and a variety of miscellaneous policies. What emerges is that insofar as the children were aware of political policies over immigration, they were aware of them mainly through the media. Powell was the politician that sprang most readily to mind (only 6 percent of the children could name any other politician, while 29 percent could name Powell), and the policies of which they were aware were (accurately) almost entirely policies of immigration control, or other restrictive measures.

Relative Deprivation and Racial Attitudes

In Chapter 3 we argued that racism was not a psychological phenomenon alone, but that it was also 'a cultural phenomenon historically rooted in social relationships, integral to the value systems of modern Western societies, and serving particular interests in existing social structures.' It is this relation between psychologically functional racism and its origin in the social structure which is of particular interest here. Merton[4] has discussed at some length how the misfit between culturally prescribed aspirations and the socially structured avenues for realizing these aspirations may produce psychological anomie.

[4] Robert K. Merton, *Social Theory and Social Structure* (The Free Press, New York, 1968).

It is the failure to achieve legitimate culturally supported goals which concerns us here, though the framework which we shall use is that defined by the concept of relative deprivation. Gurr[5] has defined relative deprivation as 'actors' perception of discrepancy between their value expectations and their value capabilities. Value expectations are the goods and conditions of life to which people believe they are rightfully entitled. Value capabilities are the goods and conditions they think they are capable of getting and keeping.' A more concise phrasing of the concept is given in Aberle's[6] definition of relative deprivation as 'a negative discrepancy between legitimate expectations and actuality'.

Relative deprivation is a psychologically uncomfortable state and the frustration experienced may become the basis of aggression which in itself can become expressed in racism and scapegoating of minority groups. This theory of frustration-aggression does not indicate that relative deprivation will necessarily result in aggression, but only that it can be the basis for such feelings. The existence of clearly stigmatized groups in society makes them suitable cues for the anger experienced by the individual at his blocked aspirations, and through this chain of events ethnic hostility can become psychologically functional.[7] Empirical support for this hypothesized link between relative deprivation and racial hostility is provided by Runciman and Bagley[8] in Britain, and Vanneman and Pettigrew[9] in the United States.

The role of the mass media in stimulating and creating needs has been the object of much debate. Galbraith and others[10] have argued that the mass media play a critical and ubiquitous function in advanced industrial societies in creating and sustaining consumer needs, and the necessary complementary values of

[5] Ted R. Gurr, *Why Men Rebel* (Princeton University Press, 1970, p. 24).
[6] David F. Alberle, 'A Note on Relative Deprivation Theory' in Sylvia L. Thrupp, *Millennial Dreams in Action: Essays in Comparative Study* (Mouton, The Hague, 1962).
[7] Cf. T. R. Gurr, op. cit. Chapter 2.
[8] W. G. Runciman and C. R. Bagley, 'Status Consistency, Relative Deprivation and Attitudes to Immigrants' (*Sociology*, 3, 1969).
[9] Reeve D. Vanneman and Thomas F. Pettigrew, 'Race and Relative Deprivation in the Urban United States' (*Race*, Vol. XIII, No. 4, April, 1972).
[10] J. K. Galbraith (1958), *The Affluent Society* (Pelican Books, 1962); Paul A. Baran and Paul M. Sweezy (1966), *Monopoly Capital* (Pelican Books, 1968); Herbert Marcuse (1964), *One Dimensional Man* (Sphere Books, 1968).

a society where production demand precedes consumer demand. Status striving is a legitimate and indeed prescribed activity with positive sanctions being supplied from for example fiction, drama and advertisements. However, it is not only the life style presented from the content of the entertainment media which reinforces the goals of acquisition and success, but even the news media may heighten awareness of these legitimate aspirations.

In recent years the government has adopted various deflationary measures, being variously called 'a period of wage restraint' and 'a prices and incomes policy'. The effect of this attempt to limit increases in pay was that all wage claims, and wage settlements, became highly newsworthy and received prominent coverage in the news media. In this situation of increasing prices and credit restriction, where there also prevails an unusual attention to the incomes of others, it is not only peers who can be the basis for comparison. For, where there is a prices and incomes policy, any pay rise in violation of this policy (real or apparent) may be regarded as a precedent relevant to each person's own case. Thus the pay rise given to the elite management of the nationalized industries, though given to a body of people far removed from the normal comparative reference groups of a manual labourer, may be expected to be perceived by him as being relevant to his case. For it is not the extent of difference in income which is relevant here, but the fact that the elite (or any group) are seen as having been awarded a pay rise which is in contravention of a policy applicable to all. Thus it is hypothesized that over time there has developed a new criterion for comparison of wages. It has become not the difference in pay between one group and another which is relevant, but rather *the difference in percentage increase in pay* awarded in a wage settlement. Thus teachers are outraged by wage settlements obtained by dustbinmen, civil servants complain of the increases given to virtually everyone in private enterprise, and everyone is outraged by pay settlements obtained by car workers. Where the criterion of comparison is percentage increase in pay, all persons receiving an income may reasonably become a comparative reference group, and the usual limitation upon choice of comparative reference group demonstrated in the research literature[11] ceases to apply. Thus

[11] See for example, H. H. Hyman, 'The Value Systems of Different Classes' in R. Bendix and S. M. Lipset, *Class, Status and Power* (Routledge and Kegan Paul, 1954). E. Stern and S. Keller, 'Spontaneous Group References in France' (*P.O.Q.* Vol. 17, 1953). W. G. Runciman, *Relative Deprivation and Social Justice* (Routledge and Kegan Paul, 1966).

in recent years, and at present, the news media have made a significant contribution to individual concern over income among differing sections of the community, middle class as well as the more traditionally cited case of the working class.[12] Through promoting the cultural values of success and acquisition, and by providing opportunity for becoming aware of relative deprivation, the mass media may indirectly exacerbate racial hostility in this country.

Given the predominantly working class nature of our sample it seemed probable that many of the adult respondents would experience feelings of relative deprivation with respect to others who were seen to be 'doing better' than themselves. In order to tap such feelings of generalized relative deprivation a modified version of the question used by Runciman[13] was put to the respondents : 'Do you think in Britain there are any other sorts of people doing noticeably better at the moment than you and your family?' (Q. 48a). 73 percent of the respondents did feel that there were others doing better and this response was not related to class or sex. However, there was a significantly greater frequency of perceiving others doing better amongst those where the net income of the head of the household was less than twenty pounds per week in comparison to those with higher incomes. The frequency of perceiving others doing better was examined in relation to attitudes toward coloured people as measured by the attitude scale and it was found that there was no significant relationship. Runciman and Bagley[14] did in fact find a positive relation between generalized relative deprivation and their measure of attitude toward immigrants. The absence of such a correlation here may well be due to the very high proportion of subjects answering 'yes' to the question and the consequently small number who said 'no' available for comparison. There is also the consideration that Runciman's question regarding perception of immigrants was phrased very similarly to the relative deprivation question, namely : 'What about foreign immigrants to this country such as the Irish or West Indians – some people think they are doing too well at the expense of British people. Do you think this is so or not?' – and this may have produced a spurious correlation between the two.

Runciman subsequently asked his respondents whether they approved or disapproved of others doing better and found that

---

[12] See for example those cited in Judith B. Agassi, 'The Worker and the Media' (Archives of European Sociology XI, 1970).
[13] W. G. Runciman, op. cit.
[14] W. G. Runciman and C. R. Bagley, op. cit.

those who disapproved were more likely to express a negative attitude to immigrants.[15] In order to obtain a broader spread of response our respondents were asked (Q. 48c) whether they thought it very fair, fair, unfair or very unfair that others should be doing noticeably better. This question discriminated well among respondents and provided a more adequate measure of the degree[16] of relative deprivation amongst those who perceived others as doing better than Runciman's measure. It was found that there was a significant but small positive correlation between resenting others doing better and having negative attitudes toward coloured people, as measured by the H scale (r=0.1453 sig @ <.05). This finding is consistent with the argument presented above, that it is probable that for many individuals feelings of relative deprivation become a source of psychological scapegoating. Indeed the data provides evidence which supports the view that this relationship is psychological rather than an expression of objective conflict, for when we look at the kind of people respondents regarded as doing better than themselves (Q. 48b), coloured people and immigrants were mentioned in only 4 percent of the cases. Even towards the end of an interview which had involved discussion of immigration and coloured people, they were seldom mentioned as being better off. Thus the relationship between degree of relative deprivation and negative attitudes toward coloured people would not seem to be based upon perceptions of realistic competition. It is also consistent that 67 percent of the few who mentioned coloured people as doing better were located in the most negative quartile of attitude scale scores. It seems that selective perception was an element even in the few cases where immigrants were seen as being better off.

The groups of people most frequently mentioned as doing better were car workers and dockers who had at the time of the interviews been involved in wage disputes. Interestingly when we examine the responses to the subsequent question: 'How have you heard or learnt that these people are doing better?' we find that the media represented 67 percent of the sources given for knowledge relating to dockers and car workers. Media sources were the most frequently given overall, being 41 percent of all sources; personal experience being the other major source with 39 percent of all sources.

Since a specific aim of our concern with relative deprivation and prejudice was to indicate how this might relate to mass

[15] W. G. Runciman, op. cit.
[16] Ibid, p. 10.

media content, two questions were used in order to tap feelings of relative deprivation in relation to characters in television drama. The questions were : 'A lot of television plays and serials are about people who are fairly well off. Do you ever wish you could have some of the things these people have?' (Q. 37), and : 'These programmes about people who are wealthy and successful could make you feel a little dissatisfied with your own lot in life. Do you ever get this feeling after seeing a programme?' (Q. 38). Responses to these questions correlated fairly highly ($r=0.585$ sig @ $<.001$), and so the scores on each were summed to make a composite 'television deprivation' score. Somewhat surprisingly only 38 percent of the sample claimed to experience no feelings of deprivation at all in relation to television characters, whilst 19 percent experienced a maximal degree of deprivation in terms of the range available on this measure. This finding in itself provides support for the hypothesis that viewers may have their store of personal dissatisfactions increased by virtue of watching particular kinds of television. 'Television deprivation' was found to relate significantly, but only slightly to negative racial attitudes as assessed by the H scale ($r=0.180$ sig @ $<.01$). This again is consistent with the proposition that personal frustrations can result in psychological scapegoating. We find that there is a small but significant positive correlation between finding television drama credible (Q. 36)[17] and experiencing relative deprivation in relation to television characters ($r=0.175$ sig @ $<.01$). This is an entirely reasonable finding since it would be psychologically inconsistent to doubt the credibility of television dramas and then experience resentment of characters in them. Rather it seems the more 'real life' the dramas are believed to be, then the more likely it is that they will serve to make viewers feel relatively deprived.

Given that both the degree of generalized relative deprivation and 'television deprivation' have been shown to be positively related to hostile attitudes, it would be reasonable to expect a positive relation between both forms of relative deprivation. In fact we found no significant relationship between 'television deprivation' and either measure of generalized relative deprivation. This, however, may be due to the fact that these measures are indeed tapping independent forms of relative deprivation. Runciman distinguished between egoistic and fraternalistic relative reprivation. The former is characterized by feelings of individual deprivation arising from comparisons of oneself with

[17] Responses to Q. 36 (a) and 36 (b) were each scored 1-4 and then summed.

others within an in-group. There is no deprivation felt concerning the in-group's position in society. Fraternal deprivation, on the other hand, is precisely the opposite in being deprivation arising from comparisons between one's in-group and other groups in society. It seems probable that the measure of generalized relative deprivation is tapping a sense of deprivation that is largely fraternalistic, whilst the 'television deprivation' is entirely egoistic. There is in fact some evidence to support this proposition. Two questions were included in the interview to tap the individual's feeling of status concern. One (Q. 49) was derived from Mizruchi[18] and the other (Q. 50g) from Kaufman's status-concern scale.[19] These two questions correlated positively, but not highly, ($r=0.391$ sig @ .001) and their scores were summed to provide a measure of status concern. It was found that this correlated positively with 'television deprivation' ($r=0.145$ sig @ .05) but not at all with the degree of generalized relative deprivation ($r=0.089$). This provides support for the view that 'television deprivation' is largely egoistic whereas generalized deprivation does not stem from such an egocentric outlook but is more related to fraternalistic considerations. Some incidental support for this last point can be found in the positive correlation between the degree of generalized relative deprivation and acceptance that Britain is lagging behind economically in comparison with other countries (Q. 45) ($r=0.155$ sig @ $<.05$). 'Television deprivation' is not significantly related to concern over Britain's economic decline.

These findings suggest that an individualistic competitive outlook tends to be related to 'television deprivation' whereas generalized relative deprivation as measured by our question is associated with a group oriented concern. These positions are not of course mutually exclusive; one may be concerned about the position of one's in-group in society and be highly conscious of one's own position within the in-group. In fact many respondents do exhibit both forms of deprivation simultaneously.

Given the somewhat *ad hoc* nature of the measures used to examine the area of relative deprivation in this study we would be foolish to draw any weighty conclusions. However, since it was a belief in the importance of this mediated relation between television content and racial attitudes which motivated the inclusion of the few questions possible, let us examine the

[18] Ephraim H. Mizruchi, *Success and Opportunity* (The Free Press of Glencoe, 1964).
[19] W. Kaufman, 'Status, Authoritarianism and Anti-Semitism' (*The American Journal of Sociology*, January 1957).

implications of the findings. We find support here for the hypothesis that feelings of relative deprivation can create the psychological stress which can become transmuted into the scapegoating of minority groups. We also have some indications that the credibility of television drama for many viewers can allow of feelings of relative deprivation in relation to dramatic characters. It seems intuitively probable, and there is some empirical support, that 'television deprivation' as we have measured it is of the egoistic variety and is related to concerns about individual status. Concern about status is in itself a symptom of a production economy where the needs of production necessitate the creation of demand. In a class society like Britain the promotion of status awareness has succeeded in establishing common values of acquisition and possession throughout all strata. The commodities pursued in different strata may differ, but acceptance of the legitamacy of the values is widespread. Where such universal goals exist they must penetrate into the culture encapsulated in the majority of television dramas where those who pursue the goals of acquisition are 'normal', and those who succeed are the heroes.

What is important about our findings is the inference they provide of an empirical connection between some of the central values of modern Western societies – particularly competitiveness and status striving – and a tendency to racial prejudice. There is the further inference that the mass media, insofar as they help to increase people's feelings of relative deprivation, may thereby indirectly make for greater hostility against immigrants. In other words they may influence the interracial situation for the worse through the values implicit in their general output and not only through the explicitly race related material that they carry. To clarify these relationships, more detailed and careful research is needed for which the present work may serve as a pilot study. Specifically more clarification of the concepts involved is needed – particularly the distinction between fraternalistic and egoistic relative deprivation[20] – and greater refinement in their measurement.

[20] Some important questions are raised by the recent work of Vannerman and Pettigrew op. cit. who suggest that two different facets of racial hostility, 'contact racism' and 'competitive racism' may be differentially related to fraternalistic and egoistic relative deprivation. The way their results are presented, however, makes the full significance of their findings difficult to appraise.

7

Race in the British Press

Our survey findings need to be seen in the light of an independently obtained description of mass media content before their significance can be fully assessed. We summarize here the results of an analysis of the treatment of race in the British national press between 1963 and 1970.[1]

Content Analysis

Content analysis of mass media has been carried out for a number of purposes and using a variety of methods, as the literature on the subject shows.[2] A description of mass media content on its own is not sufficient to be able to say anything reliable about mass media effects. For this we need 'audience' studies like the one we have reported, for there is ample evidence that selective perception and similar factors operate to produce different interpretations of the same mass media material in different kinds of 'audience'. Analysis of content should therefore be seen as an adjunct to the study of effects. Content analysis may also be used to derive inferences about the intentions and procedures underlying the production of the material. But here, too, in the last analysis, if it is production that we are interested in, then it is production that we should study. In our case we have been unable to study production processes directly, and are only able to provide a number of inferences and hypotheses about production, derived from the content analysis. These, hopefully, may be tested more directly at some time in the future.

There is good reason to think that the creation of *awareness* is one of the main effects of the news media, whereas the formation of *attitudes* and *opinions* about issues would seem to result more from subsequent face-to-face communication with

[1] Paul Hartmann, Charles Husband, Jean Clark, *Race as News: A Study of the handling of race in the British national press from 1963 to 1970*, a report to UNESCO of research carried out under a UNESCO grant. To be published shortly by UNESCO.
[2] See for instance Gerbner, G. et al. (eds.). *The Analysis of Communications Content*. (Wiley, New York, 1969).

others than from media consumption. Certainly Katz's studies[3] of voting behaviour and Rogers' work on the adoption of innovations[4] point very much in this direction, and our own survey findings support this general approach. Newspapers make people aware of certain things, and suggest the degree of importance that different events and issues have by the amount and prominence of coverage that they give them. A report of an event that is splashed across the front page tells the reader not only what happened, but also that the paper thinks it important or interesting and, by implication, that he too will (or should) find it important or interesting. In looking at the role of news in society, it may be misleading to maintain too sharp a distinction between events and issues on the one hand, and the news about them on the other. Events are reported because they are thought to be important; they are thought important because they appear in the news. The content analyst cannot claim to be studying events or their social consequences as such, nor can he claim to say much about what determines news output. He has to be content with saying something about what has been called 'events as news'[5] – that is, the versions of the world daily laid before the public as a kind of suggested agenda for their thought, discussion and action. How these images originate, and what kind of use is subsequently made of them are in themselves questions for separate investigation.

Method

In 1970 there were ten national daily newspapers. We chose the *Times,* the *Guardian,* the *Daily Express,* and the *Daily Mirror,* as being broadly representative of the British national daily press in terms of readership, political orientation, style and format. Between 1963 and 1970 these papers between them published about 10,000 issues and it was only possible to study a sample of the material. We did this by starting with a randomly selected date at the beginning of 1963 (Tuesday, 8 January) and then taking every thirteenth issue after that right through the period. The effect of this was to provide one issue of each paper each fortnight, rotated through the days of the week. The first issue was for a Tuesday, the next for a Wednesday, then the

[3] E. Katz, 'Communication Research and the Image of Society: Convergence of two traditions', in L. A. Dexter and D. M. White, *People, Society and Mass Communications* (Free Press, New York, 1964).
[4] E. M. Rogers, *Diffusion of Innovations* (Free Press, New York, 1962).
[5] See, Daniel J. Boorstin, *The Image* (Penguin Books, 1963), and James D. Halloran, Philip Elliott and Graham Murdock, *Demonstrations and Communication: A Case Study* (Penguin Books, 1970).

Thursday a fortnight later and so on, so as to average out any variations associated with particular days of the week. This gave a total sample of 193 issues of each paper, 24 each year except for 1968 which was a leap year and yielded 25 issues. Because the samples for the four papers were from the same days they may be directly compared with each other, if we can assume that all had equal access to news.

Sports pages, women's pages, the *Times Business News,* jokes book reviews and other specialized sections of the papers were ignored, but all items over $1\frac{1}{2}$ column inches in length appearing on the news pages were scanned, whether they were news stories, feature articles, editorials, letters, photographs or political cartoons. An item was read if its heading or introduction suggested that it might be about race or coloured people. It was included in the analysis if it was about coloured people in Britain or about relations between white and non-white anywhere in the English-speaking world. Passing references to race or colour in items on other subjects did not meet our criteria for inclusion; a coloured person or race had to be an explicit and substantive part of the item's main subject matter.

Main Themes and Reference Themes

Our coding schedule was designed with a view to answering two main kinds of question : How much race related material was there, and what was the material about? We aimed to discover what kind of situations and events race and colour were associated with, how the issues surrounding the question were defined, and what kind of meaning and significance questions of race and colour were given. Each item was classified initially as either British or Overseas according to whether it pertained to the situation in Britain or elsewhere. It was then classified into one, and only one, of the following categories according to its main topic of subject-matter.

1. **Housing:** This included everything about the housing of coloured people – except discrimination in housing which was classified Discrimination.
2. **Education:** Everything relating to the education of coloured people or their impact on the educational system. Most items under this topic concerned primary and secondary education, though a few referred to university provision for students from the Commonwealth.
3. **Health:** Anything about the health of immigrants, their impact on the health services or public health.

4. **Employment:** Anything about coloured people in employment or in relation to the labour market, except discrimination in employment which was classified Discrimination.

5. **Numbers:** Material about the size of the coloured population, including reports of census figures, population projections, birth rates, and so on.

6. **White Hostility:** This included assaults, hostile, derogatory or racist statements about coloured people, and the anti-black activities or right wing organizations. The hostility had to be racial in character – not personal. Material about coloured people as victims of violent crime was classified 'Normal' (see 14 below) unless there was a racial motive for the attack.

7. **Black Hostility:** As with White Hostility, this category included hostile and derogatory actions and statements, along racial lines, of blacks towards whites. 'Non-racial' assaults were classified Crime. (See 12 below.)

8. **Discrimination:** Anything which was primarily about coloured people receiving less favourable, or unfair, treatment on the basis of their colour or ethnic origin.

9. **Coloured Discrimination:** As for Discrimination, but *by* coloureds against whites. Only six items occurred under this topic.

10. **Police:** Anything primarily about coloured people and police (excluding Crime). The bulk of our material concerned coloureds entering the police service.

11. **Racial Harmony:** Any item whose main emphasis was on the lack of conflict and prejudice between races.

12. **Crime:** Coloured people accused, suspected, convicted or otherwise portrayed as participating in criminal activity.

13. **Disturbance:** Material about riots or demonstrations involving coloured people. Specific attacks by blacks on whites or whites on blacks were classified as Black or White Hostility; the disturbance needed to be of a general nature.

14. **Normal:** Material in which coloured people featured prominently through their involvement in otherwise-newsworthy events – as victims of crimes, for instance, or in 'human interest' stories. Coloureds who 'happened' to get into the news.

15. **Cultural Differences:** Material about the different cultures of coloured groups.

16. **Celebrities:** Coloured people who got into the news because of their status as celebrities – Muhamed Ali, Eartha Kitt, Sammy Davis Jnr. etc.

17. **Immigration:** Anything relating mainly to the entry of coloured people to Britain.
18. **Legislation:** Anything primarily about the various pieces of legislation (including the 1965 White Paper) concerned with immigration and race relations.
19. **Race Relations:** A broad category taking material that was primarily about relations between white and coloured, not specific enough to be classified into other categories. It included discussion about race relations as a general topic and the various steps taken to regulate race relations.
20. **Sport:** Consisted mainly of material about the events and controversy surrounding the South African rugby tour of Britain in 1969 and the (eventually cancelled) cricket tour of 1970, the (cancelled) British cricket tour of South Africa, and South African participation in the Olympic Games.
21. **South Africa:** A broad category, differentiated by the distribution of subtopics (see below), about the racial situation in South Africa.
22. **Rhodesia:** All material relating to the relative positions of white and black in Rhodesia – concerned mainly with the Rhodesian unilateral declaration of independence.
23. **Other:** Material about coloured people or race which did not fit under any of the previous topics. It was extremely varied but Civil Rights activities and black organizations in the US were distinguished as subtopics (see below).

Within the area of subject-matter represented by each of these topic headings, it was to some extent possible to distinguish more specific types of subject-matter, and each topic was divided into a number of sub-topics which made it possible to say more specifically what the material falling under any topic heading was about. Sub-topics under the general topic heading Immigration, for instance, included immigration control, coloureds refused entry, illegal entry, and Kenya Asians. Each item was classified under one sub-topic within the broader topic heading. A full list of sub-topics is given in the original report.[6] Here we make use of the data reported there in describing the subject-matter of the material falling under major topic headings.

This classification represented our main index of what the item was about, and was based on the dominant or central theme of the item taken as a whole. In addition we employed a subsidiary classification in which all subsidiary themes occur-

[6] Paul Hartmann, Charles Husband and Jean Clark, op. cit.

ring in the item were noted. This was done for the British material only. We used a list of reference themes parallel to the list of sub-topics (with some appropriate additions and omissions) and any of these occurring in the item was checked on the coding form. We were thus able to discover not only what the items were mainly about, but also what other matters were referred to in the course of the treatment of the main subject-matter. Thus an item on the Race Relations Act of 1968, for instance, would be classified Legislation as its main topic, but if it made reference also to discrimination, immigration, housing or other themes, these would be recorded as references.

The coding of main topics was carried out with an inter-judge reliability of .79 (using Scott's formula[7] for nominal scale coding). Length of items was measured in column inches, but since there was a rank order correlation of .98 between the number of items falling into each category and the number of column inches, column inches and number of items are effectively equivalent measures.

We based most of our analysis on figures for all four papers combined. There were two reasons for this. In the first place we were not concerned primarily with identifying differences between the papers, but to be able to say something about the kind of thing made available to the public as a whole. The fact that there are differences between papers does not matter greatly when there is considerable overlap among the sections of society in which the papers are read. They may still create public awareness and provide subject-matter for discussion, even for those who do not read them, provided that what they print is widely enough read to stand a chance of getting into general circulation.

In the second place, there is a good empirical reason for combining the material of the four papers, and this is that they proved to be similar in the kind of subject-matter that they carried. When numbers of column inches falling under different topic headings were ranked, the coefficient of concordance[8] across the four papers was .86. When British material only was considered, the coefficient was still high (.70). In other words, in terms of what they carried material *about,* the papers were similar to each other. This does not mean that they did not have different attitudes and advocate different policies towards the

[7] W. A. Scott, 'Reliability of Content Analysis: The Case of Nominal Scale Coding' (*Public Opinion Quarterly, Fall, 1955,* pp. 321-325).
[8] S. Siegel, *Non-Parametric Statistics for the Behavioural Sciences* (McGraw Hill, pp. 229-238, 1956).

issues surrounding race and colour – they did. But they were in close agreement about what the issues were, about what kind of thing warranted most coverage and what least, about what aspects of the situation were newsworthy. This is an important finding because it provides suggestions about news production. The similar patterns of attention to different kinds of subject-matter was partly the result of the fact that, because the papers were all from the same dates, they had the same events available to report. But this cannot completely explain the similarities. In the first place the material that they could have carried on the sample days was always far in excess of what they actually carried, and it seems that they made a similar kind of selection from what was available. But even this is only part of the explanation, for on most days there was only partial overlap in the stories and types of subject matter carried, and on some days none at all. The real similarity only emerged when the different kinds of material were aggregated over time. Then the kinds of things they thought worth printing and the amount of space they gave to different kinds of material turned out to be very similar indeed, and the picture presented did not vary much from paper to paper. We may now examine in more detail the key features of this picture.

The Overseas Picture

Table 7.1 shows the total number of items of British and overseas race related material appearing in the four papers. Between them they carried an average of over ten items per day (amounting to over two thirds of a standard newspaper page) just under half of which concerned the situation in Britain. Though the qualities carried about twice as much as the populars there was sufficient material for the reader of any of these papers to be likely to come across *something* relating to race on the average day. In other words, during the period there was a 'noticeable' amount of space given to the subject, amounting to over two thirds of 1 percent of total newspaper space and 1.5 percent of editorial space.

The majority of the overseas material came from Rhodesia, South Africa, and the United States. The topics, Rhodesia, South Africa, Sport, Disturbance, White Hostility, Discrimination and Black Hostility were the biggest topics and together accounted for 79 percent of all overseas material. The material under White Hostility, Discrimination, and Disturbance came mainly from America, while Black Hostility came from both Africa and America. Much of the coverage classified under Sport was located in Britain and concerned events surrounding the visits or proposed visits of South African sports teams to Briain but was classified as 'overseas' because it pertained to overseas situations.

The material classified under the heading, Rhodesia, consisted of a great deal of description and discussion relating to the Rhodesian declaration of independence, and material of a general nature concerning the relative positions of black and white in Rhodesia. There was also much of a more specific nature about the detention and trial of opponents of the Smith regime, about the question of African majority rule and conflict between white and black there. By no means all material carried in the papers about the Rhodesian situation was included in our analysis because we only accepted material that referred explicitly to the relationships or relative positions of white and black. Thus, for instance, much concerning the policy of economic sanctions against Rhodesia was not included because it did not meet this criterion. A similar qualification applies to the South African material which consisted mainly of discussion and description relating to South Africa's apartheid policies, reports of the detention and trial of political opponents of the regime, and the question of supplying British arms to South Africa.

Below are examples of the kind of thing that made up the bulk of the overseas material.

Rhodesia:

'RHODESIAN BRAKE ON AFRICANS' – Report of provisions of the new republican constitution making it more difficult for Africans to achieve increased Parliamentary representation. (*Guardian*, 14/1/70)

'SMITH FIGHTS A CANOE INVASION – . . . . invading terrorists . . . fighting Rhodesian army troops . . .' (*Mirror*, 18/3/68)

A cartoon in which a woman, shopping for Christmas cards, says, 'I'm looking for an adoration of the Magi with a rather prominent black King for sending to friends in Rhodesia'. (*Express*, 4/12/65)

South Africa:

'STOP BRITISH ENCOURAGEMENT OF APARTHEID' – The British Council of Churches was urged to press for action against South Africa's apartheid policies. (*Times*, 5/1/65)

'COMMUNISM CHARGES IN SOUTH AFRICA' – Seven men were charged in court at Durban with being members of the Communist Party. (*Times*, 5/1/65)

'COMMONS CLASH OVER ARMS FOR SOUTH AFRICA' – Intention of the new Conservative Government to resume the supply of arms. (*Express*, 15/7/70)

Sport:

'CRICKET TOUR FEARS AS ASHE IS DENIED SOUTH AFRICAN VISA' – The refusal to allow the black American tennis champion to play in South Africa was seen as boding ill for the proposed South African cricket tour of Britain. (*Times*, 29/1/70)

Disturbance:

'1,000 NEGROES HELD IN ALABAMA CLASH' – Account of arrests of negroes, including children, and their ill-treatment by police after mass demonstration. (*Mirror*, 4/2/65)

White hostility:

'White supremacist Jimmy Robertson was sentenced today . . . for attacking Negro leader Dr Martin Luther King.' (*Express*, 20/1/65)

Discrimination:

'MAY A CLUB REFUSE NEGRO? – The Supreme Court (USA) has reserved its decision whether a swimming and tennis club . . . was entitled to discriminate against Negro members.' (*Guardian*, 15/10/69)

Black hostility:

'BAD DEAL FOR BRITONS' – a letter recounting how the writer had experienced restrictions on freedom of speech and insults to Britain while living in Central Africa. (*Express*, 13/2/70)

Over the period, then, the British public was kept aware of the continuing situations of racial injustice and oppression in South Africa and Rhodesia. The South African situation took on particular salience over the arms question, and arrived on the British doorstep in more immediate and dramatic form, through the controversies and demonstrations over sports teams. The United States provided a picture of race riots and inter-racial hostility.

As presented in the press, the main features of relations between white and black overseas were oppression, injustice, violence and conflict between the races. For sections of the white British population the idea that Britain is a multi-racial society is a new and unusual one; for many the idea does not yet even seem to have been accepted. If the image of race overseas presented by the press has been taken as an indication of the kind of situation that it to be expected when white and black live together, it is perhaps not surprising that the entry of coloured people to Britain has been greeted with so much hostility and resentment. Obviously the complexities of British race relations cannot be explained so simply but the centrality of violence and conflict in the overseas coverage helps explain the relatively high frequency of reference to riots and trouble in our respondents' answers to the open-ended questions and the common attribution of such information to mass media sources. This illustrates how media-relayed images of race overseas may come to form part of the perspective within which race in Britain is interpreted. The existence of such a perspective would seem likely to exacerbate rather than to counter the tendencies to prejudice, discrimination and racial conflict already inherent in British society. With this overseas picture as a background we may now look at the press's picture of race in Britain.

The British Picture

Table 7.2 shows the amount of British material under different topic headings for the different papers. The seven leading topics were Immigration, Race Relations, Crime, Normal, Legislation, Discrimination, and White Hostility, which between them accounted for 70 percent of all material.

Examination of the distribution of items among sub-topics under the general heading of Immigration showed that this material was not simply about coloured people coming to settle in the country but that it had as a central theme the question of keeping them out. Material on immigration control, on illegal entry, people being refused entry, and the Kenya Asian issue, which are all aspects of the question of immigration control, accounted for 60 percent of the material under this heading.

Most of the material under the second biggest topic heading, 'Race Relations', was of a fairly general nature concerning the relations between white and black with more specific material, accounted for disproportionately by the *Guardian*, on the Race Relations Board, community relations organizations, immigrant organizations, and the appointment of social workers and others for the sake of improving race relations.

Material on crime, was about the general run of crime. Prostitution, drug and illegal immigration offences, often regarded as specifically 'coloured' crimes, formed only a small proportion of the total. In about a quarter of the items it was apparent from the headline alone that it was a coloured person that was involved in the crime – a practice for which the press has often been criticized.

'Normal' material, the next highest topic, was of two broad kinds. There were news stories in which coloured people figured prominently, as victims of accidents or crimes, for instance, but in which their race or colour was subsidiary to the central interest of the story. Secondly, there were 'human interest' stories in which the race of the people involved was sometimes incidental, but sometimes part of the 'human interest' as for instance in the report, with picture, of a coloured man working as a Santa Claus for the Christmas season. This topic heading collected material in which coloured people 'cropped up' in the general run of newspaper coverage in the same way as other people not involved in race relations do. It represented the kind of material that came closest to showing coloured people as ordinary members of society, having ordinary 'human interest', and not essentially different from anyone else.

The material classified as Discrimination consisted mainly of reports of specific instances of discrimination against blacks; that on Legislation was mainly comment on legislation by politicians, the newspapers themselves, and in readers' letters, and accounts of parliamentary debates; while the White Hostility category was mainly accounts of hostile, derogatory, or racist statements about coloured people, together with a smaller number of racial assaults and anti-coloured demonstrations. Examples of the kind of material classified under these major topics are given below.

Immigration:

'SANDYS ACTS TO CURB IMMIGRANTS' – About the intention of Conservative Opposition Member of Parliament to try to introduce a Bill to limit further the entry of coloured immigrants. (*Express*, 2/12/67)

'POLICE DISCUSS IMMIGRANTS' – A report of the intention of police throughout Britain to meet to discuss ways of breaking the international ring believed to be responsible for the smuggling of immigrants into Britain. 'They will also discuss how they can round up hundreds of illegal immigrants smuggled into Britain in the last two years.' (*Guardian*, 15/7/70)

'APOLOGY AND PERMIT FOR ASIAN' – A report of the Home Office's apology to a Pakistani father for their refusal to admit his 13 year old daughter because they believed her to be already in the country. (*Guardian*, 15/7/70)

Race relations:

'PRIMATE ASKED TO HELP RACE RELATIONS' – The Archbishop

of Canterbury was asked to convene a conference on race relations. (*Guardian*, 21/12/64)

'MULTI-RACIAL PARTY' – Christmas party for white and black children held by group interested in promoting racial harmony. (*Guardian*, 21/12/64)

An account of a sermon given by the widow of Dr Martin Luther King in St Paul's Cathedral on the subject of race relations. (*Express*, 17/3/69)

Crime:

'JURY HEARS EXTRACTS FROM TAPE RECORDING' – Report of the trial of two coloured men for murder. (*Times*, 5/11/64)

Normal;

'BABY DIES IN FIRE' – The baby was coloured. (*Times*, 7/3/64)

'THE LITTLE GIRLS THAT SANTA FORGOT' – An article with a large picture of two seven-year-old girls, one black and one white, holding Christmas presents. Race was not referred to in the text of the article. (*Mirror*, 30/1/69)

'BBC APPOINTS FIRST COLOURED ANNOUNCER' – Black radio announcer appointed. (*Guardian*, 6/7/65)

Legislation:

'DEBATE SOON ON IMMIGRANTS' – Discussion of forthcoming Parliamentary debate on the renewal of the Commonwealth Immigrants Act, 1962. (*Times*, 5/11/64)

Discrimination:

'EXPOSE COLOUR BAR FIRMS : DEMAND – An exposure of . . . firms who refuse to employ coloured labour was demanded at a meeting . . . at Wolverhampton last night . . .' (*Mirror*, 5/1/65)

White hostility:

The account of part of a radio programme being cut in which a Conservative member of Parliament indicated his distaste for the idea of 'a great big buck nigger' marrying a white girl and producing 'coffee-coloured grandchildren'. (*Mirror*, 9/4/63)

Changes over Time

The amount of race related material appearing in the press increased over the period. This was due entirely to an increase in the British material for which there was nearly twice as much in the second half of the period as in the first. This increase shows that as the coloured population increased so press attention to race related matters increased. The pattern of this increase is worth examining. The total British coverage showed an upward trend with two peaks, in 1965 and 1968, the years of major legislation on immigration and race relations. The total amount of coverage rose from 1963 until 1965 and then fell off, but not as low as it had been before 1965. It then continued to rise until 1968, the year of further legislation and Powell's speeches, and then fell off again but once again not as low as it had been before 1968. This pattern of peaks and plateaux was due mainly to the rises and falls in the categories, Immigration, Race Relations, Legislation, and White Hostility, which came into particular prominence in the years of legislation.

Other significant features of the pattern of increasing coverage emerged from a consideration of the categories that did not rise systematically. In the first place proportionately less attention was paid to the housing, education and employment of coloured people in the second half of the period, and secondly, neither the Normal category nor Crime increased in a systematic fashion. This means that the pattern of increasing news attention to race and colour cannot be explained entirely by the simple formula 'more coloured people make more coloured news'. For more coloureds in the country did not mean more 'coloured news' of all kinds. In particular, the increasing coloured population did not result in increased press attention to their relation to the major social resources of housing, education and employment, nor to their activities as 'normal' members of the society. The topics, Immigration, Race Relations, White Hostility, Black Hostility, Discrimination, Legislation and Numbers, on the other hand, did increase and accounted importantly for the total pattern of increase over the period. They showed not only an absolute rise, but taken together they accounted for a greater *proportion* of the material published towards the end of the period than towards the beginning. The press handling of race in other words showed a progressive convergence on the themes represented by these topics over the period. This leads to the inference that over the years, anything about race that could be handled in these terms came increasingly to be regarded as more newsworthy than material that needed to be handled within a different frame of reference. These themes, of course, were those that were central to political debate on the subject during the period.

Major Reference Themes

Confirmation of the existence of a particular frame of reference within which race related matters tended to be handled by the press came from further analysis that we carried out into the subsidiary themes invoked in the treatment of the subject. The results that we have summarized above show what kind of subject-matter most newspaper items were *about*. The reference themes also coded for each item allowed us to see what kinds of things were referred to in the treatment of other kinds of subject-matter. This made it possible to ask, for instance, when material on discrimination is published, are other themes also typically referred to in the course of the treatment, and what are they? Or is the subject dealt with in a relatively 'self-contained' way, without must reference to matters beyond its immediate area of subject-matter?

When we talk about a news framework or frame of reference we mean the set of inference about what is related to what, that define an area of subject-matter. Football, for instance, is commonly discussed with reference to a limited range of themes such as the league table, the scoring of goals, the rules of the game – hardly ever does the rhetoric of party politics enter the matter, for football is not presented as being related to party politics. By asking what in the field of race relations is discussed with reference to what we were able to discover a number of central defining themes that together suggest the key significance that matters of race are given in their press handling. Central to the press's picture of race were those aspects represented by the categories, Race Relations, Legislation, Immigration, White Hostility and Discrimination, and the politician Enoch Powell, who, since 1968, has emerged as a symbol of anti-immigrant feeling. Not only were these themes among those most frequently mentioned in the press but when one was mentioned there was a high likelihood that others would be mentioned as well. These were also the areas of subject-matter upon which we found progressive convergence of attention over the period. Material under the categories, Normal and Crime, on which there was no proportionate increase in attention, was by contrast handled with very little reference to other matters. So, by and large, were the topics, Housing, Education, and Employment, though these did tend to be referred to in discussion of other things; but they remained nevertheless peripheral to the picture of race presented in the press.

In an earlier chapter we noted, by way of an example, that if a drink is thought of as a beverage its taste becomes its most crucial characteristic, while if it is defined as a medicine then its curative properties become most salient. On a similar basis we can now point to the specific defining characteristics of the category 'race' as reflected in press content. Our analysis showed that the press handling of race has presented as most salient questions of immigration, particularly of keeping the blacks out, the relationships between white and black, particularly inter-group hostility, and discrimination against blacks, the legislation and machinery introduced to regulate these matters, and the views of the politician, Enoch Powell. Peripheral to this picture have been questions of coloured housing, education and employment, and the image of the black man as an ordinary member of the society.

Headlines

Additional and broadly consistent findings emerged from an analysis of headlines. Headlines are important because they are more often read than the text of items, because they have been shown to influence the reader's interpretation of the text,[9] and because they tend to provide a brief and often memorable summary of what the item contains. 39 percent of all the material that we examined (including the overseas) was signalled as race related by words such as 'race', 'colour', 'immigrant', 'Negro' in the headline. In the British material, 7 percent of headings contained 'colour/ed' and 15 percent contained 'immigrant' or 'migrant', whereas only 9 percent used a specific ethnic name such as 'Pakistani' or 'Jamaican'. This is an indication of the extent to which it is normal in Britain to refer to non-white groups in an undifferentiated way as 'coloured', and of the way in which 'immigrant' has become synonymous with 'coloured immigrant'. It closely reflects our survey finding of the un-differentiated use among our samples of 'coloured' rather than specific ethnic names and the acceptance of 'immigrant' as meaning 'coloured immigrant'.

Ten percent of headings contained violent words like 'murder', 'kill', 'shoot' or 'burn'. This was particularly characteristic of overseas material, confirming earlier indications that violence was a central theme of the overseas picture. 12 percent of headings included words like 'hate', 'crisis', 'row', 'clash', and 'threat' connoting conflict and disagreement, and 6 percent contained restrictive words like 'stop', 'curb', 'cut', 'ban', 'bar'.

[9] See P. H. Tannenbaum, 'The effect of headlines on the interpretation of news stories' (*Journalism Quarterly*, 30, 1953, pp. 189-197) and P. B. Warr and B. Knapper, *The Perception of People and Events*. (John Wiley and Sons, 1968).

When the word 'race' or one of its derivatives occurred, the heading also contained a violent or 'conflict' word about 30 percent of the time. 'Coloured' went with a restrictive word 21 percent of the time and a conflict word 14 percent of the time. 'Immigrant' went with a restictive word 12 percent of the time. Ethnic names, like 'Negro', went with violent words 16 percent of the time particularly in overseas material.

Words acquire their meanings partly from the contexts in which they are used, and these conjunctions suggest the sort of meaning that matters of race have been given in the press. The following are some illustrative headlines:

Race Hate	(*Mirror*, 21/12/64)
Racial Clash in Texas	(*Times*, 7/7/64)
Race Rumpus over Wilson	(*Mirror*, 30/4/70)
ITA Acts on race conflict outburst	(*Express*, 3/8/67)
Uproar at Race Debate	(*Guardian*, 20/1/65)
Mississippi Racial Bombing Arrests	(*Times*, 6/10/64)
Club votes for a colour bar	(*Mirror*, 22/1/69)
Tenants' threat on colour	(*Times*, 14/2/69)
Soldiers in Colour Row	(*Mirror*, 14/11/69)
Jamaican quits over migrants curb	(*Express*, 20/9/65)
Curb flow of Immigrants or face disaster: Mr Thorneycroft's proposals	(*Times*, 6/3/65)
Ban eases for last migrants	(*Express*, 2/3/68)
70 Negroes arrested at Selma: more violence	(*Guardian*, 20/1/65)
Melanie's two weeks with Negro family starts a row	(*Express*, 1/8/68)
Negro mob on rampage in New York	(*Guardian*, 19/2/65)
Gaol for man for landing Asians	(*Times*, 30/11/68)
Seven killed by Negro with shotgun	(*Times*, 22/5/64)

The kinds of meaning that race related words are likely to acquire through persistent use in these kinds of contexts are fairly obvious. For a hypothetical person whose understanding of the situation came solely from reading headlines 'race' would be likely to acquire connotations of conflict, dispute and violence in some degree at least. Specifically, race rows, rumpuses, and racial clashes would appear to be fairly common occurrences, with a good sprinkling of riots, killings, and shootings. Coloured immigrants appear as liable to be barred by the unofficial action of whites or curbed or banned by official and legislative action which itself is attended by rows and clashes. Coloured groups, mentioned by name, particularly Negroes, are depicted frequently as involved in burning and shooting, and as being arrested, jailed or deported.

A Note on Local Newspapers

A smaller scale analysis was carried out on a sample of eighteen issues each of a number of local daily and evening newspapers between March and July 1970. Some of them were from areas of high immigrant settlement (the West Midlands and West Yorkshire) and some from areas with relatively small coloured populations (Glasgow, Darlington and Teesside). The methodology was not quite the same as in the study of national papers, so the two studies are not directly comparable. Nevertheless, the analysis yielded some broad indications that are of interest.

The main finding was that, as might be expected, there was far more race related material in local papers published in 'immigrant areas' than elsewhere. While the papers in areas with a few coloured immigrants carried about the same number of items per day as there were on 'British' material in the *popular* nationals (about 0.8 per day), those in immigrant areas had over three times as many (about 2.9 items per day). This means that people in immigrant areas have greater access to news about race and coloured people than others, even though we found in our survey work that they were less dependent on the press for their information than people in Low areas. The kinds of material published did not vary much from one paper to another or from one kind of area to another. The locals were similar to the nationals in the heavy emphasis they gave to material that in the national analysis would have been classified as Race Relations and in their attention to the views of Enoch Powell. There was relatively heavier emphasis on material falling under the Crime and Normal topic headings, but less attention to the kind of subject-matter represented by the category Immigration. This probably reflects the local papers' focus on local events rather than national issues. As in the nationals, relatively little attention was paid to questions of immigrant housing, employment or education. Overall, the general drift of the coverage particularly the conflict/threat orientation, was very similar to what we found in the nationals.

Summary

In summary, the papers we examined carried, on average, something every day about coloured people in Britain or about relations between white and black in the English-speaking world. This would seem sufficient to sustain public awareness of race as a major principle of social classification. Central to the overseas material were the themes of oppression, injustice, violence and conflict. The British material was much more varied, but its main focus was on those aspects of the British situation that were central to political debate and action in regard to race and coloured people. Race in Britain was portrayed as being concerned mainly with immigration and the control of entry of coloured people to the country, with relations between white and coloured groups, discrimination and hostility between groups, with legislation, and with the politician, Enoch Powell. These were the main terms in which race was presented, and when the subject of race appeared in the press, these themes were more likely to be invoked than others. Emphasis on these themes increased systematically over the period and it would seem that, increasingly, material that could be handled in these terms was more likely to be printed than material that needed other handling. Material about coloured people involved in crime and what we called Normal material were not on the whole handled in these terms, and these topics did not increase systematically over the period, nor did attention to the housing, employment and educational circumstances of coloured people. We interpret this pattern of results as indicating the existence of a structure of inferences about the significance of race in Britain that has led to a selective emphasis over the period. One effect of this emerging news framework has been that the perspective within which coloured people are presented as ordinary members of society has become increasingly overshadowed by a news perspective in which they are presented as a problem. The emerging framework that we have identified is such that, as the number of coloured people and the social concern over race relations has increased, so attention has moved away from the relation of coloured people to the major social resources of housing, education and employment – which must be regarded as an important part of the underlying basis of interracial hostility in the country – towards the hostility itself and its manifestations, including the concern to keep coloured people out of the country and the concern to regulate hostility, by the various laws and machinery set up to these ends. We have the situation in which the press has reflected pressures that on the one hand have sought to exclude coloureds from British society and on the other have aimed to reduce discrimination against them; but has not at the same time paid proportionate attention to those factors that must be regarded as part of the underlying cause of anti-immigrant feeling and discrimination. But, most importantly – and this is the essential feature of the press treatment of race – coloured people have not on the whole been portrayed as an integral part of British society. Instead the press has continued to project an image of Britain as a *white* society in which the coloured population is seen as some kind of aberration, a problem, or just an oddity, rather than as 'belonging' to the society.

We may note here the close correspondence between what our newspaper analysis has revealed and what the survey data showed to be derived from the mass media by our respondents. On the one hand they showed awareness of the hostility, discrimination and disadvantages suffered by the coloured population and typically attributed this kind of information to media sources. The counterpart in the press is the relatively large amount of material that we classified under the headings of Discrimination and White Hostility and which we have seen were among the themes that were central to the press definition of the significance of race in Britain. Among our samples we found that, with due allowance for the effects of selective perception and interpretation, discrimination and the deprivations of coloured people were commonly viewed with concern. This we take as evidence of the vitality of equalitarian values in Britain. Such values were also well in evidence in the press where prejudice and discrimination were commonly condemned and deplored, and where much of the editorial comment in particular showed a concern to improve race relations. At the same time our subjects had a very strong sense derived from the media, that coloured people represent a problem and a threat, expressed particularly in concern over immigrant numbers, the possibility of trouble and other resentments and anxieties. This aspect, too, of their view of the world was closely paralleled in the press and was in fact the dominant emphasis of the newspaper material with its heavy attention to questions of immigration control, racial tension and the views of Enoch Powell. From 1968 onwards Powell was referred to in nearly one sixth of all newspaper items relating to the British situation. It seemed as though once Powell and his views became incorporated into the frame of reference within which race in Britain has come to be reported the press found it difficult to mention the subject without bringing Powell into it. We have seen how a considerable proportion (29 percent) even of the children knew of Powell and his views while hardly any (6 percent) could name other politicians in this context.

There is one point at which the parallel between the state of affairs as conceived by our subjects and as reflected in the press appears to break down. Respondents commonly attributed to media sources beliefs that we classified as Poor Housing ('they cause slums', etc.) while we found that this aspect of the situation was relatively neglected by the press. This disparity may be the result of selective perception, or it may be that housing has received more attention on television. (Perhaps slums lend themselves better to television than to newspaper reporting. We have been making the assumption, which we argue more fully in the next chapter, that there are broad similarities in the news and current affairs information offered by the different media.) Whatever the reason for this disparity over housing, the overall similarities between the world as seen by our subjects and the world as reflected in the press are striking, and as we have shown are consistent across a number of open-ended questions. When the adults, for instance, were asked (Q. 24) what they could recall reading about coloured people in the press; crime, riots and trouble (including the American situation), and political debate (particularly Powell) were the most frequently recalled subjects.

It is clear that the press (and the news media in general) have not merely reflected public consciousness on matters of race and colour but have played a significant part in shaping this consciousness. For this we have not only the evidence from the content analysis but also the findings of the surveys. While maintaining on the one hand the visibility and vitality of official egalitarian values, news coverage has tended to emphasize those aspects of the situation in which coloured people appear essentially as a threat and a problem. They have helped define the interracial state of affairs in a way that makes the development of attitudes of hostility among the white population more likely than acceptance. The emphasis on themes relating to immigration control, interracial hostility, tension, and conflict and Enoch Powell, represents cumulatively a perspective on the world in which the black man is seen as undesirable. In this it is of course true that the media have in part merely reflected the way the question has been defined in political circles, and this may illustrate the hegemonic nature of views held by ruling elites. The total effect of news coverage of race has nevertheless been at least partly contrary to the official egalitarian values of our society to which the media are committed, and at variance with the news media's evident intentions of opposing racism and countering racial tension.

8

The News Media and Race Relations

In order to explain the disparity between the apparent intentions of the news media and the explicitly anti-racist editorial positions that they periodically express, on the one hand, and the demonstrated effects of their coverage on the other, it is necessary to look more closely at the way the news media operate.

There are no universally accepted and recorded codes or rules applied by newsmen in the selection and production of news. Much of the journalist's professional judgment is acquired incidentally rather than through direct instruction. There are certain dictums which can be passed on verbally, but much of the judgment of the journalist is gained by 'picking up' the criteria used by established journalists, and unconsciously absorbing the value system of his fellows. The largely subjective nature of news judgment is illustrated by a statement in the report of an international conference on the problems of television news coverage.

The report says of television news reporting: 'We are not talking about a science or a technique; it is really an art which is at the fingertips of the practitioner. It depends on many thousands of personal judgments, moods and feelings . . .'[1] The subjective nature of the art of news production is also apparent from Warner's[2] account of decision making in American network television news: 'Criteria used in news selection are largely subjective; personnel in TV newsrooms have difficulty articulating them. The executive producers very frequently use the phrase "it grabs me" or "it doesn't grab me". This is a shorthand way of saying that it excites their news sense'. Newspaper editors have also acknowledged the subjective nature

[1] Quoted in J. D. Halloran et al. *Demonstrations and Communication: A Case Study* (Penguin Books, 1970, p. 25).
[2] Malcolm Warner, 'Decision-making in Network Television News' in Jeremy Tunstall, *Media Sociology* (Constable, London, 1970).

of news values and speak, for example, of having a 'feel for news'.[3]

Some of the criteria and standards by which journalists work, such as those embodied in codes of practice and professional ethics – are quite explicit and easy to apply. Others – particularly those covered by terms like 'news sense' and 'news value' – may be far from explicit and may not even be consciously identified by journalists themselves. This has implications for the way in which race is handled. The subjective nature of news judgments also makes academic criticism of news reporting and meaningful dialogue between researchers and newsmen particularly difficult, for as Evans[4] has said, 'so many of the judgments become so routine that we forget we are making them'. Because of this the journalist may find it difficult to determine in retrospect what it was that made him present a story as he did.

The largely implicit nature of many of the criteria of what makes 'news' is, however, not problematic for the journalist. Rather, news values facilitate his work by providing a habitualized approach to creating good news copy. They help him to sift the plethora of available events into those which are newsworthy and those which are not, and from the raw material provided in this way to reject some and process others into news stories. News values help further in deciding how those stories which finally make the news should be handled. The whole process is simplified and lubricated by the fact that so many of the judgments made are routine and the criteria used implicit. However, what is relevant from the point of view of a good story is not necessarily identical with social relevance. The news media operate within a commercial framework and news values evolved in a context in which the attraction of an audience was as important an objective as the provision of information. Furthermore, as Shibutani[5] has pointed out, the existence of a 'public' for information creates a demand for information of a particular kind, and this is likely to influence the kind of 'news' provided, whether this shows itself in an attempt to be more 'entertaining' or in a concern to cultivate or not to challenge particular social values. In regard to the news media's handling of race we may begin our analysis of the

[3] Examples of the subjective judgments of an American city editor are given in: Walter Gieber, *A City Editor Selects the News*, a paper given to the American Sociological Association 1961.
[4] Harold Evans, 'Positive Policy', *Race and the Press* (Runnymede Trust, 1971).
[5] Tamotsu Shibutani, *Improvised News* (Bobbs-Merrill, New York, 1966).

news process with reference to the American situation upon which a relatively large amount of work has been done, before going on to consider the British media.

The American News Media and Race

Much of the American literature on the media and race relations consists of media personnel recording their self-criticisms. In 1965 American newsmen got together to discuss 'The Racial Crisis and the News Media' and in the course of their discussion they showed a considerable awareness of their collective failings.[6] The tendency for the northern States to concentrate on the southern States as the seat of racial problems is noted by Hunt[7]; and Boone[8] and Carter[9] record the tendency within the southern press not to give adequate coverage to *local* civil rights activities. A more general criticism was that the media had failed to provide any background which might permit a better understanding of the racial crisis. The editors in reviewing the conference said 'During the three-day conference, a frequent charge was that the media have devoted too much time and space to "enumerating the wounded" and too little to describing the background problems of the Negro in America and the aims and goals of the Negro revolution' :

> What is not a crisis is not usually reported, and what is not or cannot be made visual is often not televised. The news media respond quickly and with keen interest to the conflicts and controversies of the racial story but for the most part disregard the problems that seethe beneath the surface until they erupt in the hot steam that is a 'live' news story. The media have not studied and related events in the Negro revolution to issues such as urbanization, education, automation, the anti-poverty program, the population explosion – all elements that have significant bearing on the position of the Negro today.[10]

Here we have professionals agreeing upon their failure to meet the requirements of their profession. They show awareness

[6] Paul L. Fisher and Ralph L. Lowenstein, *Race and the News Media,* (Anti-Defamation League of B'nai B'rith, 1967).
[7] G. P. Hunt, 'The Racial Crisis and the News Media: An Overview', ibid.
[8] Buford Boone, 'Southern Newsmen and Local Pressure', ibid.
[9] Hodding Carter III, 'The Wave Beneath the Froth', ibid.
[10] Paul Fisher and Ralph Lowenstein, 'Introduction and Guidelines', ibid.

that on occasions it is their own professional values which lead to their inadequacies. In the above quotation we find acknowledgement that concentration on 'live' news, a function of the professional news-sense, contributes to the inadequate coverage given to an issue that is generally accepted as being crucial in their contemporary world.

Poston[11] recounts how even such a responsible paper as the *New York Times* was unable to resist a good story when it published a report of the existence of an organization of Negro teenagers who had pledged to maim or murder every white person found in Harlem. Even though several sources refuted the existence of 'the Blood Brothers' the *New York Times* continued to follow up the story with the young membership rising from 30 to 400 and falling back to 90. Not only did the *Times* carry this story, but inevitably its competitors also took it up. When eventually the total absence of evidence became apparent the story was dropped. However, the urgent demands of good copy had made themselves felt in the acceptance and transmission of such a story. The dangers inherent in news values were also acknowledged during the conference in discussion of the news media's tendency to give coverage to those Negro spokesmen who make the most outrageous, or radical statements. In doing so they provide a false picture of the dialogue within the Negro community. To quote Poston[12] again;

> there is an increasing and dangerous tendency for Northern papers to create their own versions of negro leaders in the Harlems of this country. How do they do this? Simply by giving front page coverage to and designating as a 'leader' any non-white citizen who makes preposterous statements about race relations.

The newsmen at the conference were also aware that the relative lack of Negro staff in the American news media contributed to their ignorance of black America. The very background of white reporters often made it difficult for them to understand, and communicate with black Americans.

Not all the failings of the news-media were seen to be derived from forces within the media, for a good deal of attention was given to social and economic pressures that are brought to bear upon the small community press, and the local television and

[11] Ted Poston, 'The American Negro and Newspaper Myths', Fisher and Lowenstein, op. cit.
[12] Ibid.

radio stations. Carter talks of the desire of the Southern press 'not to alienate, not to be totally alienated from, the small communities in which one lives'.[13] A specific example of editorial policy being reversed by the weight of local anti-Negro feeling is provided by Poston,[14] and Monroe[15] quotes an instance where a publisher deliberately excluded a pro-Negro letter because the opposition newspaper was using his paper's liberalism as a sales tool against him with advertisers. Clearly the economic structure of the American news media, and the local media in particular, make them subject to pressures from powerful interest groups.

The brief outline provided above, gives some indication of the awareness of newsmen of their failings in reporting racial matters, and also of their understanding of the factors creating these inadequacies. Nor is this a unique demonstration of such awareness. In 1966 Breckner[16] delivered a critique of the media's handling of racial issues and in 1967 two further conferences[17] reiterated many of the points outlined by participants to the 1965 meeting.

Of these conference reports, perhaps the more interesting is the Columbia conference[18] for the report consists not of the formal papers, but of summaries of 'workshop' arguments. This report shows an absence of unanimity amongst the media representatives in their acceptance of criticism. Certainly self criticism is apparent, but so too is a defensiveness which hints at resentment of several years of self-flagellation. The criticisms which appear to have unanimous acceptance parallel closely those discussed in the 1965 conference. For example:

> participants in one workshop . . . both media representatives and others . . . acknowledged the habitual sensationalism of much of America's press, radio and TV and asked why race

[13] Hodding Carter III, op. cit.

[14] Ted Poston, op. cit.

[15] William B. Monroe, Jnr., 'Television: The Chosen Instrument of the Revolution', Fisher and Lowenstein, op. cit.

[16] Joseph L. Breckner, 'Broadcasting and Racial Issues' (*Television Quarterly,* Vol. V, No. 2, Spring 1966).

[17] A symposium held at the University of California in Los Angeles: published as Jack Lyle (ed.) *The Black American and the Press,* (The Ward Ritchie Press, Los Angeles, 1968).

[18] A conference on mass media and race relations held at Columbia University Graduate School of Journalism. It was conducted for the Community Relations Service of the United States Department of Justice by the American Jewish Committee, *Conference on Mass Media and Race Relations* (The American Jewish Committee, 1968, New York).

should be habitually dealt with in terms of conflict.

A thought frequently voiced was that the media must do more than cover the ghetto when it explodes, and must get beyond the usual superficial explanations ('outside agitators') for current unrest.

In 1968 criticism from within the media was supplemented by an analysis of the media from outside the profession by an army of social scientists operating under the auspices of President Johnson's National Advisory Commission on Civil Disorders. Chapter Fifteen of the published report[19] hereafter called the Kerner report, dealt with 'The Media of Mass Communications'.

The Kerner Report which resulted from the investigation into the civil disorders in American cities in 1967 came to the following conclusions about the role of the mass media:

First, that despite incidents of sensationalism, inaccuracies, and distortions, newspapers, radio and television, on the whole, made a real effort to give a balanced, factual account of the 1967 disorders.
Second, despite this effort, the portrayal of violence that occurred last summer failed to reflect accurately its scale and character. The overall effect was, we believe, an exaggeration of both mood and event.
Third, and ultimately most important, we believe that the media have thus far failed to report adequately on the causes and consequences of civil disorders and the underlying problems of race relations.[20]

The numerous similarities in the criticisms of the media's handling of race which are seen in comparing the Kerner report with the 1965 conference papers[21] is doubly interesting. At one level it indicates that external criticism has closely paralleled the self-criticism of the media professionals. What is also indicated is the sad fact that critical self-awareness in 1965 was not sufficient to prevent in 1967 the very errors of reportage that were delineated at length in 1965. The Kerner Report found instances of scare headlines, the transmission of unsubstantiated rumour, and the presentation of disturbances as black-white confrontations, rather than as the response of Negroes to basic

[19] *Report of the National Advisory Commission on Civil Disorders* (Bantam Books, 1968, New York).
[20] Ibid, chapter 15.
[21] Ibid.

problems of slum existence. The major concern of the Kerner Report was not limited to standards of riot coverage, but was concerned also with inadequacies of the media in their day to day handling of race. Yet again the failure lies in concentration on 'live' news and omission of background which could set the 'news' in perspective. The report charges the media with failing to communicate to the majority of their audience, that is white Americans, the conditions and feelings of Negroes in the United States. Further than this, the media are largely staffed by whites and this is seen in the white perspective provided by the media:

> The world that television and newspapers offer to their black audience is almost totally white, in both appearance and attitude.[22]

Now that we have reviewed some of the criticisms[23] of the media handling of race in the United States we can look more closely at the news process and seek relationships between it and the type of coverage given to race.

Throughout these criticisms there is a constant reiteration of the media's failure to provide background information, to delve beneath the news to underlying conditions. It is useful to look at this in the light of the nature of news and of the news process. Shibutani[24] says,

> news is not merely something new; it is information that is timely. . . . This transient quality is the very essence of news, for an event ceases to be newsworthy as soon as the tension it has aroused has been dissipated.

In other words, only when events are associated with a concern of 'the public' do they become newsworthy. Given the situation in the United States where the major news media are staffed by white personnel and serve a mainly white audience, it follows that the 'public' which dictates newsworthy events is a white public. The day-to-day tensions of ghetto existence, and exploitation which is a crucial concern of the coloured population is not a primary concern of the white public. Only the symptoms of these conditions such as freedom rides and social disturbances

---

[22] Ibid.
[23] See also Charles U. Daly (ed.) *The Media and the Cities*, (The University of Chicago Center for Policy Study, the University of Chicago Press, 1968). 'Journalism and the Kerner Report: a special section', '*Columbian Journalism Review*, Fall, 1968); Racism and the Media' (*Back World*, March 1971, Vol. XX, No. 5, Johnson Publishing Co. Inc., New York'.
[24] Tarmotsu Shibutani, op. cit.

impinge upon whites and hence it is only such 'events' which become newsworthy in a white press. One of the reasons for the inadequate coverage of the underlying causes of racial strain in the United States is that the condition of the negro is not in itself a matter of high interest to the white majority. Their interest in the black American is focused upon the situation in which he becomes a threat, or a problem. Such 'events' as boycotts, pickets, civil rights demonstrations and particularly Black Power and racial violence mark the points where black activity impinges on white concerns and it is, therefore, not surprising that white orientated media in seeking to satisfy the needs of their white audience reflect this pattern of attention to events.

Galtung and Ruge[25] have discussed a number of factors which they consider relevant in determining whether or not an event will become news. Many of their factors are in agreement with a commonsense appraisal of the news media. Thus, according to them, the more negative the event the more likely it is to become 'news'; and the more unambiguous the event, in the sense of the fewer interpretations of it available, the more likely is it to become 'news'.

The importance of negativeness in making news is obvious and we are habituated to a diet of conflict, tragedy and deviancy in our daily news. Such news is of course functional in the sense that conflicts within society, and deviation from societal norms, are of fundamental relevance to the continuing stability of a society. Also such news is often attractive to the audience because of its human interest or dramatic content. Negativeness as a news value in the coverage of race relations, however, has a real potential for harm. It means that positive stories of harmonious race relations are less likely to be carried than stories of racial conflict, and the negative behaviour of minority groups becomes more newsworthy than their positive achievements. The fact that the same applies to the majority population does not detract from the seriousness of this bias. For the image created of the ethnic minority is likely to be consonant with existing stereotypical conceptions about them. We have already seen how the tendency to perceive selectively may amplify the negative quality of the image presented in the mass media. There is also the point that sections of the majority population may be largely or entirely dependent on the media for their information about the minority group, and heavy emphasis on

[25] J. Galtung and M. H. Ruge, 'The Structure of Foreign News', (*Journal of Peace Research,* 1965, No. 1), reprinted in Jeremy Tunstall *Media Sociology* (Constable and Co. Ltd., London, 1970).

negative stories will inevitably lead to a distorted picture.

The tendency for the more 'unambiguous' events to become news may have similar unfavourable consequences for the reporting of race relations, for some of those events which have an unclear significance to the reporter may well be the very events that have real significance to the minority community; but because of their ambiguity they are the less likely to be reported. This amounts to a built-in tendency for the media to project a majority perspective on the world from which minority perspectives become filtered out.

A related factor that makes events newsworthy is their ability to be interpreted within a familiar framework or in terms of existing images, stereotypes and expectations. The framework and the expectations may originate in the general culture, or they may originate in the news itself and pass from there into the culture. The situation is one of continuous interplay between events, cultural meanings and news frameworks. The way events are reported helps structure expectations of how coloured people will behave or how race relations situations develop. Subsequent events that conform to the expectation stand a better chance of making the news than those that do not, and new events may be interpreted in terms of existing images even if the existing image is not in fact the most appropriate. (The use of the image of ethnic conflict derived from the American disorders of the sixties as the framework for reporting the British situation is a case in point.) The process may be illustrated from work by Lang and Lang[26] who studied the television coverage of a MacArthur Day parade in Chicago, and found a marked discrepancy between what actually happened and the television portrayal. While television presented a picture of wild enthusiasm among the crowds, on-the-spot observers found mainly curiosity, disappointment and even boredom. They show how anticipations of an enthusiastic reception for the parade, derived largely from media coverage of similar events in other cities, and shared by spectators and newsmen alike, helped to structure the television presentation so that those things which were consistent with expectations came to be emphasized, while what did not 'fit' this frame of reference was played down or ignored. Halloran and his colleagues[27] have shown how the media coverage of a

[26] K. Lang and G. E. Lang, 'The Unique Perspective of Television and its Effect: A Pilot Study' (*American Sociological Review*, XVIII, 1953, p. 3-12).
[27] J. D. Halloran, P. Elliott and G. Murdock, *Demonstrations and Communication: A Case Study* (Penguin Books, 1970).

political demonstration in London in 1968 was influenced by expectations derived from coverage of previous demonstrations. On this basis the pre-event coverage defined the coming event as likely to be violent. When it occurred it was predominantly peaceful, but it was nevertheless reported in terms of violence and other themes that had been prominent in the pre-event coverage. These authors map the emergence of a particular frame of reference or 'news framework' which served to define for the newsmen what was relevant about the event.

In the field of race relations, the findings of some American research also exemplify this kind of process. During 1968, reports began to appear in the American press of 'a new pattern of violence' in racial disturbances. Whereas the usual pattern of civil disorders was that of spontaneous and uncoordinated outbreaks of violence directed at property rather than at people, triggered by some precipitating incident (such as an arrest) in an area already characterized by tension and grievance, it was said that a new pattern was emerging of deliberately planned and coordinated attacks on the police by strategically placed snipers. A series of incidents were reported in these terms in which conspiratorial planning and systematic sniping were said to have been the key features, with the spectre of Black Power in the background.

Researchers at the Lemberg Centre for the Study of Violence investigated 25 such reports, and found little evidence either of planning, organizational affiliation of participants, or of sniping. Twenty-two people hit by gunfire in three incidents turned out to be the victims of just three shotgun blasts, and yet in many cases these casualties were presented by the press as being the result of systematic single-round sniping. Knopf[28] interprets her findings as the result of expectations generated by predictions of a 'change from spontaneous to premeditated outbreaks resembling guerilla warfare', based on unconfirmed reports and the rhetoric of black militants. These expectations then served to shape the way incidents were reported and interpreted. Knopf wrote, 'unwittingly or not, the press has been constructing a scenario on armed uprisings'.[29] What she has described would seem not to be a case of deliberate distortion by the press so much as an example of the way a 'scenario' or news perspective may come to shape perceptions and interpretations. Our own

[28] Terry Ann Knopf, 'Sniping – A New Pattern of Violence' (*Trans-action,* Vol. 6, No. 9, Whole No. 47, July/August 1969, pp. 22-29).
[29] Ibid, p. 29.

finding[30] of a tendency for race-related news in the British press to be reported with reference to a limited number of themes upon which attention has converged over a period would seem to be another instance of a news framework, or 'inferential structure' influencing news production.

The majority of the news media are adapted to a diurnal rhythm; they expect to provide 'today's news'. It has been argued that events which occur within this time perspective are more likely to be reported.

> A murder takes little time and the event takes place between the publication of two successive issues of a daily, which means that a meaningful story can be told from one day to the next.

> Correspondingly, the event that takes place over a longer time-span will go unrecorded unless it reaches some kind of dramatic climax (the building of a dam goes unnoticed but not its inauguration).[31]

There is an obvious analogy here with the on-going ghetto conditions, and the exploitation and frustration of the Negro which is not dramatically different day by day, and which remains unreported in daily news. However, the violence and political rhetoric that arise from this experience are more amenable to the habitual time scales of the news media and are more easily reported.

The news media are predisposed to handling discrete events – a court case, a riot, a speech – which can readily be fitted to the time schedules of their production process. Realities which are not independent, 'one off' occurrences, but which are evolving, interdependent conditions and processes – like ghetto existence, poor education, exploitation on racial grounds – are not so suited to the format imposed on realities by the news media's routinized processes of news collection and treatment.

What Galtung and Ruge called 'personification' refers to the tendency of the news media to present events in a way which sets persons or groups of people as the focus of attention and enables the events to be explained as resulting from the actions of individuals. The alternative is to discuss events in terms of such abstractions as 'social forces' and 'structural features of society'. Not only would such a style of reporting be unintel-

---

[30] See Chapter 7, and Paul Hartmann, Charles Husband, Jean Clark, *Race as News: A Study of the handling of race in the British national press from 1963 to 1970* (a report to UNESCO of research carried out under a UNESCO grant. To be published shortly by UNESCO).
[31] Galtung and Ruge, op. cit.

ligible or unacceptable to the audience, but a 'structure-centred' approach would impose strains on traditional modes of news presentation. For example, personalized events can be illustrated with photographs or film of the participants but 'social forces' or 'institutional racism' is much more difficult to present simply. The fact that the Kerner Report[32] was more critical of television than the printed media for their failure to analyse the underlying reasons for civil disorders probably reflects the greater difficulty of the visual media in handling such material. It is comparatively easy for television to cover a riot, for action shots make for 'good television', but it is much more difficult to televise the underlying causes of racial disturbances where adequate coverage demands some attempt at treatment on a 'structure-centred' basis which requires abstract conceptualization.

The use of visual illustration is not the only feature of news presentation making for a personification of events. Tuchman[33] has argued that one of the 'strategic procedures' used by newspapermen in their claim to objectivity is their 'judicious use of quotations and quotation marks to remove the reporter from the story'. She argues that newsmen use quotation as a means of providing 'facts' to substantiate the report. Also they relieve the reporter of responsibility for the views expressed even though he may have chosen the quotation because it is what he would have liked to have said.[34] The personification of events is a style which assists in the use of this tactic.

Philip Elliott[35] has pointed out that newsmen develop routine channels for news gathering and that this involves the use of 'experts' and informed sources. The newsman comes to see events in terms of human actions and so uses personalities and experts to provide him with material. When a story breaks his routine will send him in search of the key individual, the witness, the expert; and his 'personality frame of reference' will make him tend to explain events predominantly in terms of personal ambition, conspiracy, 'outside agitators' or other personal motivations.

[32] *Report of the National Advisory Commission on Civil Disorders*, op. cit.

[33] Gaye Tuchman. 'Objectivity as Strategic Ritual: An Examination of Newspapermen's Notions of Objectivity' (Paper Presented at the 66th Annual Meeting of the American Sociological Association, 1971).

[34] Hohenberg provides supporting evidence for Tuchman's argument, see John Hohenberg, *The News Media: A Journalist Looks at his Profession* (Holt Rinehart and Winston, Inc. 1968, p. 88).

[35] Personal communication. See also Philip Elliott, *The Making of a Television Series* (Constable, London, 1972).

If personification, use of visual illustration and other news production processes operate to suppress analytic journalism, there are also pressures which encourage sensational and conflictful journalism and the antithetical to the presentation of reasoned background information. In part this pressure stems from the audience who demand 'exciting' news. As Boorstin[36] says, 'There was a time when the reader of an unexciting newspaper would remark: "How dull is the world today!" Nowadays he says: "What a dull newspaper!" ' The effort to put 'pep' into the news means that the slightest disturbance is likely to be headlined 'More Violence Flares' and a dispute over political policy as 'A Race Row'. Not only headlines but the selection of events to be covered and items to be published is also influenced by the need to titillate, hold, and if possible increase the audience. 'The news media respond quickly and with keen interest to the conflicts and controversies of the racial story but, for the most part, disregard the problems that seethe beneath the surface . . .'[37] Conflict and controversy are the essence of 'newsworthiness' and their significance as criteria in news selection is as apparent in the coverage of sport as it is in politics and race. The subjective skills of the newsman when applied to the reporting of race produce an emphasis on conflict, negativeness and the unusual that again sets 'newsworthiness' at odds with reporting underlying trends and background information. It is the discrete event which is more able to encapsulate the elements of conflict and excitement, and which can be condensed into a forceful news story. The underlying processes of urban living and the 'reasons' for prejudice and discontent are on these criteria less amenable to manipulation into good news items than are manifestations of violence, crime, and individual tragedy which are the more visible symptoms.

To explain the handling of race in the American news media it is not necessary to invoke the personal prejudices and racist beliefs of individual reporters, though prejudiced and racist newsmen undoubtedly exist.[38] The very forces and values which underlie news production would appear to constitute a built-in tendency to provide a distorted picture of race relations. Attention has been focused upon the potential failings of the

---

[36] Daniel J. Boorstin, *The Image* (Penguin Books, 1963, p. 19).
[37] Paul Fisher and Ralph Lowenstein, 'Introduction and Guidelines', op. cit.
[38] For example see Whitney M. Young, Jnr, for reference to Southern racist news outlets. 'The Social Responsibility of Broadcasters' (*Television Quarterly,* Vol. VII, No. 2, Spring 1969).

news media, and upon the part played by news values in producing these shortcomings. There are professional standards which guide news production and these do provide checks against overly biased and irresponsible reporting. However, what we have been arguing is that much of the reporter's skill is subjective, and that there are dangers inherent in the news values which guide his behaviour. Concern for responsible journalism does not directly or inevitably produce adequate coverage of race-related topics.

The American News Media as Apologists for the Status Quo

In apparent opposition to some of the news values discussed there is another feature of the news media which disposes them to play down social conflict or at least to obscure its nature. This is a restraint embodied in the ideal of 'responsible journalism'. The responsibility is to the society and local community. Breed[39] reviews earlier writers' conceptions of the socializing function of the media thus: 'By expressing, dramatizing, and repeating cultural patterns, both the traditional and the newly emerging, the media reinforce tradition and at the same time explain new roles. Members of the society thus remain integrated within the sociocultural structure. As a form of adult socialization, the media are seen as guarantors that a body of common ultimate values remains visible as a continuing source of consensus, despite the inroads of change'. Breed adds the corollary that the media achieve the same positive ends through omission; 'they omit or bury items which might jeopardize the sociocultural structure and man's faith in it'. There is a good deal of evidence to support this view of the media. Thus, for example, studies of the American community press[40] have shown an avoidance of controversy over local issues. Olien et al[41] in their study conclude that 'this study supports the observations of some social scientists that the community press frequently tends to protect community institutions rather than report the disruptive side of life'.

[39] Warren Breed, 'Mass Communication and Sociocultural Integration' in Lewis Anthony Dexter and David Manning White, *People, Society and Mass Communications* (The Free Press, New York, 1964).
[40] Morris Janowitz, 'The Community Press in an Urban Setting' (Free Press Glencoe, Ill., 1952); Arthur J. Vidich and Joseph Bensman, *Small Town in Mass Society* (Princeton University Press, New Jersey, 1958).
[41] Clarice N. Olien, George A. Donohue and Philip J. Tichenor, 'The Community Editor's Power and the Reporting of Conflict' (*Journalism Quarterly*, Vol. 45, No. 2, Summer 1968).

The way in which the press may unintentionally reinforce the authority and credibility of local government is shown most perceptively in a study of the daily paper in an American city.[42] The authors show how, by following his habitual news values and journalistic procedures, the reporter imbues the activities of the city council with a sense of responsibility, rationality and concerned efficiency which would not be confirmed by actual attendance at council meetings. The consequences for the coverage of race relations of this tendency toward consensus maintenance may be eventually disfunctional for society. Given that the news media are staffed and controlled almost exclusively by the majority group – then it follows that the consensus which is maintained is that of the predominant sub-culture. The disfunctional aspect of this bias emerges when the realistic concerns of minority groups are ignored as being irrelevant or threatening to the majority population. An example of suppression of information which might prove threatening to the community is the manner in which the local press in America have handled racial conflict. Coverage of such conflict is threatening in two ways. At one level reporting the conflict may amplify it by informing potential demonstrators or boycotters of the activity already under way and thus encourage them to take part in it. At another level, reporting the conflict encourages speculation as to its causes, and in a society which both lauds equality and institutionalizes discrimination this can be potentially disruptive.

Paletz and Dunn[43] in a study of the press coverage of civil disorders found that coverage of the disorder was almost entirely in terms of legitimate authority suppressing blatant lawlessness. Significantly they found very few reports of the disturbance from the perspective of the black participants. By presenting those engaged in protest as 'hoodlums' who were atypical of the majority of local Negroes, the press may have eased the worries of the local white population, but they also failed to inform them of the real feelings of the black community. In this study both strategies of consensus maintenance are apparent; in the positive indentification with law and order, and in the failure to report the reality of the disorders and their causes. The

---

[42] David L. Paletz, Peggy Reichert and Barbara McIntyre, 'How the Media Support Local Governmental Authority' (*Public Opinion Quarterly,* Vol. XXXV, No. 1, Spring 1971).
[43] David L. Paletz and Robert Dunn 'Press Coverage of Civil Disorders: Winston-Salem 1967' (*Public Opinion Quarterly,* Vol. XXXIII, No. 3, Fall, 1969).

conflict is shown as an aberration caused by deviant and lawless elements in an essentially integrated and just society. The possibility that social injustice and a conflict of interests between social groups in inherent in the structure of the society is effectively obscured. Speculation as to whether there really is equality of opportunity for black and white is discouraged by this kind of handling.

Gieber[44] in a study of California newspapers records a similar failure of the press to report adequately local events concerning civil rights. His finding and those of Paletz and Dunn, apply to local press reporting. Though such factors as the stronger social constraints upon the local press and economic considerations imposed by a restricted financial base, may make the local news media more prone to conflict management there is every reason to believe the same forces operate in the news media with a wider audience. For example, in a report of a conference on mass media and race relations attended by representatives of national as well as local press, and television news agencies, one of the suggestions was that 'editors might brief civil-rights activists on what will get their stories into the news, much as they now brief the heads of community fund-raising campaigns. . . . . *However, discretion must be used in choosing the groups to whom such help is extended*'.[45] (Authors' italics.) Apparently there are some activists who should not be given coverage. One is tempted to suggest that the Black Panthers, a group that does question the essential justice and equality of American society, would fall into this category. An account of a network news programme on the Panthers recounted by Sales[46] shows how selective interviewing and editing can be used to 'manage' such groups. In the CBS – TV programme in question, careful intercutting of interviewees made it possible for the Panthers to be presented as self-contradictory. Also the tone of interviewing adopted with the Panthers, a police chief, and a 'moderate Black' made it possible for the last two to be identified with the interviewer who discounted the significance of the Panthers. The use of a 'moderate Black' enabled the link man to imply that the majority of Blacks did not take the Panthers seriously. This

[44] Walter Gieber, *Gatekeepers of News of Civil Rights and Liberties: A Study of the Fate of Local News Stories* (Department of Journalism, University of California, Berkeley, 1958).
[45] The American Jewish Committee, 1968, *Conference on Mass Media and Race Relations,* conducted for the Community Relations Service of the United States Department of Justice.
[46] William Sales, 'The News Media: Racism's First Line of Defence' (*Black World*, March 1971. Johnson Publishing Co., New York).

example provides a cameo illustration of how a potentially disruptive group may be presented in such a way as to diminish their perceived potency and threat. Such a programme is doubly effective in maintaining 'sociocultural consensus' for by showing the inconsistencies of the Panthers and stating their peripheral position in Black politics their image in the Black world is damaged. At the same time, the anxiety of the white community is reduced and their acceptance of the status quo reinforced, since these critics of society are seen as marginal militants whose very actions render their arguments ridiculous.

THE BRITISH NEWS MEDIA

British journalists on race in the press

Less has been written on ethnic reporting by British journalists than by their American counterparts but a recent publication[47] contains the views of four eminent newspapermen.

> I subscribe wholeheartedly to the UNESCO Declaration in Paris, of 1967, which runs :
> 'Because mass media reach vast numbers of people at different educational and social levels, their role in encouraging or combating race prejudice can be crucial. Those who work in these media should maintain a positive approach to the promotion of understanding between groups and populations. Representation of people in stereotypes and holding them up to ridicule should be avoided'.
>
> *Clement Jones*[48]

> The attitude of the mass media is a crucial element in race relations. Public opinion on immigration or colour prejudice can be materially affected by the way newspapers, television and radio handle stories concerning them.
>
> *P. W. Harland*[49]

> This paper starts from a basic assumption which, if one had pretensions to science, would need to be proved rather than stated. It is clear to students of race relations that there is a strong connection between race reporting and racial attitudes among the public; that the newspaper treatment of race relations has an important bearing on the quality of race

[47] *Race and The Press* (Runnymede Trust Publication 1971).
[48] Ibid., p. 13.
[49] Ibid., p. 21.

relations on the ground; hence, that newspapers, when dealing with race, have a peculiarly delicate responsibility.

Hugo Young[50]

I believe it matters intensely the way newspapers, radio and television report race relations. Spectacularly in India, the Ahmedabad riot was touched off by rumours given the veracity of print; stealthily in Britain, the malformed seeds of prejudice have been watered by a rain of false statistics and stories.

Harold Evans[51]

Here three editors and an assistant editor declare their appreciation of the important role which the news media may have on race relations. Not only do they acknowledge their power and responsibility but like their American counterparts they also show that they are fully aware of the failings of professional journalism in its treatment of race.

Young goes straight to a fundamental problem for British journalism when he declares that race related news is seen by journalists within a frame of reference which starts from an assumption that colour is a problem. He says that:

By and large, unless a very conscious attempt is made to do otherwise, race only earns its place in the news to the extent that it is bad news. When coloured people behave or are treated in a normal, unexceptional manner, the fact goes the same way as the millions of normal, unexceptional events happening to millions of people in Britain : out of the news. But when something slightly outside normal behaviour – such as a pub fight – happens to them, it is treated differently from such an event happening between white people. *This is because everything to do with coloured people takes place against an underlying premise that they are the symbols or the embodiments of a problem.* Whether we like it or not, that is the state of public opinion as perceived by news editors; and that is what tends inevitably to influence professional news judgment.

The result of this, however, is well-known and harmful to race relations. It means that, *if newspapers judge by news value alone, they cannot avoid reinforcing the view that race is more of a problem than it really is.*[52]

50 Ibid., p. 29.
51 Ibid. p. 42.
52 Ibid., p. 31.

This statement was made by a journalist and shows that criticism of the press handling of race is not a preserve of academics and others who lack the journalist's professional background. Here we have the assistant editor of a major national newspaper pointing to 'news value' as a potentially dangerous criterion for determining the handling of race related issues. Young states what our content analysis indicates that news values tend to result in an undue emphasis on colour as a problem. Harold Evans in his article also points to an unwarranted conflict orientation in coverage of racial stories:

> So many racial stories – street brawls, housing disputes, overcrowding and so on – are there in print for the same reason. Not because there is any real news, but because the race tag hints at conflict, the traditional bread and butter of news. And this kind of news judgment breeds its own justification because it plants the idea in the reader's mind that there is a conflict of interest between different ethnic groups.[53]

We have here examples of senior British journalists who are aware of the dangers inherent in applying traditional news values to race related events. We have already discussed the subjectivity of news values, their partially unconscious acquisition and the ubiquity of their influence. Some instances of the kind of 'news judgment' referred to by Evans will help to make the point.

Conflict Journalism and Race in the News

In 1962 there was a smallpox outbreak in Bradford[54] which was the occasion for the *Yorkshire Post* to produce a paradigm of conflict reporting. The paper's first big story carried the headline 'Pakistanis blamed in Smallpox City: Anger in Bradford'. This front page headline immediately focused attention upon the Pakistani community and implicitly supported the notion that *blame* could be allocated. In fact the outbreak originated with a nine year old Pakistani girl who died of the disease. She had been vaccinated and it seems futile to attach blame to any individuals when the disease is an enemy to all. Although the headline spoke of Bradford as a 'Smallpox City' there were only 14 cases in the entire outbreak. The text of the story contained some remarkable copy more calculated to inflame than inform. For example:

[53] Harold Evans, ibid., p. 47.
[54] For a full description of this see: Butterworth, Eric, 'The Smallpox Outbreak and the British Press' (*Race,* Vol. VII, No. 4, 1962).

Bradford was an uneasy city last night . . . It was an angry city, too, and all over the city, in public houses, clubs and on the buses, there was open evidence that the public as a whole was blaming the Pakistani population. Up to last night there had been no physical incidents involving whites and coloured in Bradford – a town long noted for its tolerance towards coloured immigrants – but conversation was mainly centred on the lines of 'Send them home'.[55]

As the Bradford *Telegraph and Argus* pointed out the next day, the *Post* could not have sent out sufficient reporters to justify such a definite statement of feeling in Bradford. They also reported that over the weekend there had only been seven letters on the subject of immigrants whilst there were 2,000 entries for a *Telegraph and Argus* quiz. To quote the *Telegraph and Argus'* own editorial conclusion on these respective figures : 'this hardly suggests angry Bradfordians seizing an immediate opportunity to express their anger . . .'[56]

Not only did the *Yorkshire Post* sensationalize its reporting of events but it was also able to find conflict in non-events : 'Up to last night there had been no physical incidents involving whites and coloured in Bradford'. Public anticipation of violence may well become a self-fulfilling prophecy. For the *Yorkshire Post* it certainly was, in the sense that such minor instances as did occur were reported by the *Post* in subsequent issues.

The *Yorkshire Post* had a general anti-immigration stance and was an advocate of the 1962 Immigration Bill. In a situation where the immigrants and the indigenous population faced a common threat in the smallpox, the *Post*'s coverage stressed the conflict between the groups and focused attention upon violence, potential and actual.

This example, admittedly a fairly extreme one, shows how the location of race within a conflict-problem framework can produce distortion. It is, however, easy to find similar if less obvious manifestations of the same thing.

For example, consider the press treatment of two different statistics, one consistent with the conflict definition of race, one not so suited to that news framework.[57] The first figures were the Registrar General's returns of 10 March 1970 which showed

---

[55] Ibid., p. 352.
[56] Ibid., p. 354.
[57] Earlier discussed in Paul Hartmann and Charles Husband, 'The Mass Media and Racial Conflict' (*Race,* Vol. XII, 3, 1971).

that the birth-rate among immigrants was higher than the national average. This was obviously well suited to the 'numbers game' which, following on Enoch Powell's anti-immigration campaign had become an established feature of the press coverage of race in Britain. The other statistic was the announcement by the Home Secretary on 14 May 1970 of the immigration statistics which showed that the rate of immigration was decreasing and that the number for the previous quarter was the lowest on record. These immigration statistics were obviously contrary to the problem oriented 'numbers game'. Let us compare press coverage of these two statistics for the days of 10 March and 15 May respectively; that is, the days on which the news was first carried.

Seven of the eight national dailies carried the birth figures, only four reported the reduction in immigration. Five of the papers carried the birth figures on the front page whilst the immigration figures appeared on only one front page. The average headline for the birth figures occupied four times as much space as the average headline for the immigration figures. There was about five times as much news-space given to the birth figures and reactions to them as to the immigration figures. A contribution to this greater coverage was the fact that five of the seven papers carried Enoch Powell's reaction to the birth figures. Only the *Times* attempted any balance by eliciting reactions from other sources. Invoking Powell in the reporting of the birth figures is consistent with the practice of reporting new events in relation to known arguments and personalities. Powell's relationship to the birth figures through his previous utterances is unquestionable but the shift in presentation through his inclusion is important. The *Sketch* in its front page article carried the assertion that 'the report adds fuel to Mr Enoch Powell's previous warnings of the rapid breeding rate among coloured families'. These figures may have been consistent with Mr Powell's predictions about fertility rates, but do we, like the *Sketch*, have to accept his interpretation of the figures as inevitably threatening, and as a cause for concern? The *Telegraph*'s front page carried the statement that 'there was no sign of panic over the fact that nearly 12 percent of the 405,000 babies . . . were conceived by mothers born outside the United Kingdom'. This passage shows the penetration of the conflict framework into the *Telegraph*'s coverage of the birth statistics : this coupled with Powell's response to the figures produces a report which is neither objective nor neutral. The idea that coloured people constitute a social threat has become one of the unspoken assumptions of the news framework. The birth statistics provided material that was amenable to easy interpretation within this framework and so got big play. The immigration statistics were not so conducive to that mode of presentation and became relatively submerged. However, even in the reporting of the decrease in immigration, the problem-conflict theme emerged in that all four papers that carried the story also reported the Home Secretary's determination to keep the figures low. In this way the threat element was kept alive.

Such is the appeal of news items that fit the existing news framework on race that stories can become news more because of their news value than reliability. Young[58] quotes the example of the *Daily Telegraph* which during its coverage of the 1968 Kenyan Asian immigration carried the front page headline on 14 February : 'Kenyan Asian Exodus Numbers Double – 100,000 may enter Britain by end of year'. This headline which in the context of events at that time was a very serious escalation of the debate was not based on any official projections; not even on the opinion of the *Telegraph*'s Nairobi correspondent; it was the calculation of unidentified 'airline officials'. This dubious source was declared low down in the report where its significance might easily be overlooked.

A similar event took place in 1972 when a story originating from one man gave rise to reports that the British Government was easing its policy on the entry of unqualified immigrants into Britain. The story blew up over 41 Asians who, on arrival in Britain without the correct papers, had been allowed to remain as visitors for a period of three months after immigration office headquarters had considered their case.

The *Daily Express* on Thursday 6 April 1972, carried the headline 'Stay-on "illegal" visitors start a row', and began the 18 column inch article with : 'Immigration officials were up in arms last night over what they regard as a new Government policy that could allow thousands of illegal immigrants into Britain without fear of deportation'. On the same day the *Guardian* had the front page headline 'Kenya Asians slip through Britain's net'. The introduction to the 24 column inch article stated that : 'Immigration officers are concerned at the number of Kenyan Asians being allowed into Britain. Officers have strict instructions not to talk to the press – but an

[58] Hugo Young, 'The Treatment of Race in the British Press' *Race and the Press* (Runnymede Trust, London, 1971, p. 36).

"official leak" from immigration sources claimed that the British Government's attitude towards the shuffling of immigrants from one country to another would mean that thousands of immigrants would have to be let into Britain.'

These quotations show that two papers, generally considered to be of different political complexion, both printed similar stories which implied that there had been a shift in Government policy regarding immigration, a consequence of which would be 'thousands of "illegal" immigrants' entering Britain.

However, what the *Guardian* chose to label an 'official leak' originated from a Mr Bill Pryke who was an interpreter employed by the Home Office at Heathrow. It was the *Sunday Times*[59] which exposed what had been a sloppy piece of journalism in their article entitled 'How the Colonel started fears of an immigrant flood' ('the Colonel' was the nickname by which Mr Pryke was known):

> Claiming to represent immigration officers – who unlike him are civil servants and barred from talking to the press – he [Mr Pryke] met Mr Ray Watts, news editor of the airport news agency, Brenard's, and told him of what he called the officers' softer attitude and of their fears that thousands more immigrants would have to be let into Britain.

As the *Sunday Times* pointed out, the story was not followed up by Britain's national news agency, the Press Association, because it 'could not obtain confirmation'. Their own enquiries of Mr Alan Spence of the UK Immigrants Advisory Service at Heathrow elicited as part of his reply, 'There are 400 immigration officers and 50 chief officers and I don't know how one or two can claim to be representative'.

It seems that the instant fit of this news item into the race news framework was so compelling that the normal journalistic routine of adequately checking sources was not carried through. As a consequence four national dailies gave considerable prominence to an event which was in itself insignificant, but which through their acceptance of it and elaboration upon it became yet another immigration scare, a further statement of coloured immigrants as threatening.[60]

[59] *Sunday Times,* April 1972.
[60] For another example of the predominance of news values in structuring the news coverage of race, to the extent of submerging vitally relevant evidence, see: Louis Kushnik. ' "Black Power" and the Media' (*Race Today,* Institute of Race Relations, London, December 1970).

The Interdependence of the News Media

Before going further we should comment on the fact that in this chapter it is the press which is most frequently used to provide instances. One obvious reason for this is the permanent nature of their product which allows those sufficiently interested to check their memories against back-numbers of any paper. Television and radio news, on the other hand, are more ephemeral and unless you deliberately record all the output, you are forced into relying on memory. Another reason is the expense of recording television and radio news broadcasts over a long period.

This emphasis upon the press in a discussion of all news media is not, however, too great a handicap, for the very close ties between the different media ensure a continuity. The press has been a traditional training ground for television and radio news staff, and established journalists from the national press are recruited to television and radio journalism. In this way the common professional socialization establishes a considerable homogeneity in acquired news sense across the different media.

A similarity in news content is further maintained by the very interdependence of the news media. We are all familiar with the daily ritual of hearing the morning newspapers echoed in the morning radio news, paraphrased in 'The World at One', and then regurgitated almost unchanged throughout the day. In the same way the news on television overlaps considerably with what is carried by the papers and the radio. Of course all the news media have the same range of events to draw upon and the same or similar sources of information upon which to rely. However, it is also the incestuous mutual monitoring of the others' output which contributes to the appearance of a news item in one news medium and then another.

Harland[61] provides an account of the operation of this incestuous process. In May 1968 an individual councillor in Birmingham was widely reported in the national press as advocating a restriction on the number of immigrants living and working in the centre of the city. He also wished to restrict movement in and out of that area. The *Yorkshire Evening Post* followed up this story and obtained the opinion of the Leader of the controlling Conservative group on Bradford City Council. His agreement with the views of the Birmingham councillor was reported on the *Post*'s front page. This was seen by BBC Television in Leeds who decided to follow it up and invited the

[61] P. W. Harland, 'Reporting Race: Some Problems' (*Race and the Press*, Runnymede Trust, 1971, p. 24).

Bradford alderman to Leeds where he repeated his views for 'Look North'. This in turn was followed up by BBC national television news and BBC sound news programmes for the rest of that evening.

Not only did this process escalate the views of one alderman to national prominence but as Harland reports :

Unfortunately, in translation the item became garbled and was presented to the nation not as one man's *opinion* but as a *decision* by Bradford City Council to implement the restriction.

The very homogeneity of what comes to be defined as news, a consequence of a common process of professional socialization and of the practice of incestuous reporting, increases the power of the news media through diminishing the alternative definitions of events. It also makes our own reliance on the press for examples less problematic.

The News Media and Legitimate Beliefs

We have already discussed the mass media's function of sustaining socio-cultural consensus in relation to the American situation. The same function can be identified in the British mass media. Let us remind ourselves of what Breed said on the matter :

As a form of adult socialization, the media are seen as guarantors that a body of common ultimate values remains visible as a continuing source of consensus, despite the inroads of change.... they omit or bury items which might jeopardize the socio-cultural structure and man's faith in it.[62]

The role of the news media in Britain has been examined by Downing[63] who points to various ways in which news about industrial relations is handled so as to maintain consensus on the nature of the social structure and economic system. He argues that in industrial disputes the employers and employees are presented as having equal power and in interviews the interviewer is presented as a disinterested representative of the 'national interest' who seeks to guide their debate. But Downing points out that the concept of the national interest contains in

[62] Warren Breed, 'Mass Communication and Sociocultural Integration' in Lewis Anthony Dexter and David Manning White. *People, Society and Mass Communications* 'The Free Press, New York, 1964).
[63] John Downing, 'Class and "Race" in the British Mass Media', a paper given to the Working Convention on Racism in the Political Economy of Britain, London, December 1971.

itself an acceptance of the status quo, and preempts any consideration of whose economy it is, and what power relations and interests are involved. In the case of a dock strike, for instance, the issue was discussed in terms of the effect of the strike (national interest), rather than by examining the causes of the strike, an approach which might have brought into prominence the question of whether industrial conflict is intrinsic to our society or merely some kind of occasional aberration.

Our concern with the news media is to examine its consensus maintaining function in relation to race in Britain and to determine what values are relayed and sustained through the media. One value which is frequently confirmed through the news media is the essential *tolerance* of British society. This is usually done by direct statement. For example when dealing with current immigration the past examples of British tolerance to various refugee groups is presented as evidence of our tolerant credentials. These sentiments are also to be found in social science :

> For many centuries Britain has been a favourite asylum for refugees and a country of increased opportunity for immigrants. Wave after wave of hunted and poverty-stricken men have sought refuge on these shores, and more often than not have been accepted.[64]

There are two points of concern about this parading of Britain's tolerant record.

At a general level, the quotation from Krausz must be accepted as accurate in that refugees have been admitted to this country, but without qualification this kind of statement can be very misleading. Britain has not been an open sanctuary; and in recollection there has been a tendency to focus upon the laudable features of our past tolerance while ignoring or diluting those facts which might detract from this good image. In 1938 Britain was fully aware of the plight of Jews in Germany and the press clearly condemned German anti-semitism. Sharf says :

> Initial reactions to the 'Crystal Night' were not unexpected. It can never be emphasized too often that the dominant note struck by the British Press in the presence of Nazi anti-semitism was one of genuine moral outrage.[65]

[64] Ernest Krausz, *Ethnic Minorities in Britain* (MacGibbon and Kee, London, 1971, p. 55).
[65] Andrew Sharf, *The British Press and the Jews under Nazi Rule* OUP, London, 1964, p. 58).

Yet what was the response of the British Government to the gross violence perpetrated against Jews throughout Germany and Austria on 'Crystal Night' and the progressively harsher official measures which followed? Krausz provides a concise summary:

> A few days after the 'Crystal Night' pogrom in 1938 the British Government announced plans to cope with a limited number of refugees and called on its allies to investigate together with Britain the possibility of settling refugees in various colonies. The Government proposed to admit some 'selected' adults and a limited number of children to be trained for re-emigration. It was argued that to do more would lead to 'a definite anti-Jewish movement in the country'.[66]

Britain did in fact admit refugees – Sharf quotes 65,000 as the total number[67] but these were intended to re-emigrate. Seen in relation to the experience of the Jews left under Nazi rule, and the millions who were exterminated, how 'tolerant' were we?

Not only does the categorical statement of the British record of admitting refugees spare us the less comforting specifics which might contradict our tolerant self-image, but it has the further benefit of not going beyond the fact of admission. The typical response to an influx of aliens, whether refugees or immigrants, has been one of hostile suspicion or worse. The entry of thousands of Huguenots to Britain in the seventeenth century is often quoted as an example of Britain's historic record of 'tolerance' and yet they met with much resentment and even violence. Similarly the nineteenth century immigration of Irishmen and later of European Jews was greeted with considerable bitterness and prejudice.[68] The reality of Britain's ethnocentrism has more recently been evident in the massive popular prejudice elicited by the arrival of coloured immigrants. Only a 'British' interpretation of our record of tolerance could paint such a favourable picture, and then it requires a 'British' audience to find such an interpretation credible. Predictably, when *Colour and Citizenship*[69] was published in 1969, out of all

[66] Ernest Krausz, op. cit., p. 63.
[67] Andrew Sharf, op. cit., p. 155.
[68] See for further discussion of British attitudes to immigration: Paul Foot, *Immigration and Race in British Politics* (Penguin Books, Harmondsworth, 1965).
[69] E. J. B. Rose et al., *Colour and Citizenship* (OUP, 1969). We have already commented on this attitude survey in Chapter 1.

the detailed analysis the book provided documenting the position of coloured people in Britain, the media chose to focus mainly on the finding from the attitude survey that most of us were 'tolerant' or 'tolerant inclined'.

The media may also help to sustain sociocultural consensus by what they omit from the news. Humphrey,[70] himself a journalist with specialist experience in the area of race relations, describes the failure of the established Liverpool press to report adequately two cases where blacks were acquitted of drug offences. In both cases the accused based their defence on the argument that the drugs were planted on them by the police; and they were acquitted! This took place at a time when police harassment of the black community was causing great concern, and here the Liverpool press had an opportunity to open a public debate on police-black relations. This they failed to do. In Humphrey's words – 'under their very noses in local courts a series of dramatic cases, important to the individual and the community, is ignored.'[71] Such reporting would have involved questioning the integrity of the British police and this would certainly have been to go against the consensus. Another factor which perhaps contributed to the press reticence in following up these cases is their dependence upon the police for information relating to crime.[72]

Television too has failed to report adequately upon police-black relations and Downing[73] gives the example of a 'News at Ten' report, on 8 July 1970, on the black march on Caledonian Road police station to protest at police harassment. The report:

> simply rehearsed the charges (obstruction, abusive words, wilful damage, assault on a police officer), together with the courtroom shouts of 'fascist pig' and Black Power salutes. No explanation; no black person involved.[74]

Downing's analysis of television news coverage of race relations found explanations of underlying conditions and grievances to be 'very unusual in news media reporting'.

In January 1971 several petrol bombs were thrown through the window of a house in London where some black people

---

[70] Derek Humphrey, *Police Power and Black People* (Panther Books, London, 1972).
[71] Ibid., p. 20.
[72] Cf. Paul Croll, 'The Deviant Image' in James D. Halloran (Ed.), *Violence and the Mass Media* (Davis-Poynter, forthcoming).
[73] John Downing, op. cit.
[74] John Downing, op. cit.

were at a party; several people were burned, some very seriously.[75] This incident was given very little coverage in the national press. Could such an attack, causing serious personal injury to black individuals, really be as insignificant as the coverage it received indicated? The attack *and* its meagre coverage was certainly of significance to the black community. It is possible that it was played down lest reporting it would instigate further violence. Perhaps sensational coverage could have had that consequence, but here was an opportunity for the press to analyse clearly, and with concern, the nature of racism and relate it to this frightening example of racism's potential. Their response was virtually to ignore the event and, rather than outlaw racism, they preferred to maintain the embargo on discussing it.

In the press treatment of another manifestation of racist violence, which became labelled 'Paki-bashing', we can again discern the natural bias of white, British journalism when faced with racism. Firstly, what importance did the press attach to Paki-bashing? Meredith[76] in a study of Paki-bashing during April 1970, when it had reached the columns of the press, found only one instance when Paki-bashing reached the front page, and then it was a third of a column in the *Daily Express* for a murder! '2 am Skinhead murder hunt after Pakistani dies' – *Express* 11 April 1970). Yet the discovery of forty illegal immigrants in a Bradford cellar had conspicuous coverage in seven national dailies with the *Daily Express* front page head-line being 'Police find forty Indians in "black hole"' (2 July 1970). Further comparative evidence is provided by Meredith in an example from the *East London Advertiser* on 24 April 1970. She records that a report of a 17 year old Paki-basher who had been fined £30 for assault and grievous bodily harm received only 1.5 column inches of print, halfway down page six. In the same edition there was a report of a Pakistani who was given a three months suspended sentence and £25 fine for carrying an open penknife which he claimed was to protect himself against Paki-bashers. This was front page news and occupied five column inches. Here is an apparent reversal of news values, for surely an assault involving grievous bodily harm ought in itself to be a better negative, conflict story than merely possessing an offensive weapon? One feels that here there

---

[75] See *Black Voice* (Vol. 2, No. 1, London).
[76] Patricia Meredith, *'Here Comes Old "Arry Krishna"': Paki-Bashing as Depicted in the Press,* Dissertation in partial fulfilment of B.A. in Social Administration, Birmingham University, 1972.

must be other considerations. An Asian carrying a weapon constitutes a double threat. There is a summation of negative connotations provided by his basic definition as a threat or problem, as well as the possession of a weapon. Paki-bashers on the other hand were seen as an adolescent hooligan fringe, rather than a reflection of racism exacerbated by a high density, low income urban environment. This viewpoint was reinforced by police opinion, which discounted claims that they failed to protect Asians against assault. Chief Inspector Roberts, Liaison Officer for Stepney was reported as saying: 'We've always had an element of hooliganism, today we don't look on this as anything new. As far as we're concerned there's no increase in assaults or hooliganism which warrants an increase in Police patrols.[77] This presentation of the situation was consistent with the established dogma of British tolerance and by defining Paki-bashers as hooligans even those cases of racially motivated assaults which become news were capable of being discounted.

One of the features of the reporting of the Paki-bashing in 1970 was that although the attacks had been going on for a long time[78] their frequency was not reflected in the press. It took the murder of Tausir Ali on 6 April to make Paki-bashing a national concern. Speaking of this time Humphrey and John said: 'For two years the Pakistani community in London had been insisting that they were being attacked in the streets on a scale which exceeded normal street crime rates. The politicians, the police and the press ignored their cries, arguing that there was always a certain amount of "mugging" on the streets of the Metropolis but no one was picking on Pakistanis in particular.'[79]

Following Tausir Ali's murder the first report of the Paki-bashing incidents concerned the intention of the Community Relations Officer for Tower Hamlets to set up a bureau to combat the attacks. His intention was 'to take community action rather than civil or criminal action'. The Pakistani Workers' Union called a meeting and voted to form self-defence groups since the police had proved unwilling or inadequately staffed, to prevent the attacks. Only the day previously, at a mass meeting of Pakistanis where they had called for 'immediate

---

[77] 'Race War Threat in London's East End' (*The Scotsman*, 25 April 1970).

[78] See for example, statements by: Gulam Taslin, *The Times*, 3 April 1970; Staff of the London Chest Hospital, *The Times*, April 7th 1970: Pakistani Students Federation, *The Times*, 16 April 1970.

[79] Derek Humphrey and Gus John *Because They're Black* (Penguin Books, Harmondsworth, 1971, 'It takes a death to convince', p. 49.

and adequate measures to protect the life and the property of
the law-abiding and peace-loving Pakistanis',[80] they had been
told by the divisional police chief that:

> 'The police here are not concerned whether a man is black
> or white or where he was born' – 'You are all treated equally' –
> 'Hooliganism and damage to property is on the increase in
> Britain' – 'For every one attack against a Pakistani there are
> many more against white people.'[81]

Again the refusal to see racial assaults for what they are, and
the insistence that hooliganism is the correct interpretation of
the attacks. Just as American racial troubles have commonly
been discounted as the work of 'outside agitators' or 'fringe
militants' so white British racism was written off as hooliganism.
The image of British 'tolerance' remained intact and the need
to ask questions about the nature of British society was avoided.
Faced with this situation, elements of the Pakistani community
threatened to form vigilante patrols unless the police increased
their activities against the assailants.

It seems likely that it was this statement of their intention to
protect themselves, coupled with the murder, which was the
catalyst necessary to get Paki-bashing into the national press.
However, the manner of reporting these events further demonstrated the commitment of the press to consensus values. As
Meredith reports, 'surprisingly little emphasis is laid on the
failure of the police to combat the attacks'.[82] Rather there was
a concern that the Pakistani community threatened to usurp the
role of the police, and the *Daily Express,* in particular, spoke
up against them and warned 'Danger – When a man strikes
back' (8 April) and 'Pakistani patrols warned – you must obey
the law' (10 April). Meredith on the basis of her analysis of the
press at the time said, 'other papers did not condemn the
vigilante groups quite so forcefully, but even so the emphasis
was on them rather than the attacks or the police'.[83]

It seems that the chronology of assaults against the Asian
community as treated in the press is that for up to two years
their existence was largely ignored; when they were acknowledged they were attributed to a hooligan fringe; and when they
eventually received conspicuous coverage, this was *because the*

[80] Humphrey and John, ibid., p. 51.
[81] Humphrey and John, ibid., p. 51.
[82] Patricia Meredith, op. cit., p. 12.
[83] Meredith, ibid., p. 12.

Pakistani community put the law in jeopardy. Serious discussion of popular racism and of police apathy which would have questioned the consensus belief in British tolerance and British law was side-stepped. However, the community action threatened by the Pakistanis became an issue on which the integrity of the police and the adequacy of law was the basis for criticism of the Pakistanis. Surely this is a paradigm of reporting which maintains sociocultural consensus. Not only does it 'bury items which might jeopardize the sociocultural structure and man's faith in it' but it complements this omission with a reiteration of the 'common ultimate values' of faith in British justice and tolerance.

The great tradition of tolerance so often presented by the news media is an essential element of our national self-image. Tolerance and one of its corollaries, individual freedom, are values widely held in British society. Indeed it is a British dilemma that tolerance should be so highly prized whilst discrimination is so widely practised. Of course one solution to the dilemma is to determinedly deny its existence, through constant verbal expression of our tolerance. This has a double benefit, for not only does it sustain the national conceit about our liberalism, but by obscuring the realities beneath a consensus acceptance of our tolerance, it provides a screen for the pursuance of discriminatory behaviour, which by popular judgment and official connivance is *de facto* impossible in a tolerant society.

British Ethnocentrism in the Press: a historical perspective

The findings of our content analysis show how closely press coverage of the recent coloured immigration to Britain has reflected the ethnocentrism of British culture. The extent to which such tendencies are entrenched in British journalism can be seen from a brief look at the press's past record on this area. Postgate and Vallance in their review of 'The English People's Opinion of Foreign Affairs as reflected in their Newspapers since Waterloo'[84] illustrate how this ethnocentrism has taken on different forms under the changing situations of international relations throughout our history. They also show how events can bring particular nations and ethnic groups into the domain of national relevance; and how, once this focus is achieved, these national and ethnic categories come to be associated with stereotypical comment. Their discussion of the coverage of the Dutch in the Boer War period and of the Germans in the First World War illustrates this process well.

[84] Raymond Postgate and Aylmer Vallance, *Those Foreigners* (Harrap & Co. Ltd., London, 1937).

With the declaration of war in South Africa in 1899 the *Daily Mail* in predicting an inevitable British victory provided a veritable check list of biased conceptions and stereotyping :

> The superb expansion of the British Empire and the dwindling of the Dutch throughout the world have proved that, brain for brain, body for body, the English-speaking people are much more than a match for the Dutchman, despite the superior trickery and cunning of the men of the Low Countries . . . Doubtless at first we may suffer, but we have suffered before, and in the end the Boers, their shareholders, company promoters, German and Celtic hirelings, will receive the punishment which their insane attempt to perpetuate an almost barbaric system of Government in the 19th century most thoroughly deserves.[85]

This passage illustrates the beauty of ethnocentric bias in allowing one both to have one's cake and eat it. Having stated that 'English-speaking people' are superior to 'the Dutchman' in brain and body the writer then allows that the Dutchman is superior in some respects : in those negative skills of 'trickery and cunning'. Also while the 'superb expansion of the British Empire, proves our superiority to the Dutchman, it is their very attempt to rule in South Africa which justifies the punishment they will receive. But then, of course, the expansion of the British Empire is 'superb', whilst this Dutch attempt at *imperialism* is an 'insane attempt to perpetuate an almost barbaric system of Government'. It is also of interest that the Dutch share-holders and company promoters are mentioned as amongst those who will receive a just punishment. For this would seem to suggest that the Boers are motivated by mercenary interests, whilst we must assume that British interest is in overthrowing the said 'almost barbaric system of Government'.

The force of such ethnocentric writing lies in the fact that, to the reader who shares the cultural assumptions of the writer, the question of double standards, or bias, does not arise. Particularly is this so when the contemporary international situation is conducive to the acceptance of such writing, in as much as it explains and legitimates the action to which the Government and the country is committed.

The excesses which may be achieved in ethnocentric journalism, and still meet with general acceptance amongst the audience,

[85] Ibid., p. 195.

is illustrated in the contents of *John Bull* during the First World War. Postgate and Vallance say of this period :

> John Bull was the first to begin the deliberate working up of anti-German hatred. By the end of the war, as a result of systematic and ceaseless atrocity campaigns, English public opinion had been convinced that the Germans were sub-human.[86]

It is worth noting that these authors report that the type of article found in *John Bull* during this period was not opposed by any 'influential organ of public opinion'. In fact the malevolent influence of Bottomley's *John Bull* was apparent throughout the English press of the period.

The highly emotive fiction which was part of the style of *John Bull* may be illustrated from the issue of 3 October 1914 :

> It is our bounden duty to call up before the eye of imagination the scenes of butchery, rape and rapine which everywhere have marked the progress of the German arms. . . .

> Close your eyes and picture these things. 'Is that the wail of a child you hear? Ah, friend, it is that promising boy of yours – the one you were beginning to be so proud of – the one who had all those good qualities – spitted on the bayonet of a blood-drunken German soldier – the little face, that you loved to kiss, tortured in the agony of death. And that slipping mass upon which you stumbled as you ran? Take a long look at it, for you will make nothing of it at first. Ah! You have recognized it now. Out of the hideous mass of severed and bleeding limbs you have reconstructed that curly-haired little prattler at your side, still alive and merry, thank God! For, of course, you were only dreaming; and the fleet is in the North Sea.'

Later in the article[87] the reader is encouraged to imagine the rape of his wife as further 'evidence' of the bestiality of German soldiery.

This certainly must rank among the most emotive material ever placed in print in the British Press. However, it should be remembered that *John Bull* merely provides an extreme example of a more general phenomenon. For example, in 1914, the *Daily News,* one of the papers commended by Postgate and Vallance for their restraint in wartime reporting, started a

[86] Ibid., p. 235.
[87] Ibid., p. 237.

series of news stories called 'Under the Heel of the Hun'.

The above examples are of ethnocentric reporting in time of war, and it must be acknowledged that war creates special pressures within a society, and a crucial redefinition of the characteristics of participant nations; with allies becoming more favourably defined and the enemy more negatively defined. History has given us ample opportunity to note how the characteristics we impute to different national groups are found to be conveniently changeable when a shift of alliance demands a redefinition of our conceptions of national characteristics. Thus, for example, the American stereotype of the Japanese changed considerably following Pearl Harbor. Seago[88] found in November 1941 that the Japanese were regarded as courteous, ambitious, tradition loving and, the only characteristic showing awareness of Japanese activity in the war, aggressive. However, after Pearl Harbor, the traits courteous and ambitious disappeared from the stereotype and the salient traits became, deceitful, treacherous, sly and extremely nationalistic. Similarly, before American entry into the Second World War the war in Europe had not had a great impact on the American stereotype of Germans which included, scientifically minded, industrious, extremely nationalistic, and stolid. However, after the American entry into the war the traits aggressive, cruel and arrogant were added.[89] Also Guillaumin[90] records how in the Algerian war of liberation against France:

> Over the period from 1960 to 1962, the terms 'terrorists', 'bandits' and 'killers' gave way to 'the army'. Algerian soldiers had ceased to be 'shot down', instead, they were 'killed'.

Here the initial complacent outrage of colonial France was shifted toward respect as the success of the Algerians made it embarrassing to contemplate being defeated by 'terrorists' and 'bandits'.

These changes in stereotypes demonstrate the validity of Duijker and Frijda's[91] statement that 'we may expect to find

[88] D. W. Seago, 'Stereotypes: Before Pearl Harbor and after' (J. of Psychol., 1947, 23. 55-63).
[89] See D. W. Seago, ibid. and N. Schoenfield, 'An experimental study of some problems relating to stereotypes' (*Arch. Psychol.* 1942, 38).
[90] Collette Guillaumin, 'The popular press and ethnic pluralism: the situation in France' (*International Social Science Journal*, Vol. 23, No. 9, 1971).
[91] H. C. J. Duijker and N. H. Frijda, *National Character and National Stereotypes* (North Holland Publishing Company, Amsterdam, 1960, p. 126).

some correlation between stereotype content and stereotype function'. For the French in the early stages of a war to suppress a revolt in a colonial population it was useful to regard the rebellion as the activities of a few terrorists or bandits. For such labels imply that the rebellion is not legitimate in having popular support among the Algerian population. However, with the victory of the rebels imminent, it is then useful to change tactics. To demean the legitimacy and credibility of the opposition is functional in legitimating one's own aggression. But acknowledging both their effectiveness and legitimacy is the necessary pose to adopt when they begin to look like winning. Similarly for Americans involved in a war against Japan it would have been somewhat incongruous to have continued to regard them as courteous. The addition of the negative traits to the stereotype is a positive contribution to stabilizing a wartime mentality. Just as adding the traits aggressive, arrogant and cruel to the stereotype of the Germans helped to rationalize entering a war against them.

If stereotypes are 'undifferentiated judgments', thumbnail sketches simplifiying our world and our understanding of it, then it is reasonable that, as the relationships between nations change, then the stereotypes we hold of them also change so that the world continues to make sense to us. These examples of wartime journalism show how changes in intergroup, or international relationships set in motion a redefinition of not only that relationship, but also of the participants. Wartime journalism also demonstrates the processes of labelling and stereotyping discussed in Chapter 3 which so often operate within the news media, though in a less apparent form. Ethnic groups, like national groups, are subject to the same process of labelling and stereotyping. Here again stereotyping descriptions change with changes in intergroup relations, though frequently such changes are variations upon existing stereotypes and not completely novel in their content.

Jews as an ethnic group with a distinct and continuing culture have been in Britain for centuries and there has always been an undercurrent of anti-Semitism which has on occasion become more visible as internal conditions in Britain have provided the conditions under which anti-Semitism could prosper. British anti-Semitism came to the surface in the 1920s when the Protocols of the 'Elders of Zion' had a brief notoriety. These were supposedly secret documents which contained the plans of a Jewish conspiracy to achieve world domination. In fact, they were a complete fiction concocted by the bastardiza-

tion of a subtle argument for liberation written in the reign of
Napoleon III in France.[92] In 1920 an English translation of
the 'Protocols' was published and attracted much attention. It
is worth noting at this point that the 'Protocols' themselves are
not easy reading, or indeed consistent in any intelligent way as
can be ascertained today by reading them in Cohn's excellent
book. Cohn himself says:

> And what a document! Anyone who has spent long hours
> trying to make some sense of their nonsense can only feel
> baffled to read, in what was one of the most sophisticated
> of British weeklies [*Spectator* 15 May 1920], that 'the "Proto-
> cols" are of very great ability', 'brilliant' in (their) moral
> perversity and intellectual depravity' and indeed 'one of the
> most remarkable productions of their kind'.[93]

It is an indication of the potency of the latent anti-Semitism
in Britain that those 'Protocols' should have been taken so
seriously and given coverage in the British press. Cohn quotes
The Times from their issue of 8 May 1920:

> What are these 'Protocols'? Are they authentic? If so, what
> malevolent assembly concocted these plans, and gloated
> over their exposition? Are they a forgery? If so, whence
> comes the uncanny note of prophecy, prophecy in parts
> fulfilled, in parts far gone in the way of fulfilment? Have we
> been struggling these tragic years to blow up and extirpate
> the secret organization of German world dominion only to
> find beneath it another, more dangerous because more secret?
> Have we, by straining every fibre of our national body,
> escaped a ' Pax Germanica' only to fall into a Pax 'Judoeica'?
> The 'Elders of Zion', as represented in their 'Protocols', are
> by no means kinder taskmasters than William II and his
> henchmen would have been.

This from the respectable and authoritative *Times*! Not
surprisingly the right wing *Morning Post* showed even less
restraint and carried eighteen articles expounding the Judeo-
Masonic conspiracy. That the idea of such a conspiracy should
have been taken so seriously is indicative of the latent anti-
Semitism in Britain. That it should have been based on such
evidence as the 'Protocols' shows how important the pre-existing

[92] For an account of the history and origins of the 'Protocols', see
Norman Cohn, *Warrant for Genocide* (Pelican Books, 1970).
[93] Ibid., p. 156.

conceptions relating to Jews were in facilitating the perception and *reporting* of such specious material as possibly valid.

Evidence that the 'Protocols' were false became available and in August 1921 *The Times* published the proofs that they were indeed forgeries. Following this the 'Protocols' disappeared from the pages of the British press and from the concerns of the British public. That they could fade so easily was probably a reflection of the fact that at that time there were no social forces operating within the country to supply the demand for maintaining the myth.

In the 1930s anti-Semitism again found expression under conditions which were more conducive to its development. During this period the emergence of the Nazis in Germany created a progressively increasing emigration of Jews from Germany. Though at first German persecution of the Jews was not fully comprehended in Britain, from 1935 onwards the British press had given increasing coverage to the plight of German Jews.

In 1933 the response to Jewish flights from Germany was generally sympathetic and it is not surprising that this should be so for . . . 'by December 1933, there were only 3,000 Jewish or other refugees in Britain, while by the following April their number had decreased to 2,000'.[94] However, even in 1933 there was press opposition to the immigration on the grounds that it constituted a threat to the native labour force, though Sharf points out that this was largely confined to the local press. In the period between summer 1938 and the outbreak of war, when Britain admitted approximately three quarters of her final refugee population of about 65,000 (mostly intended for re-emigration), opposition became more widespread. Though the press showed sympathy with the plight of the Jews, it also argued that Britain could not accept unrestricted entry of refugees.[95] The limited help offered to German Jews and the grudging and complacent attitude of both press and public towards them illustrates the distorting morality of anti-Semitism. Only anti-semitism and the focusing of attention on their Jewish identity could make such complacency possible in view of what was known about their treatment in Germany at the time.

The point about the press handling of the Jewish refugee

---

[94] Andrew Sharf, *The British Press and Jews Under Nazi Rule* (OUP, London, 1964, p. 157).
[95] Ibid., p. 167 ff. for examples.

problem in the period 1938-39 is its remarkable and prophetic similarity to the coverage of the Kenya Asians in the late 1960s: as for example in the 1938 headlines, with the *Daily Mail's* – 'Aliens Pouring into Britain' and the *Daily Mirror's* (Manchester) – 'Smuggling of Exiles Alarms Britain'.

Sharf[96] provides an example from the *Sunday Express* of 19 June 1938 which has a familiar ring to anyone acquainted with press coverage of recent coloured immigration.

> In Britain half a million Jews find their home. They are never persecuted and, indeed, in many respects the Jews are given favoured treatement here. But just now there is a big influx of foreign Jews into Britain. They are overrunning the country. They are trying to enter the medical profession in great numbers. They wish to practise as dentists. Worst of all, many of them are holding themselves out to the public as psycho-analysts. A psycho-analyst needs no medical training, but arrogates to himself the functions of a doctor. And he often obtains an ascendency over the patients of which he makes use if he is a bad man . . . Intolerance is loathed and hated by almost everybody in this country. And by keeping a close watch on the causes which fed the intolerance of the Jews in other European countries we shall be able to continue to treat well those Jews who have made their homes among us, many of them for generations.

In this item we find the successful submerging of potential inconsistency that we noted earlier. First we establish our own unquestionable liberal credentials by reciting our positively preferential treatment of the 'half million' Jews already here. We then use this liberal loathing of intolerance as an argument for restricting the entry of more Jews since it is only by preventing refugees from overrunning the country that we can 'continue to treat well those Jews who have made their homes among us'. In his analysis of the press of the time Sharf[97] says:

> . . . one basic assumption emerged, whether all its implications were consciously understood or not. If more Jewish refugees means, or might eventually mean, more anti-Semitism in host countries, then the cause of anti-Semitism was – the Jew. And since anti-Semitism, at least in its more virulent form, was clearly wrong and barbarous, the only course was to prevent any notable increase in one's own Jewish population.

96 Ibid., p. 168.
97 Ibid., p. 170.

This formulation re-emerged in its entirety in the 1960s, the only change being that colour prejudice replaced anti-Semitism, and coloured immigrants replaced Jewish refugees.

In 1972 the same argument has been resurrected in defence of Britain's reluctance to accept Ugandan Asians. *The Times* leader of 14 August 1972 had this to say:

> Immigrants already settled here stand to suffer more than anyone else from a rate of new immigration greater than the social body of the host country can digest, or than its prejudices can tolerate.

Over 30 years later the old double-think is being employed without embarrassment or question. Now it is Amin's racism which is vilified, and the argument persists that it is because of our concern for tolerance that we must refuse to accept more coloured immigrants. It is true that in a racist society a greater number of coloured immigrants will probably increase the frequency, and possibly the degree, of racialism, as our attitude findings suggest. But no one has suggested that the problem lies not with coloured immigrants, but in white racism. The respectability of white prejudice has been enshrined in the acceptance of claims that certain cities can take no more Asians, for reasons that barely trouble to disguise blatant hostility. It is to the Government's credit that it did accept the Ugandan Asians. With the exception of the *Daily Express*, the British national press acknowledged British responsibility for them. These sentiments were, however, largely confined to the leader columns. On the news pages the papers predictably accepted unquestioningly 'the problem' which the Asians are held to constitute.

The *Daily Express* of 5 August 1972 made abundantly clear its belief that Ugandan Asians constituted a problem; its first report was front page news and carried the headline 'New Asian Threat'. It then informed its readers that 'Britain was threatened yesterday with a flood of Asians from East Africa'. Again the imagery of threat, of floods of immigrants, which was apparent in 1938 and which was developed to the state of an art in the polemic of Enoch Powell in relation to Kenyan Asians is once more brought forth.

If other papers avoided the paranoia of the *Express* they still conveyed the 'problem' definition of events through their unquestioning acceptance of the belief that the entry of the Asians constituted a threat to social services, housing, education and, of course, good race relations. The impression was reinforced through the prominence given to the utterances of local figures who claimed that their community could accept no more Asians, or only a few.

Nor was it only in the information provided that the press conveyed the 'problem' image, it also largely failed to reveal or give prominence to facts or viewpoints which might confound that definition. So, for example, David Lane of the Home Office was much quoted as saying : 'We are already a crowded island and immigration must and will remain strictly controlled' – the implication being that immigration is the cause of over-population. Yet a feature of this country for a decade and more has been a net *emigration*. In the midst of the panic over the Asians, official Government statistics became available which confirmed that in 1971 emigration exceeded immigration by over 20,000. This statistic was remarkable for its relative invisibility in the press. It did not contradict the anti-immigrant argument, but it certainly was not evidence for it. The reliance of the British medical services on Asian doctors has similarly not been regarded as a significant fact in a debate about Asian immigrants; and the finding of Jones and Smith[98] that coloured immigrants make less of a demand upon the social services than the indigenous population still remains one of the submerged facts about immigration.

Once again, the press failed to acknowledge and analyse British prejudice; rather it obscured it behind a superficial concern for tolerance. In its coverage of events, it accepted uncritically those items which were consistent with its habitual perception of coloured immigrants as a problem, while it submerged contrary facts.

[98] K. Jones and A. D. Smith, *The Economic Impact of Commonwealth Immigration,* (OUP, July 1970).

9

The Entertainment Media

Our empirical work has shown how, although the news media have been effective in maintaining the visibility of anti-racist and egalitarian sentiments, they have at the same time helped to define the racial situation in Britain in a way more conducive to the development of hostility towards coloured groups than to acceptance of them. They have communicated a view of the situation broadly consistent with the traditional ethnocentric and racist values of British culture, in spite of their affirmation of contrary values, and often in spite of their apparent intentions.

In the previous chapter, we argued that this state of affairs comes about because in the last analysis the mass media serve the social function of maintaining faith in the existing social order by ensuring – in Breed's words – 'that a body of common ultimate values remains visible as a continuing source of consensus'. This entails explaining or obscuring contradictions in the value system of the society or between value ideals and social practice. To say this is not to make any statement about the motives or good intentions of media personnel. It means only that the news media operate under constraints that make the kind of outcome we have mapped likely, if not inevitable. These constraints derive from a number of features of the way the news media are constituted and related to the wider society. They show themselves most noticeably in prevailing conceptions of what kind of thing makes 'news', what treatment is appropriate to particular kinds of news, the kind of news sources and spokesmen utilized and so on.

The commercial context in which the media operate in particular produces a tendency for what is thought newsworthy to be weighted towards what sells papers or attracts audiences, and away from any questioning of cherished cultural assumptions. The fact that the media are staffed almost entirely by whites also increases the likelihood that they will project an essentially white perspective on the world in which the traditional ethnocentrism of British culture will more readily find a place than alternative conceptions. Finally, when it is borne in mind that the sections of society in which ownership and control of the mass media is concentrated are closely associated with the same interests that stand to benefit most from a climate of opinion in which discrimination against non-whites and exploitation of the Third World are accepted as normal, then it is hardly surprising that the traditional 'white man's' view of the world should predominate in the mass media's treatment of race. In this chapter we argue that parallel processes operate in the entertainment media.

Blacks in the Cinema

Once again we need to take account of American media output, both because of the work that has been done on the topic in America and because we import so much of our television fare from there. A recent content analysis of one week's viewing[1] found that nearly 42 percent of the non-white characters seen in British television drama appeared in programmes imported from America. Of the non-white characters seen in feature films on British television, 67 percent were in American films.

Since American films may play such an important role in disseminating an image of non-whites, it is worth reviewing some content studies of American films. Because many of the films transmitted on television are not recent productions, studies dating to the 1940s will be examined.[2] A study of 100 films involving either Negro themes or Negro characters of more than passing significance was published in 1945.[3] This found that, with regard to their treatment of Negroes, 75 percent of these films should be classified as stereotyped and disparaging, 13 percent as neutral or unobjectionable, and 12 percent as favourable. In 1950, 20 feature films were analysed,[4] and it was found that 95 percent of those characters who received 'sympathetic', *i.e.* favourable, presentation were white Americans.

[1] *Non-Whites on British Television* (BBC Audience Research Department, 1972).
[2] The criteria used for categorization are not identical in all the studies cited but are sufficiently comparable to permit their use for the argument developed here. The significance of content analysis should not be exaggerated; it is no substitute for critical appraisal but an empirical complement to it.
[3] Columbia University, Bureau of Applied Social Research. *How Writers Perpetuate Stereotypes* (Writers' War Board, 1945 Pamphlet).
[4] Shirley Auer and Martin S. Allwood, 'The Social Characteristics of the Movie Dream World', in M. S. Allwood, ed. *Studies in Mass Communication* (Geneva, NY: Department of Sociology, Hobart and William Smith Colleges, 1951).

This echoed the findings of Jones[5] whose study carried out in 1941-42 reported that 81 percent of the sympathetic main characters in the 100 feature films analysed were white Americans. A 1959 study of heroes and heroines in 20 feature films[6] found that not one of these was a Negro.

These studies of the American films produced in two decades indicated the infrequency with which coloured people appeared in the cinema, and also demonstrated the predominance of mainstream white Americans as the category of person given sympathetic treatment. Goodrich[7] in summarizing content studies of several American media, including the cinema, over the same period concluded that :

> Mass-media man has, for the most part, been a 100 percent American – a white Protestant English-speaking native-born American without any hint of foreign or minority-group ancestry. From slightly more than 7 to as many as 9 out of 10 of the characters in the mass-fiction world have been 100 percent Americans.

> If, although the odds have been against it, media man has been a minority ethnic, a deviant from the 100 percent American standard, the greatest likelihood is that his ethnic affiliation has been with some European country. American-born ethnics, such as Jews and Negroes, have appeared less frequently than ethnics with European background.

Goodrich's work shows that the content of the American cinema in the 1940s and 1950s did not differ greatly in its treatment of coloured people from television, the radio, or short stories. Summarizing the research he points to the close relationship between the attitude toward minority ethnic groups in America and their treatment in the media :

> The media world's closest contact with the actual world has been on the cultural level. Certain widely held ethnocentric and nativist attitudes and beliefs in the real population have been mirrored in the fictional world, often at the expense of the objective facts.

One instance of this fictional-cultural correspondence has been

---

[5] Dorothy B. Jones, 'Quantitative Analysis of Motion Picture Content' (*Public Opinion Quarterly*, 6, 1942, pp. 411-28).
[6] Donald G. Arnstine, 'The Aesthetic Dimension of Value Education' Doctoral Dissertation, University of Illinois, 1960).
[7] Herbert Goodrich *Man and Society in Mass-Media Fiction: The Pattern of Life in the Mass Media as Revealed by Content Analysis Studies* (Ph.D. Thesis, University of Illinois, 1964).

in connection with the widely held American preference for native-born white Protestant Americans and the widespread antipathy for deviants from the pure white American standard. The antipathy in media society as in the real population has generally varied according to the remoteness of the ethnic minority from the 100 percent American standard, with the most readily observable basis of ethnic differentness, such as race, leading to the greatest disfavor.[8]

This close reflection of the dominant culture in the entertainment media is not simply a consequence of these cultural values being held by writers, directors and producers within the media. Colle[9] points to some more concrete forces which operate. When a TV drama series, 'Playhouse', sponsored by Philco, put out a play in which Sidney Poitier had a major role, the consequence was the cancellation of distributorships by Philco franchise holders, and threats from consumers never to buy Philco goods again.

That was in 1955. Several years later when NBC launched the 'Nat King Cole Show', the first television series to have a Negro star performer, they found that advertising support was not forthcoming and the show was cancelled before it was half-way through its planned season. Economic forces were also a factor in the American film industry where the Southern market was seen as representing a threat to any producer whose liberality caused offence. The content of the American entertainment industry in this period reflects not only dominant cultural values in the beliefs and perspectives of writers, directors and producers, but these values held at grass root level in significant sections of the audience were able to impose themselves upon the entertainment media because of the economic veto which this audience was seen to constitute.

The roles occupied by coloured people in American and British films until the 1960s were very largely supporting parts, or they were extras. Quite often their presence was justified because of the geographical location of the film. For example, in films set in the American Deep South they were cast as maids, butlers, field workers and slaves. In the North they would occupy service jobs like train attendants, waiters, or shoe-shine boys. A predominant part of the Negro image in the cinema of the '30s, '40s and '50s was a reiteration of the Sambo stereo-

8 Ibid., p. 195.
9 Royal D. Colle, 'Negro Image in the Mass Media: A Case Study in Social Change' (*Journalism Quarterly*, Spring 1968).

type. Boskin[10] quotes a description of the Sambo characteristics provided by Robert Penn Warren.[11]

> He was the supine, grateful, humble, irresponsible, unmanly, banjo-picking, servile, grinning, slack-jawed, docile, dependent, slow-witted, humorous, child-loving, child-like, watermelon-stealing, spiritual-singing, blamelessly fornicating, happy-go-lucky, hedonistic, faithful black servitor who sometimes might step out of character long enough to utter folk wisdom or bury the family silver to save it from the Yankees.

Elements of that description ring true for many of the films seen at the cinema, and which now continue to appear on television. True, the cinema 'Sambo' seldom exhibits the full array of Warren's description in any single film, but reflection calls forth innumerable instances where variations on the theme have heavily impregnated Negro roles. Whether in a Marx Brothers comedy, where we witness a display of dancing and the spontaneous musicality of the Negroes as amidst a flurry of happiness and flashing teeth they sing 'Who dat man?', or in many less memorable sequences in formula dramas, the contented, simple musicality of the Negro has been imprinted upon us all. In other contexts it has been the superstition of the nannies, and the child-like fear attributed to coloured servants which have received emphasis. Boskin[12] quotes some classic examples of such fear as, for instance, when a frightened Negro outran people and animals in his haste to escape and shouted 'Git out de way an' let a man run what can run'. Such examples may represent an extreme end of the range, but in subtler forms these stereotypes have been ubiquitous in their penetration into the cinema portrayal of the American Negro.

British Films

In most cases, the coloured person's status in British films has been bounded by the internal logic of the location. In Africa he was often the faithful 'boy', quick to obey 'Bwana', or in safari dramas Africans were the porters who carried the equipment and who could be relied upon to run off at some point because of their abject terror at the prospect of entering a taboo area. The superstition and temerity of the natives was often used as a valuable counterpoint to the rationality and courage of the

[10] Joseph Boskin, 'Sambo: The National Jester in the Popular Culture' in Gary D. Nash and Richard Weiss, *The Great Fear: Race in the Mind of America* (Holt, Rinehart and Winston, Inc., 1970).

white man. Coupled with the prescribed inferior status of the African, this juxtaposition further contributed to the equation of non-white with inferiority.

In India, the range of themes again tended to result in Indians being cast as extras to fill in background as market traders, tribesmen or soldiers. Even when the part carried some status such as a rajah or prince, it was seldom a major role in the context of the film. In the event that an Indian occupied a substantial part, then there was a strong likelihood that the actor would be a suitably made-up white. The films set in India were, as Halliwell[13] puts it 'mainly of the military kind' and this itself greatly influenced the way in which Indians were presented. Typically, troops of 'loyal' Sepoys were led by their white officers against Indian tribesmen, the latter being presented as variations on the theme of the 'wily Pathan', fierce, skilled mountain fighters, and particularly treacherous.

In many of the British films located in India and Africa, the justifying assumptions of colonialism were writ large though seldom made verbally explicit. For successive generations of cinema-going youngsters, the North West Frontier provided a venue for the celebration of human fortitude and courage. Few of us who enjoyed such films could have felt any disquiet that the protagonist with whom we were invited to identify was always white. Nor did it seem strange that we were presented so often with the same scenario, of British forces *defending* themselves against attack, often against the background of a broken treaty. No less frightening is the sense of gratification experienced when the British troops retained their control of the territory. For one of the strengths of these films is the assumptions they can take for granted in their audience, who found the presence and activities of the British in the colonies entirely acceptable and understandable. A British education in itself was sufficient to provide a suitably ethnocentric conception of history. Nor was there ever anything in the film which suggested that right might not lie with might, and certainly there was nothing which floated the idea that the British were in fact aggressors in a conflict aimed at imperial exploitation. It is the closed circle of an ethnocentrically biased film being directed at an audience with exactly the same biases which makes such films an effective means of reinforcing all the nationalistic and racial

[11] Robert Penn Warren, *Who Speaks for the Negro?* (Random House Inc., New York, 1965, p. 52).
[12] Joseph Boskin, op. cit., p. 178.
[13] Leslie Halliwell, *The Filmgoers Companion* (Paladin, London, 1972, p. 505).

conceits which are nurtured in our history and everyday beliefs.

More recently, these same assumptions have been revitalized on location in Kenya and Malaya. How natural and immediate was the acceptance of the settlers in Kenya, and the rubber planters in Malaya, as the heroes, the 'good guys'. Equally, how easy it was to believe in the animal savagery of the Mau Mau, where once more the superstition of the African was apparent in, for example, the oath-taking ceremonies. For the British characters, however, the same fortitude which had enabled them to survive the North West Frontier and penetrate the Dark Continent in earlier films was now manifest in concentrated form in Malaya and Kenya. In these locations it was the isolated individual and his family who dared to defy the 'terrorists'. The terrorists frequently even lacked the courage to attack during the day, although the occasional Mau Mau houseboy was known to do a hatchet job on the wife and family while the husband was at his work. In one film the victims were struck down by an animal's claw held in the assailant's hand.

A feature which such films have in common with the earlier ones about Africa and India is their entirely 'British' perspective. The physical location of the action and an approximate statement of the time in history is normally enough to prime the audience sufficiently for them to supply the appropriate perspective. The presence of the British in India or Kenya does not need explanation – the audience knows they were there, and that their presence was a part of our great history.

In films we have fought battles in foreign parts where the concern was the victory, not the purpose of the war. The typical story-line has mitigated against the exposition of political realities. The political situation has largely been a taken-for-granted back-drop against which the heroes and heroines pursued their personal destiny. The internal time span of the story atomizes history so that our concern is one brief period of time where the actions of individuals occupy our attention.

Perhaps it is not reasonable to expect a commercial enterprise like the film industry to strive for a more objective version of history when our school text books have not yet emerged from the mystifying glow of our colonial glory,[14] and when decolonization has not substantially altered the economic relationships between Britain and her ex-colonies. Broadly speaking, the British cinema has reflected and sustained our natural ethnocentric perspective on the world.

[14] See for example F. Glendenning, 'Racial Stereotypes in History Textbooks' (*Race Today*, February, 1971).

It is not only the ethnocentric view of history inherent in films which must concern us, but also the stereotypes of non-British groups which are woven into the narrative. These stereotypes are presented in two distinct ways. In the first place, conventional biases are perpetuated through the low status roles that non-whites commonly occupy. Negroes are typically servants doing menial jobs, and Africans are porters or savages. Secondly, stereotypes are transmitted through the kind of behaviour typically associated with particular groups. Negroes are associated with musicality, and dull-witted, eyeball-rolling simplicity, and Africans are presented as being superstitious by nature. It is because these characteristics come to seem *natural* in non-white groups that they are so dangerous. Stereotyping in film roles and behaviour is entirely consistent with the normal human tendency to stereotyped thinking and it is this that makes the association of particular characteristics with particular races all the more powerful.

The predisposition of audiences to think in stereotypes is doubly reinforced when the categories and stereotypes used in the film are identical to those already held by the audience as part of the dominant cultural beliefs of the society. Films on television are viewed by large audiences and it is important that their content does not reinforce views of reality which should be anathema in a multi-racial Britain.

American Television Drama and the Presentation of Blacks
The study referred to earlier[15] showed that in a week of British television 42 percent of the non-whites appearing were in programmes from the United States. Of American television Dominick and Greenberg wrote in 1970:

> Before the most recent TV seasons the black American was the 'invisible man' of US television. Although there are more than 20 million Negroes in this country, the TV industry had managed to overlook them almost entirely. True, blacks appeared on television before the last year or two, but those instances might properly be called rare events.[16]

This both indicates the absence of black actors from television

---

[15] *Non-Whites on British Television* (BBC Audience Research Department, 1972).
[16] Joseph R. Dominick and Bradley S. Greenberg, *Three Seasons of Blacks on Television*, (Communication Among the Urban Poor, Report No. 11, May 1970, Department of Communication, Michigan State University).

before 1967, and implies that things were getting better by that date. These authors carried out a content analysis of 'Three Seasons of Blacks on Television' in which they studied a full week's output in 1967, 1968 and 1969. For dramatic shows (situation comedies, Westerns, action and adventure – the kind of material that we take most of from American television) they found an increase in the number of programmes containing at least one black – from 34 percent of drama programmes in 1967 to 52 percent in 1968 and 1969. However, they also found that whereas 63 percent of blacks appearing in 1967 were in major roles, only 20 percent were in major roles in 1969. In other words, the numerical increase represented an increased concentration of blacks in minor and background roles. Other findings of these authors show an increasing tendency for blacks on television to occupy roles reflecting white rather than black American values and life-styles, as judged by style of dress and language.[17] The greater number of black faces on the screen did not therefore carry with it an increased exposure of black American culture. It would seem that blacks in American television drama are not functioning as representatives of any distinctive black culture; rather they are merely black skins in white roles. Their presence does not add materially to the nature of the values which are displayed; they could in all honesty be replaced by white men.

Having on the whole ignored the existence of blacks in the past, American television sought a remedy in hiring black actors rather than in creating black parts. The attempt to inject blacks into American TV succeeded, but if any conscious attempt to inject a black perspective based upon the black experience was made, it failed because white ownership and white production could not know what constituted that experience. A black perspective would result in black characters voicing the values of black Americans, derived from their experience of oppression and their growing sense of identity.

Thus, even in a period when a burgeoning civil rights movement made American television painfully aware of its inadequate treatment of blacks, and when an improved grass roots understanding of past prejudices made change possible, the tremendous inertia of the television industry was evident. Even when deliberate efforts are made to improve the presentation of

[17] Joseph R. Dominick and Bradley S. Greenberg, *Blacks on TV Their Presence and Roles* (Communication Among the Urban Poor, Report No. 8, June 1969, Department of Communication, Michigan State University).

coloured people in television programmes, an inadequate analysis of the problem yields an inadequate solution. In an industry staffed by whites, it was not surprising that the problem was conceived of as being mainly a matter of frequency of appearance rather than the need for greater expression of black values and culture through television.

This definition must have been easy for media professionals to accept for its solution required no major revision of habitual procedures. If the problem is quantity, then hire more black actors. Any other definition of the problem would have required more fundamental changes to provide a solution. One of these would have been increased control of the medium by black representatives, and this might have led to a greater voice on television for dissident, alienated black America. This however would have amounted to a questioning of the consensus and a challenge to white hegemony.

The consensus maintaining function of American television drama is readily evident in many of the programmes imported to Britain. Of the 1968 sample studied by Dominick and Greenberg, they reported that 'most blacks were shown as a member of some type of law enforcement agency'.[18] That is, they are seen to uphold the law of the land, a law which still fails to guarantee their rights and has been used as an instrument of political repression.[19] Perhaps the best example of this particular stratagem is the black character, Mark, in 'Ironside', the popular series shown on BBC television. Not only is he the prodigal delinquent brought home to serve the paternal Chief Ironside in fighting crime, but he is also a law student. Although he has latitude to identify with the underdog, in the end he always accepts the rule of law and Ironside's justice. The same function of a black character sponsoring 'all American values' can be seen in 'Julia' in which the lead character in the twin roles of nurse and mother reflects wholesome American womanhood in the mundane toils of middle-class existence.

The problem facing the American television network is the inevitable failure of a white dominated medium trying to serve the needs of a black audience. There are two major factors which contribute to this failure. One is the real problem of the white

[18] Dominick and Greenberg, 1969, op. cit.
[19] See for example George Jackson, *Soledad Brother,* Penguin Books, Harmondsworth, 1971. Paul Chevigny, *Police Power,* Vintage Books, New York, 1969. Angela Davis, *If they come in the morning,* Orbach and Chambers Ltd., London, 1971.

media professional. As an individual he is identified by his employment with a dominant white elite and its sub-culture, and his problem lies in trying to comprehend the values and needs of a minority group whose very existence is influenced by its subjugation at the hands of the white group. His income will be such as to remove him physically from contact with the majority of black Americans, and his life-style will be totally different from theirs. On top of this, the very fact that he continues to command a high status position in the television industry indicates his compliance with the implicit consensus politics of big business, status quo America. This compliance will have of necessity numbed his capacity for critical appraisal of social realities, since commitment to ideals outside of the industry would have proven counter-productive in the past. Therefore, after years as a media man, he will have accommodated to media values; had he not, he would no longer be there.[20]

The other factor is more fundamental. It is that to allow full freedom of expression to an exploited minority group would be to endanger the existing social structure and people's faith in it. Such freedom would give a platform, not only for black culture, but also for a black critique of white society. Documentaries about blacks made by blacks for a black audience can hardly be expected to have the anaesthetizing blandness which so often characterizes documentaries about blacks made by whites for a white audience. Mild self-flagellation motivated by guilt might be replaced by incisive criticism driven by resentment and frustration.

This discussion of the American television industry is relevant to Britain because, at one level, we suffer from the failings of the American medium through our imports of its products, and at another the American situation stands as a cautionary tale for Britain. Although there are differences in structure and ownership, the two systems are similar in being white monopolies, in a society dominated by white economic interest and shaped by a culture which contains strong racist underpinnings. The comments we have made regarding the relative exclusion of black American interests from access to the medium can, of course, be applied to a greater or lesser extent to the position of any social group whose lack of economic and political power

[20] See Sander Vanocur, 'How the Media Massaged Me: My Fifteen Years of Conditioning by Network News, (*Esquire*, January 1972, p. 82 ff). This provides a case history of the adjustments necessary and the pressures that induce them.

render it liable to exploitation and denigration by a dominant group. A parallel argument could probably be made in respect of women, the trade union movement, and national minorities both in the United States and Britain.

Non-whites on British Television

The content study[21] of a full week of British television that we referred to earlier showed that across all three channels, only 8 of 34 dramatic programmes[22] contained non-whites in any parts; 648 white characters were identified in comparison with only 35 non-whites; 368 white characters spoke while only 9 non-whites had speaking parts. Coloured actors represented 5.1 percent of the characters in dramatic programmes, but even of this low number their percentage of speaking parts was lower than for whites, namely 25.7 percent as against 56.8 percent for white characters. Of the 35 non-whites there were only three who had major roles; two of these were Hawaiian policemen in 'Hawaii Five-O' and the other was a West Indian who was co-lead in a British 'Play for Today' on BBC-1. All other parts were minor or background roles, including a black African waiter, a West Indian bus conductor and a West Indian messenger boy.

A similar picture emerged from a study of our own of the output of ITV and BBC-1 over one week.[23] We found one major role for a non-white actor – an African student political leader in an episode of a British dramatic series. Of the four minor roles observed, one was the high status executive in 'Department S' and the others were a building labourer, an oriental servant, and an Indian priest. All the other non-whites were in incidental background parts. Taking dramatic, music and variety programmes together, non-whites were found to appear most frequently as musicians or singers. (The BBC study[24] found that four of the 16 variety programmes in the week contained one or more blacks.)

These studies confirm what must be obvious to any regular viewer of British television, namely the relative absence of non-whites from dramatic programmes and the predominantly minor parts they have when they do appear. Their characteristic casting

[21] *Non-Whites on British Television* (BBC Audience Research Department, 1972).
[22] Dramatic programmes were defined as – situation comedies, westerns, the detective shows, the plays.
[23] This was carried out by the authors in the week 24-30 April 1971, and used categories comparable to the BBC study.
[24] Op. cit.

in low status roles as servants or bus conductors is consistent with prevailing stereotypes of coloured people, as is the frequency of their appearance as musicians or singers.

An aspect of this situation which calls for special comment is that the stereotypical roles occupied by television blacks may be defended as being only a reflection of the actual situation of blacks in British society. To some extent this is true. The very fact that much of the media stereotype does reflect the social reality makes for a dangerously closed system. The media disseminated stereotype reflects and reinforces the association of blacks with inferior occupations and this helps to sustain the processes of discrimination which prevents their moving to other occupations. We find again that closed circle of belief so common to racialism : blacks are believed to be inferior on racial grounds, and their manifest occupational inferiority justifies this belief. The persistence of the myth of racial inferiority legitimates discriminatory behaviour and renders its consequences largely invisible by making the limited social achievement of blacks appear normal. This close link between fact and stereotype also imposes a limit on the extent to which a 'liberalization' of media drama could upgrade the roles allocated to blacks. Any consistent upgrading would strain dramatic credibility *because* it presented a fake image of reality. Again it is apparent that real changes in the media presentation of blacks must be accompanied by a radical change in their position within the society itself.

Comedy is perhaps the area in which the television handling of racial matters has attracted most attention. There seems to be a widespread acceptance that humour is entirely benevolent in its influence and that racial humour is especially cathartic. In the case of television comedies, this belief is highly questionable. 'Till Death Us Do Part' was a British comedy series which portrayed mindless racial prejudice and ethnocentrism in the words and deeds of Alf Garnett. That this series was intended to demonstrate the pettiness and illogicality of such people in no way insured that this would be the effect. There is a literature which describes the failure of programmes which sought to eradicate prejudice,[25] but which on occasions actually had the opposite effect. 'Till Death Us Do Part' would seem to fit exactly into that category. For many viewers Alf Garnett's comments would have been regarded as the rabid outpourings of an ill-educated bigot. But it seems probable that to many more

[25] See for example: E. Cooper and H. Dinnerman, 'Analysis of the Film "Don't be a Sucker": A Study in Communication' (*Public Opinion Quarterly,* Vol. 15, No. 2, 1951).

his outbursts were seen as only excessive over-statements of basically sound ideas. He was not an unsympathetic character, and his pain and bewilderment in the face of a world of changing values would have found understanding among many. What is certain is that many coloured people, and coloured organisations, objected strongly to the series and community relations officers commented upon its deleterious effect in areas of immigrant settlement.

If 'Till Death Us Do Part' was at least justified by the standard of writing and the real humour that it contained, a successor by the same writer, 'Curry and Chips', had much less claim to merit. In this programme a white man, blacked up, played the part of a Pakistani-Irishman nicknamed 'Paki-Paddy' – a caricature of the obsequious, eager to please immigrant. He became the butt of a great deal of humour directed at characteristics associated with his ethnicity, and the presentation was such that laughter *about* incongruities associated with immigration and ethnic differences readily shaded over into laughter *at* immigrants and Pakistani culture.

'Curry and Chips' is important, not only because of the possible harm it may have had among the white audience through its reiteration of working class racial bias, but also because it is symptomatic of the insensitivity of the 'white man's perspective' underlying television production. After the concern expressed over 'Till Death Us Do Part', and during a period of racial tension reflected in Powellism, 'Curry and Chips' represented a remarkable disregard for the coloured audience of British television. It would be naïve to pretend that there is some simple criterion for distinguishing between 'harmful' and 'harmless' ethnic humour. The best that can be hoped for is greater sensitivity, and awareness of what may be involved from those who produce television entertainment. In the case of any particular programme or joke it is necessary to ask : Who or what is being laughed at, and what cultural assumptions are being capitalized upon for the sake of producing humour? The dangers in the 'Curry and Chips' type of programme are two-fold. In the first place they may increase the sense of resentment and alienation among the coloured audience, and in the second they may reinforce racial stereotypes and encourage and confer respectability on racial hostility among the white population. It should be remembered that comedy series typically attract large audiences, and this must constitute a temptation to broadcast them with the minimum of critical appraisal. The compliance of the white working class is a necessary factor in the exploitation of the coloured work force. It is therefore important to question whether such comedies mediate this exploitation through sustaining white working class colour prejudice. Any current judgment must bring in a verdict of 'not proven', and for this reason we can only hope that greater concern will be directed towards obviating the harmful potential of such series.

Drama is not only entertaining; it is also an opportunity for non-purposive, latent learning.[26] Facts can be acquired and beliefs modified as an incidental by-product of viewing a programme for enjoyment. Such learning may be particularly effective precisely because it is non-purposive, and people come to it with their defences down. By accepting without question popular stereotypes and assumptions and then using these as the basis for drama, television adds to the legitimacy of these beliefs. The 'assumed reality' which is taken as the basis for drama becomes translated by the viewer into a dramatic portrayal of 'actual reality'. Beliefs which started as widely shared stereotypes become slowly and unconsciously transformed into 'facts'. Good race relations ought to merit sufficient concern for gratuitous social risks to be avoided, and the fostering of better race relations to be a matter of conscious policy.

A further feature of British television that needs to be mentioned is the tendency to accept the definition of the situation provided by the news media as the basis for the production of entertainment. Those themes that have been central to news coverage of race are fastened into and elaborated in dramatic form so that the picture of reality provided by the news is reinforced and cemented in the public mind through drama. This is true particularly of the conflict/threat image of the coloured population that we noted in news output. Thus, in the past few years 'The Saint', 'Softly Softly' and 'The Strange Report' have all had episodes in which the story line concerned illegal immigration. In one of these the illegal immigrants were the cause of a smallpox scare which led to street scenes with people, including the aged, going to a mobile clinic for inoculation. A similar instance occurred in an episode of 'Z Cars' where an Indian woman doctor treated an English friend and wrongly prescribed a treatment which nearly killed him. On top of the fact that her position in the British medical system meant that

[26] For a discussion of the significance of non-purposive learning see Herbert E. Krugman 'The Impact of Television Advertising: Learning Without Involvement' (*Public Opinion Quarterly*, XXIX, 3, Fall 1965); Herbert E. Krugman and Eugene L. Hartley, 'Passive Learning from Television' (*Public Opinion Quarterly*, XXXIV, 2, Summer 1970).

she should not have treated him in the first place, we had a graphic presentation of her inadequacy, which was then generalized to Indian doctors as a group. This story was presented in a country where patients already refuse treatment by black doctors on racist grounds alone, and where the usual justification is their supposed incompetence. To press the message home, an authority figure was introduced into the story – a consultant who said in her defence that she could hardly be blamed as her Indian qualification was markedly inferior to its British equivalent. A deliberate attempt to promote hostility against the coloured doctors upon whom the Health Service depends so heavily would not have needed to be very different from this programme.

Instances like this illustrate how, where race is involved, the normal professional concern for a good story and a polished production is not in itself sufficient guarantee of programme merit, for dramatic excellence and dramatic license may act as anaesthetics to social responsibility. Not all television entertainment that relates to race is as tendentious as some of these examples, of course, and British television has broadcast material to which no champion of multi-racialism could take exception. But this does not detract from the seriousness of the dangers represented by the more stereotyped and ethnocentric output. It is not a matter of balance. A prejudiced statement exists in its own right and cannot be counterbalanced or cancelled by an unprejudiced statement.

We have concentrated on television as the main entertainment medium. Others have examined other media.[27] Jenny Laishley[28] has shown how over the past ten years children's comics have continued to present 'colonial' stereotypes of Third World countries and have failed to reflect the increasingly multi-racial character of British society. Much the same may be said of the other media. (The reader might ask himself how much popular Asian music he has heard played by Radio One disc jockeys. We cannot recall any, though there must be a large potential audience among the immigrant population.) Like the news media, the British entertainment media reflect on the whole a white man's world in which coloured people,

[27] Janet Hill (Ed.), *Books for Children: The Homelands of Immigrants in Britain* (IRR, 1971); Felicity Bolton and Jennie Laishley, *Education for a Multi-Racial Britain* (Fabian Research Series 303, Fabian Society, 1972).
[28] Jennie Laishley, 'Can comics join the multi-racial society?' (*Times Educational Supplement*, 24 November 1972).

if they are visible at all, tend to have a marginal or subordinate position or to strike a discordant note in an otherwise harmonious world. We must conclude, also, that where race is concerned, the usual conception of 'entertainment value' is not on its own a sufficient guide to the production of entertainment in a multi-racial society, any more than the pursuit of news value on its own is sufficient to produce unbiased news.

10

Conclusion

At one point in the preparation of this book we were asked why we were calling it *Racism and the Mass Media* rather than, more simply, *Race and the Mass Media*. Our choice of title stems directly from the way we have come to understand the British racial situation. At the outset of the project we thought of ourselves as studying the question of race, and *Race and the Mass Media* would have expressed accurately what we thought we were examining. It soon became clear, however, that this was a misleading approach, implying as it does that what we are concerned with is a problem of race. Race in itself is a matter of no social importance; it is a biological fact as peripheral to essential human nature as differences in height or eye colour. Race as a means of *classifying* people socially, however, is important. This is another way of saying that race is important because people think it is important. It is not race that is the problem but the negative symbolism and meaning which is attached to it, and it is this in turn which makes race a crucial criterion in individual perception and collective action. When people think that differences of race constitute differences in social entitlement you have racism; and *racism* not race is the basis of the British 'racial problem'. Hence we have entitled the book *Racism and the Mass Media* rather than *Race and the Mass Media* in order not to seem to give credence to the idea that Britain has a race problem. Britain has a problem of racism.

The nature, origins and dimensions of this problem have been developed in earlier chapters. In particular we have shown how the negative symbolism and meaning surrounding blackness, with its deep historical roots in British culture, forms the interpretive framework within which interracial situations are perceived in Britain. Throughout this book also we have emphasized that 'the dynamics of intergroup relations cannot be reduced to the laws of individual psychology'. For prejudiced attitudes not only serve the function of bolstering up the psychological inadequacies of the individual, but more importantly they maintain whites as a group in an advantageous position relative to blacks. It remains for us to summarize our conclusions regarding the role of the mass media in the British racial situation, and to emphasize again that the elements of racial conflict in British society and the impingement of the mass media upon this process cannot be understood apart from the structure of the society as a whole and the major conflicts of interest that govern its course.

The crucial conflict of interests in British society is that between capital and labour, between employers and employees. The profit accrued from the exploitation of labour is the central dynamic of our social system. British racism creates a perspective on the world which reduces the visibility of injustice and exploitation and creates a cultural environment in which inequality and repression can continue to serve the economic and political interests of the dominant groups in British society – specifically employers, the owners of capital.

The employment of blacks in jobs which whites are no longer prepared to take has the benefit of filling the 'dirty' and less attractive jobs in our society but it also has the effect of preventing the cost of labour for these jobs from rising to the level which would otherwise be necessary to attract labour to them. Discrimination in employment is thus a process which creates a reserve pool of cheap labour for jobs which would otherwise fail to attract labour. Because blacks have difficulty in obtaining employment they are targets for exploitation in the forms of labour which they must be prepared to accept, and in the levels of payment they are able to command. The connivance of British trade unionism in this system of exploitation makes it all the more effective.[1] Through a misguided protectionism white British trade unionists assist in the exploitation of the black labour force and ultimately of themselves.

Prejudice, however, not only serves the economic interests of the power elite of white society. It has a further function which we have already outlined. Racism permits those who are alienated in their labour, economically exploited and denied political potency to blow off steam in a way which is harmless to the real beneficiaries of the social system, through scapegoating of pariah groups. In attaching responsibility for poor housing, inadequate social provision, and low wages to 'the immigrants',

---

[1] The *Report of a Committee of Inquiry into a dispute between employees of the Mansfield Hosiery Mills Limited, Loughborough, and their employer*. (HMSO London, 1972) in spite of its tendency to gloss over the racialist aspects of the situation, provides an interesting contemporary case study of this process.

the indigenous white working class actively contributes to its own deception. Resentment is therefore dissipated against the wrong groups and symptoms become mistaken for the real problems. The political exploitation of race in the last decade clearly shows the advantages to be obtained from promoting pseudo-problems while maintaining vested interests in the political and economic status quo. Again it is worth repeating that the endemic racism of this society forms the necessary basis upon which racial exploitation and scapegoating can be built. In any study of race relations in Britain, racism must be taken as a given. What we have been concerned to examine is the translation of the latent racism into visible hostility. It is from within the framework of British society at large that we sought to understand the role of the mass media.

In this book we have analysed and discussed the mass media treatment of race, and we have examined through survey data the response of white Britons to coloured immigration. In outline, our main findings may be summarized as follows.

Our findings on the white British response to coloured immigration have shown the importance of situational factors based on the local area, and the specific neighbourhood within the area, as determinants of feelings toward coloured people. Area and neighbourhood norms which develop in relation to specific features of the local situation appear to be important determinants of these evaluative, affective attitudes toward coloured immigrants. It is mainly these feelings toward coloured people which vary between areas with differing levels of coloured population.

The similarities between areas, however, are to be found in the concerns and issues which define the nature and meaning of coloured immigration into Britain. Given the considerable variations in geographic location, level of immigration, and local conditions – including, for example, levels of employment – there is remarkable overall consensus in the definition of the situation throughout our samples. There may be general differences between areas in how individuals feel about immigrants and immigration but to a considerable extent they are responding to a common definition of the significance of race and immigration in Britain.

Beliefs and ideas that are derived mainly from media sources are very heavily weighted toward definitional, conceptual beliefs, rather than affective response. Beliefs typically derived from the media may have varying overtones of hostility or friendliness, approval or disapproval, but more than anything they are statements of what is going on, of what the general state of affairs is. This is particularly apparent in comparison to the kind of thing typically attributed to first hand experience which, by contrast, is distinctly affective/evaluative. These media-derived ideas were also found to be very similar over areas. Even in different areas, where situational and attitudinal differences produce a tendency towards selective perception, individuals appear to be deriving essentially similar pictures of the world from the media.

This media definition has two main facets. On the one hand people have been kept aware of the hostility and discrimination suffered by coloured immigrants. In this respect, in not allowing social injustice and hardship to go unnoticed and in maintaining the visibility of egalitarian and anti-racist values, the media have performed a valuable function. On the other hand, and simultaneously, people have derived from the media a perception of the coloured population as a threat and a problem, a conception more conducive to the development of hostility towards them than acceptance.

Finally, there is agreement between the definition of the situation apparent in the responses to our open-ended questions, and the definition observed in the content analysis of the press.

The fit of these various findings taken together lead us to conclude that the mass media have played an important part in defining for the white public the nature and meaning of the black presence in Britain. We would also say that this definition is entirely consistent with the attitudes and perspective on race provided by the entertainment media which continue to reflect traditional cultural assumptions about race.

The prevailing negative definition of the significance of race in Britain, which is to an important extent disseminated and reinforced by the mass media, limits the significance that should be attached to individual attitudes of hostility or acceptance. We have seen that individual attitude does have some mediating influence upon the perception of race relations in Britain, but such is the impact of the media definition that this selective individual influence operates within a limited range set by the essentially negative media definition. The individually prejudiced may find this definition consistent with their attitudes and find in it legitimations for their behaviour, while those who lack individual hostility may find themselves endorsing discriminatory action against coloured minorities because this appears reasonable from within the perspective contained in the media definition.

To somewhat overstate the case, the conclusion can be presented anecdotally in terms of two adolescent respondents whose measured attitude differed widely, one being very 'tolerant' and the other decidedly hostile; yet they both accepted the same definition of the situation in that the issues and concepts which constituted their understanding of race in Britain were the same. Both regarded race as 'a problem', felt that there were 'too many coming in', and anticipated 'trouble' as an inevitable consequence. The significance of this similar definition of the situation lies in its potential for imposing constrants on the tolerant individual, whilst at the same time permitting the racist youth to perceive himself as a virtual moderate.

One of the immediate implications of our findings must relate to the adequacy of research on social issues where the only research tool has been the attitude scale. Clearly studies which rely upon attitude scales as the only means of testing the social consensus are providing only a partial statement of the reality, for the definition of the situation within which these attitudes operate may radically modify the behavioural implications of such attitudes.

The Mass Media

Though many comments typically reserved for conclusions have been expressed explicitly and implicitly in individual chapters there remains a responsibility for us to state our own recommendations on the basis of the research. As we indicated earlier prejudice is not a phenomenon of the individual alone. Though prejudice may serve psychological functions for the individual, as for example in attenuating the stress of deprivation, it is also socially functional in maintaining a traditional system of power relations, particularly through its manifestation in discrimination. Because of this dual nature of prejudice there are two categories of solution which may be pursued. One is largely cosmetic and is concerned to minimize the expression and impact of prejudice where it exists. The other solution is more fundamental and is concerned to attack the structural basis of prejudice in our society.

It is apparent from our analysis of the news media that to demand that journalists be more professional does not solve the problem of reporting race relations. For much of the bias in race related news would seem to stem from the habitualized 'news sense' which is integral to their professionalism. This professionalism, however, would also seem to include a capacity to face and evaluate criticism of journalistic practice. We believe that a conscious questioning of the relevance and implications of the usual journalistic procedures when applied to the coverage of race should be sufficient to show that when reporting racial issues the current procedures are not adequate. Indeed distinguished journalists have themselves acknowledged this and suggested changes in practice which would improve the news media's coverage of race.

The Code of Conduct evolved by the Seminar on Reporting Ethnic and Communal Tensions[2] contains many such recommendations, which are of the cosmetic variety, and which would in themselves have a considerable beneficial effect upon the reporting of race in Britain if they were consistently implemented. This code of conduct points out, for example, that 'Factual accuracy in a story is no substitute for the total truth. A single story which is factually accurate can none the less be misleading.' This warning links with another of the recommendations which urges journalists to check their own material from time to time to see how far they are themselves initiating enquiries and how far they are merely reacting to events and to the statements of politicians. Journalists must be more critical of their own performance and be aware of the dangers involved in culling the newsworthy aspects of events while failing to give a sufficiently detailed analysis of the nature of the event itself; of its background and significance. In relation to this, though journalists may resent some of the specifics of our comments upon the inherent dangers of relying upon 'news sense', we would hope that they could accept the general argument and use this as a basis for increased self-awareness in their professional role. Critical self-monitoring would, of course, be difficult because of the nature of the skills being applied and the institutionalized pressures under which journalists operate. At the same time such self-criticism is a necessary adjunct to the acceptance of any code of practice such as that mentioned above.

Some changes in practice would seem, however, to be relatively simple to achieve. The unnecessary racial identification of individuals which is still widespread could and should be stopped. There are few instances where such identification is justified and frequently this practice is conducive to sustaining dangerous racial stereotypes.

Similarly the sensational treatment often given to race related stories is perhaps merely a reflection of a general journalistic

[2] Reprinted in *Race and the Press*, (Runnymede Trust, 1971).

foible, but its consequences in exacerbating racial tensions, and perpetuating exaggerated misconceptions make it an unjustifiable luxury.

Journalists should also adopt a positive attitude toward improving race relations and deliberately seek to publish material which challenges prevailing false stereotypes. This requires investigative journalism which sets out to establish the background to racial situations rather than merely reporting events as they occur. Where there are widely-held misconceptions surrounding the role of blacks in Britain the news media have a responsibility to correct these rather than tacitly supporting them through neglect of contrary information. Too often material which has not been consistent with current stereotypes and perspectives has been ignored or buried.

The news media also have a positive role to play in attacking racial inequalities and exploitation, and this cannot be achieved without a deliberate intent to seek out such injustices and expose them. Our own findings have shown how the media have been instrumental in maintaining public awareness of racial injustice and in appealing to values of equality and fair play. We suggest that their potential role in this direction remains far from being fully exploited. An exceptional example of positive journalism of this kind was provided in the *Guardian* campaign against the exploitation of black South African labour by British firms. The front page headline of 12 March 1973 was 'British Firms Pay Africans Starvation Rate' and the coverage left the readers in no doubt as to the importance of the issue. The extent and detail of the coverage which the *Guardian* gave to this chronic exploitation compelled other papers and news media to follow their lead. In this instance, well researched, positive journalism produced visibly positive results in changing the policy of at least some of the British companies concerned. It also brought before the public conscience matters which otherwise would not have been known, and which the public may well have preferred not to know about. This detailed critical analysis of British exploitation of South African labour illustrated what a positive approach to the reporting of race can mean. What is needed is more journalism of this calibre, with the focus on issues in Britain as well as abroad.

At present the news media, like the British white population, have still to accept that Britain is a multi-racial society. For this reason they have been able to give emphasis to 'immigration' and 'immigrants' while ignoring the fact that increasingly the people characteristically labelled 'immigrants' are in fact British. They speak with British accents and have all the credentials of British nationality, except white skin. Our content analysis showed that as the number of coloured people, and the consequent concern over race increased, so the relationship of coloured people to the major social resources of housing, education and employment became increasingly overshadowed in the press by the symptoms of intergroup hostility. The British news media have failed to report adequately on the underlying bases of racial conflict in this country, and in so doing have assisted in the scapegoating of coloured immigrants : in this their conflict framework has played a facilitating role. In saying this we are not suggesting that 'conflict' racial stories and information uncomplimentary to coloured groups should be ignored or suppressed, only that the handling of racial news should not be based on the uncritical acceptance of prevailing cultural assumptions about colour and 'the colour problem'. 'Racial' news should be presented so as to discourage simple racist interpretations on the part of the audience. It is vital that the news media should debate the background to conflict and not confine itself to monitoring the symptoms. Ignorance of the nature of the real sources of social tension can be countered by a more determined responsible journalism. Such a policy is, however, outside the range of cosmetic solutions, for adequate discussion of the role of immigrant labour in the British economy, or of the structural reasons for unemployment and housing shortages would ultimately remove the buffer of scapegoating and lay bare the actual social inequalities. Given the current pattern of ownership and control of the media and their close identification with those interests that gain most from social inequalities and from the 'management' of conflicts rather than their removal, it remains unlikely that such a radical change in policy can be achieved.

It is possible though that enlightened self-interest may provide sufficient motivation to allow at least a partial shift toward such a searching journalism. It seems probable that if the news media do not attempt to make known to white Britain the personal cost of prejudice to the black British, then black alienation may in the long run breed violence and conflict that is not readily 'manageable'. The news media are spoken of as 'setting the agenda' for the population's concerns. If they fail to include the possible consequences of racism and discrimination on that agenda then they may ultimately destroy the status quo they seek to protect.

The possibility of improving race relations in this country

through a campaign of advertising has been suggested[3] and advertising has been used in at least one London borough.[4] However, we believe that advertisements for increased racial tolerance provide too great a scope for selective interpretation, particularly when the ubiquity of racial prejudice creates a wide-spread predisposition among the audience to neutralize the intent of the advertisements. Not only may such advertising be ineffective, but it may have the opposite effect of producing resentment and increased hostility.[5] The excessive expense of advertising, (for example a one minute slot on television may cost between £200 and £3,000 depending on the hour of trans-mission for the London area alone) makes realistic campaigns, as opposed to token gestures, financially unviable. The massive sums of money involved would have a greater potential if directed toward community projects where the involvement of residents in a community may not only improve the physical environment, but in the process of doing that may ease local tensions as well.

Advertising campaigns to promote racial tolerance, further-more, do not necessarily challenge the basic social injustices; and to the extent that they confuse tolerance with justice they will be pursuing the wrong goal. In this country we do not want a situation in which the white population is tolerant of the black population. What is required is justice and equality for all. To the extent that advertisements are based on the assumption that prejudice is a matter of misinformation that may be corrected by the provision of appropriate information, or propaganda, they are inevitably inadequate. This is because, as we have frequently reiterated, prejudice serves the function, among other things, of maintaining whites in an advantageous position relative to blacks. Therefore, prejudiced attitudes can-not be changed significantly independently of the structural relationships to which they relate. Ultimately it is only when economic exploitation of Third World resources abroad, and coloured labour here ceases; and when institutionalized dis-criminatory practices are outlawed that we can expect any true shift in inter-racial attitudes. Equality in power relations

[3] See *Race Today*, January 1970, p. 28 for discussion of an imaginary campaign floated by the Institute of Practitioners in Advertising.
[4] Alan Marsh, 'Posters Against Prejudice'. See *Race Today*, October 1970, p. 371, for discussion of a poster campaign in Camden.
[5] See for example, Eunice Cooper and Marie Jahoda, 'The Evasion of Propaganda: How Prejudiced People respond to Anti-Prejudice Pro-paganda'. *The Journal of Psychology*, 1947, 23, pp. 15-25.

between groups is the best basis for equality in status.

The purpose of this book has been to examine the contribution of the mass media to the state of race relations in this country.

Clearly in important respects the effects of the mass media are to some degree determined by characteristics found in the audience. At another stage removed these characteristics can be seen to be related to features of the society itself. In a society which has in recent years had an example set by Governments passing discriminatory legislation on racial grounds, and where scapegoating is a necessity for disguising the real conflicts within the social system, it is not surprising that overt racism is rampant. Therefore, though we should continue to be critical of mass media performance, we must not expect too much of the mass media if we fail to criticize the society in which the media operate.

Having said this we cannot neglect the implications of our research. Hopefully those responsible for mass media performance will seriously consider their responsibilities; while those who make up the audience for the media should exercise a constant critical vigilance.

Appendix I

CHILDREN'S INTERVIEW SCHEDULE

1. Could you tell me what you think are some of the problems in Britain today?
(Prompt with 'anything else?' until you are sure that you have all that springs *easily* to mind. Do *not* push child.)

2. (Take the first problem mentioned, unless it is race-related, in which case take the second problem, and ask):
How do you know about this?
Where did you learn about it from?
(Explicitly probe family, peer, school, as sources. Don't mention media.)

3. (If race-related issue mentioned in Q. 1, repeat Q. 2 for this, without probes.)

4. You may know that there has been immigration into Britain recently. Do you know what is meant by immigration? (Define as 'people coming to live here from other countries'.)
Can you tell me some of the countries from which immigrants to Britain have come? (If less than 3 produced, prompt: 'Any others?' Don't push).

5. Now I would like you to think particularly about coloured people. Can you tell me what you know about coloured people living in Britain today?
(Record each item, even if it is opinion rather than fact. Then repeat for each item in turn.)
'You say that. . . .' How do you know that? Did anyone tell you about it, for instance? Where did you learn about it from? What makes you think that? or similar.

6. Do you think that there are any problems connected with coloured people living in this country?
(Mention each problem in turn and ask: 'How do you know about this?' etc.)

7. How does the fact that coloured people have been coming to live in Britain affect you now?

(Record each item and then ask : 'What makes you think that?' etc.)

8. How do you think that the presence of coloured people in this country might affect your life in the future?
What makes you think that? etc. As before.

9. Do you think anything should be done about coloured immigration to Britain? What do you think should be done? Can you tell me where you got that idea from?

10. What proportion (or fraction) of the population of Britain are coloured people? Which of these would you say was right?
(Urge to guess if necessary.) SHOW CARD.

1 in 200	1 in 100	1 in 50	1 in 20	1 in 10	1 in 5	No answer

11. *Rating Scale* (see next page)

(a) Present chart
Say : Now I'd like to know how *you* feel about coloured people.
Explain chart, and ask him to show 'how you feel about coloured people'.

(b) Generally speaking, how do you think *most* of the other (white) children in your class at school feel about coloured people? Can you show me on this line?
(If necessary, ask him to say '*on average*' how they feel, and to make a guess.)

(c) How do you think your *mother* feels about coloured people?
Can you show me on this line?

(d) *Father*

(e) How do you think most of the people who live near you feel about coloured people?

Rating Scale

(a. SELF)

| I LIKE them very much | I LIKE them a little | I neither like nor dislike them | I DISLIKE them a little | I DISLIKE them very much |

(b. SCHOOL PEERS)

| THEY LIKE them very much | THEY LIKE them a little | They neither like nor dislike them | THEY DISLIKE them a little | THEY DISLIKE them very much |

(c. MOTHER)

| SHE LIKES them very much | SHE LIKES them a little | She neither likes nor dislikes them | SHE DISLIKES them a little | SHE DISLIKES them very much |

(d. FATHER)

| HE LIKES them very much | HE LIKES them a little | He neither likes nor dislikes them | HE DISLIKES them a little | HE DISLIKES them very much |

(e. NEIGHBOURS)

| THEY LIKE them very much | THEY LIKE them a little | They neither like nor dislike them | THEY DISLIKE them a little | THEY DISLIKE them very much |

12. When you talk about coloured people, do you have people from any particular countries in mind or are you just thinking about coloured people generally?
(Record countries, or 'gen.')

13. If you got new neighbours who were immigrants, would you prefer them to come from:
The West Indies and Jamaica OR India OR Pakistan OR would you feel that there was no reason to prefer one over the others?
(If a choice is made, ask : 'Why would you prefer.........s?')

14. Do you know what any of the politicians – Members of Parliament, for instance – have said about coloured immigration into Britain?
(Probe for names and policies).
Where did you hear about that?

15. About how many coloured people who go to this school do you know to talk to?

    None   1 or 2   3-10   More

16. Are there any of these people that you know from school that you also meet and talk to outside of school?

              YES   NO

17. Where do you meet them?

18. Apart from people from school, do you know any coloured people of about your own age to talk to outside of school? How many?

    None   1 or 2   3-10   More

19. Where do you meet them?

20(a) Have you spoken to coloured people who are grown-up (adults)?

    How many?
    None   1 or 2   3-10   More

  (b) Who were (are) they? *or* Who was (is) this person?
(Prompt: 'Anyone else?')

21(a) Are there any coloured boys or girls that you would say are good friends of yours?

              YES   NO

  (b) Have you ever visited any of the coloured boys or girls that you know at their house?

              YES   NO

  (c) Have any coloured boys or girls ever visited you at your house?

              YES   NO

22. (Ask first years only)
(a) What school did you go to before you came to.........?
....

(b) Were there any coloured children at that school? Were there any in your class during your last year there? How many?

23. Have you ever read about coloured people in the newspaper? Can you tell me what you can remember reading about them?
(Probe – 'Anything else?' etc.)

24. Have you ever seen a coloured person or coloured people in a film – either in the cinema or in a film on television? What sort of part were they playing? (Probe for as many as he can remember. Obtain role description.)

25. Have you ever seen a coloured person, or coloured people in a television play or serial? What sort of part were they playing? (Probe for as many as he can remember.)

26. Apart from plays and serials, have you ever seen a coloured person, or coloured people appearing in any other television programmes? What were they doing? What was the programme about? etc. (Probe for as many as possible).

27. Do you think that in general the newspapers are fair to coloured people in what they have to say about them? Or do they give too favourable, or too unfavourable a view of them?

| Papers too favourable | Fair | Too Unfavourable |

28. Do you think that in general the television is fair to coloured people in what it shows? Or does it give too favourable or too unfavourable a view of them?

| TV too favourable | Fair | TV too Unfavourable |

29. *The H Scale*
Now I'm going to read you some statements – things different people have said. I want you to tell me whether

219

you agree or disagree with what they have said, and also how strongly you agree or disagree.

(SHOW CARD) I want you to tell me whether you agree strongly or agree a little, or disagree strongly or disagree a little. These are things people have said : (Read items)

Response Categories: Agree Strongly, Agree a Little, Disagree a Little, Disagree Strongly.

1. Everyone in this country should be treated equally regardless of their colour.
2. It is reasonable for people *not* to want to have coloured people as neighbours.
3. Coloured people are naturally just as intelligent as white people.
4. Coloured people are more often trouble-makers than white people.
5. Coloured people in Britain should be encouraged to mix with white people as much as possible.
6. Coloured people should not be put in positions of authority over white people.
7. Coloured immigrants should be able to get council houses in the same way as English people do.
8. This country would be better off if there were no coloured immigrants living here.
9. Coloured immigrants should only be given jobs that the English don't want.
10. Coloured people should be allowed to come and settle in Britain.

30. Now I'd like you to think about something quite different. I'd like you to think about the usual kind of television play or serial, like *Z Cars, Dr Who, Coronation Street, Softly Softly* – programmes that tell a story. I know they are all different, but I want you to try to think about this sort of programme *on average*.

(a) On average, do you think that the people in most of these kinds of programmes are like real people? How much like real people would you say they usually are? (SHOW CARD)

Very like real people	Fairly like real people	Not very like real people	Not at all like real people

(b) Do you think that the sort of things that happen in

these kinds of programmes are believable? Would you
say: (SHOW CARD)

Nearly	Fairly	Only	Very
Always	Often	Sometimes	Seldom

(c) Do you think that the sort of stories told in these
kinds of programmes really do happen in real life?
Would you say they happen: (SHOW CARD)

Very	Fairly	Only	Very
Often	Often	Sometimes	Seldom

(d) By watching stories like these on television how much
do you think you can learn about life and how people
live? Would you say you can learn: (SHOW CARD)

A great	A certain	Only a	Little
deal	Amount	Little	Very

31. On ordinary school days, do you ever listen to the radio
in the mornings before coming to school?
(If 'YES' establish whether it's ever the Radio 4 News
and how often, for schooldays only)

32. In the afternoons and evenings after you get home from
school do you ever hear:
(a) The 6 o'clock news and radio newsreel on Radio 4.
How often?
(b) Newstime at 7.30 on Radios 1 and 2.
How often?
(c) The 10 o'clock news programme on Radio 4.
How often?

[These and the following four questions were appropriately
modified when news programme times and titles changed.]

33. On ordinary school days, not weekends, how often do you
watch the television news, at 10 or 6 or thereabouts, either
on the BBC or ITV?

34. What about the BBC television news at 10 to 9. Do you
ever watch that during the week? How often?

35. Do you ever see the 'News at Ten' on ITV at 10 o'clock?
How often?

36. Do you ever see 24 hours on BBC? How often?

37. Can you tell me if there are any daily newspapers that you regularly look at? When no more forthcoming, ask: Do you regularly read an evening paper other than the papers you have mentioned? (After recording papers check frequency of looking at each.)

> NATIONAL DAILIES
> *Daily Mirror*
> *Daily Express*
> *Daily Mail*
> *Sun*
> *Daily Telegraph*
> *Daily Sketch*
> *Times*
> *Guardian*
> Local Dailies
> Local Evenings

38. Are there any Sunday newspapers that you look at on most Sundays?

> *News of the World*
> *People*
> *Sunday Times*
> *Sunday Express*
> *Sunday Telegraph*
> *Sunday Post*
> *Observer*
> *Sunday Mirror*
> Other (specify)

39. When you are looking at a newspaper, about how much of the time do you spend on things like sport, the woman's page, cartoons, hobbies, things about films and television and so on – rather than on other things? (Make sure child understands. SHOW CARD.)

Most of the time	A little less than ½ the time	A little more than ½ the time	Hardly any of the time	No answer etc.

40. Do you think the news that you read in newspapers can be believed to be an accurate account of what actually happened? Would you say: (SHOW CARD.)

	Always	Nearly Always	Quite Often	Only Sometimes	No answer etc.

41. Do you think the news that you hear on the radio can be believed to be an accurate account of what actually happened? Would you say: (SHOW CARD.)

	Always	Nearly Always	Quite Often	Only Sometimes	No answer etc.

42. Do you think the news that you see on television can be believed to be an accurate account of what actually happened? Would you say: (SHOW CARD.)

	Always	Nearly Always	Quite Often	Only Sometimes	No answer etc.

Appendix II

CHILDREN'S WRITTEN QUESTIONNAIRE

(Each item was read out and explained to the children as a group and individual help given where needed.)

WHAT DO YOU LIKE TO DO IN YOUR SPARE TIME?

1. Here is a list of things that people do in their spare time. Look down the list and find the one that you usually like doing best. Put a '1' in the box next to that one. Then find the one that you like second best. Put a '2' in the box next to that. Continue like this until you have numbered them all.

   Reading books
   Listening to the radio
   Watching television

   A hobby – like making things or collecting things

   Going to the cinema

   Listening to records
   Playing some kind of sport
   Talking to or playing with friends
   Going to Scouts, Guides, a Youth Club or something like that
   Reading comics or magazines

2. If you were in *a good mood*, which of the following things do you think you would feel most like doing? (Underline the *one* that seems right for you.) *Same list as for question 1.*

3. If you were feeling *unhappy* which of the following things do you think you would feel most like doing? (Underline the *one* that seems right for you.) *Same list as for Question 1.*

4. Do you have a television set at home?

   YES   NO

5. If you have a television set, which channels can it receive?
   ITV   BBC-1   BBC-2

224

6. Here is a list of television programmes. There are **two** questions to answer about each of them.

Next to the name of each programme is a space for you to answer each question:

(1) How often do you watch it?   (2) How much do you like it?

Programmes: Top of the pops   Doctor Who
         Panorama   This Week
         World of Sport   Blue Peter
         The Tuesday   World in Action
         Documentary   Z Cars

Response Categories:

(1) How often do you watch this programme?

| Most times it is on | About half the times it is on | Less than half the times it is on | Never |

(2) How much do you like it?

| I like it a lot | I like it a little | I neither like it nor dislike it | I dislike it a little | I dislike it a lot |

7. Below you will see a scale showing hours and half-hours, that goes from 4 o'clock in the afternoon to 11.30 at night. Will you put a line to show what time you usually get in from school, and another to show the time during the week when you usually go to bed. Then between these lines will you shade in the hours you usually spend watching television, remembering this is for weekdays only.

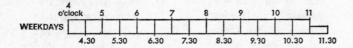

Are there any weekdays (Monday to Friday) when you see a lot less television than you have shown above? If there are any, write them here : ....

Are there any weekdays when you see a lot *more* television than you have shown above? If there are any, write them here : ....

Now shade in the hours you watch television on Saturday, and Sunday.

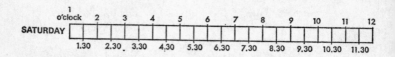

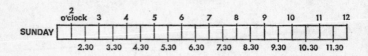

8. Please write below the names of any comics or magazines that you get regularly.

WHAT SORT OF TELEVISION PROGRAMMES DO YOU PREFER?

9. We want you to think about the different *kinds* of programmes that you see on television. The questions below are about which kinds of programmes you prefer. Only give *one* answer to each question. In general, what sort of programmes do you mostly prefer?

(a) Programmes that are easy to watch without thinking about them   OR   Programmes that make you think

| Greatly Prefer | Prefer a Little | | Prefer a Little | Greatly Prefer |

(b) Programmes about things that are quite new to you   OR   Programmes about things that you already know something about

| Greatly Prefer | Prefer a Little | | Prefer a Little | Greatly Prefer |

(c) Programmes that leave you to draw your own conclusions   OR   Programmes that provide a conclusion for you

	Greatly Prefer	Prefer a Little	Prefer a Little	Greatly Prefer

(d) Stories with people in that OR Stories with people in
you have not seen before   that you have seen before

	Greatly Prefer	Prefer a Little	Prefer a Little	Greatly Prefer

(e) Stories in which it is easy OR Stories in which it is not
to tell who are the good   easy to tell who are the
people and who are the   good people and who are
bad people   the bad people

	Greatly Prefer	Prefer a Little	Prefer a Little	Greatly Prefer

(f) The sort of story in which OR The sort of story where
the good people always   the good people don't
win   always win

	Greatly Prefer	Prefer a Little	Prefer a Little	Greatly Prefer

10.   WHAT DO YOU THINK?

Response Categories:

Strongly Agree	Agree a Little	Disagree a Little	Strongly Disagree

Items: (These were read out to the children)

(a) People should be less concerned with pleasure and more concerned with good hard work.

(b) There are two kinds of people in the world: those who are right and those who are wrong.

(c) There is only one right way to do most things.

(d) No normal, decent person could ever think of hurting a close friend or relative.

(e) Someone who loves animals could never be cruel to an animal.

(f) There is *one* right answer to most problems.

(g) It is a glorious thing to die for one's country.

What is your name? ....

Name of School   ....

Which form are you in? ....

227

Appendix III

PARENTS' INTERVIEW SCHEDULE

I would first like to ask you about life in ....(name postal district)

1(a) How long have you lived in ....(name postal district)
     All your life or how long?
     IF 10 OR LESS YEARS ASK (b) and (c)

(b) Where did you live before coming here?
    WRITE IN NAME OF TOWN AND COUNTRY : ....

(c) How long did you live there?

2. Thinking of all the people you know in.....................
   (name postal district), how many do you know well enough to stop and talk to in a street or shop?

3. Of these people you know in...............(name postal district) how many do you thing of as actually being your friends?

4. If you were asked to describe a successful person in......
   .... (name postal district), how would you do it?

5(a) Have you ever thought of leaving .... (name postal district)?

    IF 'YES'
(b) Would you say you have thought of leaving...............
    READ OUT Only once or twice, Not very often, Often, Don't know.
    I would now like to talk to you about some of the problems we are faced with in Britain today.

6. Could you tell me what you think are the main problems in Britain today (PROBE : anything else?)

7. One of the things about which there has been a great deal of talk is immigration; that is people coming to live here from other countries. Can you tell me the main countries from which these immigrants to Britain have come? (IF LESS THAN THREE COUNTRIES NAMED, PROBE 'Any others that are important?')

8(a) Now I would like you to think particularly about coloured people. Can you tell me what you know about coloured people living in Britain today?

FOR EACH ENTRY AT (a) ASK: ....

(b) You say that .... Do you remember where you learned or heard about that from? DO NOT PROMPT.

9(a) Do you think there are any good things that result from coloured people living in this country?

IF 'YES'

(b) What are these good things?

FOR EACH ENTRY AT (b) ASK:

(c) You say that .... is a good thing. Do you remember where you first learned or heard that? DO NOT PROMPT.

10(a) Do you think there are any problems connected with coloured people living in Britain?

IF 'YES'

(b) What are these problems?

FOR EACH ENTRY AT (b) ASK:

(c) You say that .... is a problem. Do you remember where you learned or heard that from? DO NOT PROMPT.

11(a) Does or will coloured immigration into Britain affect you personally?

IF 'YES'

(b) How does or will it affect you?

FOR EACH ENTRY AT (b) ASK:

(c) You say you are (will be) affected by .... Can you tell me where you heard or learned that this does (will) affect you personally? DO NOT PROMPT.

229

12(a) Have you talked with anyone about coloured immigrants?
IF 'YES'

(b) Who was it you spoke to

people at work	neighbours
my children	other people (record)
other members of my family	can't remember?

FOR EACH TYPE OF PERSON TALKED TO :

(c) When you talked with ...., would you say you learned some new facts about coloured immigrants or were you airing your opinions to each other?

13(a) Do you think anything should be done about coloured immigration to Britain?

IF 'YES'

(b) What do you think should be done?

(c) Can you remember where you first heard or learned that idea?

14. What fraction do you think coloured people make up of the total British population? Looking at this card, which statement would you say shows the right proportions?
SHOW CARD.

```
1 coloured person for every 200 white persons
1 coloured person for every 100   "      "
1 coloured person for every  50   "      "
1 coloured person for every  20   "      "
1 coloured person for every  10   "      "
1 coloured person for every   5   "      "
```

15(a) As far as you know, are there any coloured people living near your home, for example, in the streets around here?
       Yes   No   Don't know
IF 'YES' *ask* (b) to (e)

(b) Do you have any coloured people as neighbours, that is, living next door, opposite, or backing on to your house and garden?
IF IN BLOCKS OF FLATS, ASK : Do any coloured people live on the same floor as you or immediately above or below you?

Yes   No   Don't know

(c) Do any coloured people live 2-4 doors away?
IF IN BLOCKS OF FLATS, ASK : Do any coloured people live on other floors of the block?

Yes   No   Don't know

(d) Are there any coloured people living in the rest of the street?

Yes   No   Don't know

(e) Are there any coloured people living in the other streets near your home?

Yes   No   Don't know

16. How do (would) you feel about having a coloured family as neighbours?
Do (would) you feel........................... (READ OUT)
   Very happy about it   No feelings either way
   Quite happy about it   Quite unhappy about it
            Very unhappy about it

17. How do (would) most of the people who live near you feel about having a coloured family as neighbours? Do (would) they feel.............................. (READ OUT)
   Very happy about it   Quite unhappy about it
   Quite happy about it   Very unhappy about it
   No feelings either way   (Don't know)

ASK QUESTIONS 18-20 OF WORKING INFORMANTS ONLY

18(a) Does the organization you work for employ coloured people?

Yes   No   Don't know

IF 'YES'
(b) Do you yourself come into contact with any coloured people employed there?

Yes   No

19. How do (would) you feel about working with coloured people? (READ OUT)............
   Very happy about it   Quite unhappy about it
   Quite happy about it   Very unhappy about it
   No feelings either way   (Don't know)

20. How do (would) most of the other people where you work feel about working with coloured people? (READ OUT)

Very happy about it   Quite unhappy about it
Quite happy about it   Very unhappy about it
No feelings either way   (Don't know)

ASK ALL INFORMANTS

21(a) In the last two months, how many coloured people have you met to talk to?

None   1 or 2   3-10   More   Don't know

IF '1 OR MORE' TALKED TO, ASK (b)

(b) Where did you meet these people?

22. Are there any coloured people that you would say are your friends?

Yes   No

23(a) If you got new neighbours who were immigrants, which of the countries on this card would you prefer them to come from? SHOW CARD B.

FOR COUNTRY SELECTED AT (a) ASK (b)

(b) Why would you prefer ....'s as neighbours?

24(a) Have you ever read about coloured people in the newspapers?

Yes   No

IF 'YES'

(b) Can you tell me what you can remember reading about them? (PROBE: anything else?)

25. Do you think that, in general, newspapers are too much in favour, too much against or are they fair in what they have to say about coloured people?

Too much   Too much   Fair   (Don't know)
in favour   against

26. Do you think that, in general, television is too much in favour, too much against or is it fair in what it has to say about coloured people?

Too much   Too much   Fair   (Don't know)   (Never see
in favour   against   television)

27.   Now I'm going to read you some things people have
said to us.
Please tell me from this card (SHOW CARD C) how much
you agree or disagree with each one.

Response Categories: Agree strongly, Agree a little, Disagree a little, Disagree strongly.

(i)   Everyone in this country should be treated equally
regardless of their colour.

(ii)   It is reasonable for people to object to having
coloured people as neighbours.

(iii) Coloured people are naturally just as intelligent
as white people.

(v)   Coloured people are more often trouble-makers
than white people.

(iv)   Coloured people in Britain should be encouraged
to mix with white people as much as possible.

(vi)   Coloured people should not be put in positions
of authority over white people.

(vii) Coloured immigrants should be able to get
council houses in the same way as English
people do.

(viii) This country would be better off if there were no
coloured immigrants living here.

(ix)   Coloured immigrants should be allowed to come
and settle in Britain.

(x)   Coloured people should only be given jobs that
the English don't want.

28(a) Do you own or have access to a radio you can listen to
frequently?

Yes   No

(b)   And do you own or have access to a television you can
watch frequently?

YES   NO

IF NO TO BOTH (a) AND (b) SKIP TO QUESTION 39
I would now like to ask you some questions about the
radio and television.

ASK ONLY OF THOSE HAVING ACCESS TO A RADIO ....

29.   On average how many Radio 4 news broadcasts do you
hear on the radio each day – that is on the old 'home'
service, not Radio 1 and 2?

None   One   Two   Three   Four or more   Don't Know

ASK QUESTIONS 30-38 ONLY OF THOSE HAVING ACCESS TO
A TELEVISION

30(a) On average, how many times each day do you see the news on television?

(b) And how often each week do you watch the local news programme *after* the 6 o'clock news?

None   One   Two   Three   Four or more   Don't know

31. Thinking back over the last 12 months, how often have you watched any of these weekly programmes?

(a) First of all 'The World in Action'. Would you say you watched it .... READ OUT

Most times it is on	About half the times it is on	Less than half the times it is on	Or, that you never watch it	(Don't know)

REPEAT (a) FOR PROGRAMMES

(b) Panorama   (c) This Week   (d) The Tuesday Documentary

32. (a) Normally on how many nights per week do you watch television for longer than half an hour?

None   One night   Two nights   Three nights   Four nights   Five nights   Six nights   Seven nights

ASK ONLY THOSE WATCHING 1 OR 2 NIGHTS ONLY:

(b) Are either of these nights on a weekday?

YES   NO

ASK ONLY THOSE WATCHING ON WEEKDAYS

33. Thinking only of the weekday nights on which you watch television, on average for how many hours do you watch a night?

ASK ALL INFORMANTS

34. Looking at this card, could you tell me which statement is most true for the way you watch television? SHOW CARD

Nearly always watch BBC	Nearly always watch ITV	Mostly watch BBC	Mostly watch ITV	Watch BBC and ITV about the same	(Don't know)

35. Thinking of the advertisements on ITV, how often do

234

you actually watch them when they come on? Would
you say you watch them .... READ OUT
Very often Quite Often Seldom Never (Don't know)

36. A somewhat different kind of question now. I would like
you to think about the usual kind of television play or
serial; programmes like 'Z Cars', 'Coronation Street' and
'Softly Softly', for example. Programmes and plays that
tell a story.

(a) In general do you think that the people in most of
these kinds of programmes are like real people?
Would you say they are .... READ OUT

Very like	Quite like	Not very	Not at all	(Don't
real people	real people	like real	like real	know)
		people	people	

(b) Do you think that the sort of stories told in these
kinds of programmes really do happen in real life?
Would you say they happen .... READ OUT

Very often	Fairly	Only	Very	(Don't
	often	sometimes	seldom	know)

37(a) A lot of television plays and serials are about people who
are fairly well off. Do you ever wish you could have
some of the things these people have?

Yes   No

IF 'YES'

(b) How often do you see programmes that make you feel
this? Would you say .... READ OUT
Often Sometimes Seldom Very Seldom (Don't know)

38(a) These programmes about people who are wealthy and
successful could make you feel a little dissatisfied with
your own lot in life. Do you ever get this feeling after
seeing a programme?

IF 'YES'

(b) Do you feel this .... READ OUT

Very	Seldom	Occasionally	Quite often	(Don't
seldom				know)

Turning now to newspapers:

39(a) Can you tell me if there are any *daily* newspapers, either
national or local, that you regularly look at?

       IF 'YES' : Code papers read. PROBE : any others?

(b) And are there any evening papers you regularly look at?
       IF 'YES' : record papers read. PROBE : any others?
       FOR EACH PAPER CODED ASK (c)

(c) On average, on how many days a week do you look at
       ....(name paper)?

40. Are there any Sunday newspapers that you look at on most Sundays?
       IF 'YES' : code papers looked at

News of the World	*Sunday Telegraph*
People	*Sunday Post*
Sunday Times	*Observer*
Sunday Express	*Sunday Mirror*
	Other (state)

ASK ONLY OF INFORMANTS LOOKING AT AT LEAST ONE PAPER A WEEK

41. When people look at a newspaper there are some types of news they just glance at and others they pay a lot of attention to. For the following types of news, can you tell me which you pay a lot of attention to and which you just glance or never look at?

       (a)   First of all – sport
       (b)   The women's page
       (c)   Overseas news
       (d)   National British news
       (e)   Local news

Response categories: pay a lot of   glance at/
                       attention to   never read

ASK ALL INFORMANTS :

I want now to ask you some general questions about the news reported in newspapers, on the radio and on television.

42. How often do you think the news you read in newspapers can be taken as a fair and accurate picture of what actually happened? Would you say .... READ OUT

Always	Nearly always	Quite often	Only sometimes	(Don't know)

43. How often do you think the news you hear on the radio can be taken as a fair and accurate account of what actually happened? Would you say .... READ OUT

Always   Nearly   Quite   Only   (Don't
           always   often   sometimes   know)

44. How often do you think the news you see on television can be taken as a fair and accurate account of what actually happened? Would you say .... READ OUT

Always   Nearly   Quite   Only   (Don't
           always   often   sometimes   know)

45. Would you agree with the statement that, generally speaking, Britain is lagging behind economically in comparison with other countries in the world. Would you say..................READ OUT

Definitely, On the   On the Definitely, (Don't
  Yes   whole, Yes whole, No   No   know)

ASK QUESTIONS 46-47 OF WORKING INFORMANTS ONLY

46(a) Would you say that people like yourself should be paid more?

       Yes   No   Don't know

IF 'YES'

(b) Why do you think that people like yourself should be paid more? RECORD FULLY.

47. Apart from the pay you get, how satisfied are you with your job itself? Would you say you are : ....
READ OUT

Very   Quite   Neither   Quite
satisfied   satisfied   satisfied nor dissatisfied
                 dissatisfied

Very   (Don't know)
dissatisfied

ASK ALL INFORMANTS :

48. (a) Do you think in Britain there are any other sorts of people doing noticeably better at the moment than you and your family?

       Yes   No   Don't know

IF 'YES', ASK (b) to (d)

(b) What sort of people do you think are doing noticeably better? RECORD FULLY

(c) What do you feel about that? I mean do you think this is .... READ OUT

Very fair Fair Unfair Very Unfair (Don't know)

    (d) How have you heard or learnt that these people are doing better?

Television	Magazines	Friends/acquaintances
Radio	My children	Personal experience
Newspapers	Other members of family	Other

49. How important is it to you personally to get ahead in life? Would you say it was .... READ OUT

Very Important	Fairly Important	Not very Important	Definitely not Important	(Don't know)

50. Here are a few more things that different people have said. Once again I'd like you to tell me whether you agree or disagree with what they have said. Looking at this card, please tell me how strongly you agree or disagree. SHOW CARD. (*Response categories*: Agree strongly, Agree slightly, Neither, Disagree slightly, Disagree strongly, Don't know.)

    (a) Obedience and respect for authority are the most important things children should learn.

    (b) Army life is a good influence on most men.

    (c) In the end, parents generally turn out to be right about things.

    (d) People should be less concerned with pleasure and more concerned with good hard work.

    (e) It usually helps the child in later years if he is forced to follow his parent's ideas.

    (f) There is only one right way to do most things.

    (g) The raising of one's social position is one of the more important goals in life.

CLASSIFICATION

SEX: AGE: (Exact age)   MARITAL STATUS
NUMBER OF CHILDREN: (Write in exact number)

HOUSEHOLD STATUS OF INFORMANT:
  Head of household   Housewife   Other

HOUSEHOLD COMPOSITION:
 (i) No. of people, including informant, in household

(ii) No. of people, including informant, in paid employment (at least 10 hours a week)

ACTIVITY STATUS OF INFORMANT AND HEAD OF HOUSEHOLD (IF NOT INFORMANT) :
Working full time. Working part time. Temporarily out of work. Retired. Student. Non-working housewife. Other unemployed.

OCCUPATION OF INFORMANT : (if temporarily out of work, sick or retired give last main occupation)
Job title: *Description:*   *No. of people working under him/her:*
Training/qualifications: *Self-employed or not:*   *Industry:*

OCCUPATION OF HEAD OF HOUSEHOLD IF NOT INFORMANT :
Job title: *Description:*   *No. of people working under him:*
Training/qualifications: *Self-employed or not:*   *Industry:*

INCOME OF INFORMANT AND HEAD OF HOUSEHOLD (IF NOT INFORMANT) :
Total net income per week from *all* sources. SHOW CARD.

> Nil
> Up to £5
> Over £5, up to £10
> Over £10, up to £15
> Over £15, up to £20
> Over £20, up to £25
> Over £25, up to £30
> Over £30, up to £40
> Over £40, up to £60
> Over £60
> D.K./refused

EDUCATION OF INFORMANT :
(i) Age informant left school :
(ii) Type of school last attended :

Independent	Comprehensive
Direct grant	Secondary Modern
Grammar	Overseas
Technical	Other

(iii) Further education :

University	Other Colleges
Technical College	Evening Classes

HIGHEST EDUCATIONAL QUALIFICATION OBTAINED

No qualification	GCE 'A' Level/Higher school
Full industrial apprenticeship	cert./Intermediate/HNC

239

School leaving certificate
GCE 'O' Level/Matric/
school certificate/ONC/
City & Guilds

Teacher's cert./Membership
of professional institute
etc.
University degree/full medical training/Higher degree
Anything else (specify)

TENURE OF INFORMANT'S ACCOMMODATION :

Owner occupied
Renting from council

Renting privately
unfurnished
furnished
Other

CAR OWNERSHIP :

Do you or other members of your household own or have full use of a car?

Yes   No

Appendix IV

MEASURES USED IN THE SURVEYS

Attitude to coloured people – the H scale

In order to measure favourability of attitude towards coloured people, that is the affective/evaluative dimension of people's consciousness of the matter, we set out to produce a short measure of conventional type, balanced for direction of scoring, containing items of relevance to the present British situation, suitable for use with eleven-year olds as well as older people, and having acceptable psychometric characteristics. The result was the H Scale, a ten item Likert Scale shown as Item 29 of the children's interview schedule and Item 27 of the adults' schedule. Subjects were required to respond 'Strongly Agree', 'Agree', 'Disagree', or 'Strongly Disagree' to each item which was scored 1 to 4 with the more hostile responses getting the highest score. Full details of this scale have been given elsewhere.[1] Here we summarize its main features.

The ten items of the scale were selected by item analysis techniques from an original pool of seventeen items given to an initial sample of 104 white secondary school children. Factor analysis of inter-item correlations of responses to the ten items used in the present investigation yielded a first principal component accounting for about 40 percent of the variance and loading well on all items. The next two factors accounted for about 10 percent of the variance each and their statistical significance was dubious. The scale thus has a high degree of unidimensionality, and a high level of internal consistency (corrected split-half reliability – children, .79-.82; adults, .85-.86). These characteristics remain essentially the same whether they are calculated on the children or the parents, on the High, Low or No area samples, or on combined samples. It would appear to be measuring very much the same kind of thing whatever group it is used on, within this study. Its relationships with other measures suggest strongly that more than anything else it is tap-

---

[1] Paul Hartmann and Charles Husband, 'A British Scale for Measuring White Attitudes to Coloured People' (*Race*, XIV, 2, pp. 195-204, 1972).

ping a pro- or anti-coloured sentiment. Among the children, for instance, it correlated .55 with their rating of their liking of coloured people on the rating scale (Question 11 (a), and parents' H scores correlated .22 (mothers) and .19 (fathers) with the child's rating of parents' attitude on the same rating scale. High H scores were also closely correlated with strong opposition to coloured immigration (Question 9) among both children and parents. There was a close link between H score and whether or not people claimed to have coloured friends, for both parents and children, and with attitudes to having coloured people as neighbours or workmates among the adults. In brief it appeared, from every point of view, to be a good measure of its type, and we feel justified in concluding that it may be accepted with high confidence as measuring, in Thurstone's words,[2] 'the degree of positive or negative effect associated with some psychological object', the psychological object in this case being 'coloured people'.

'Authoritarianism' – (a) The Children's Measure

In Chapter 3 we discussed the theory of the authoritarian personality and its relationship to racial prejudice, and mentioned also the variant on this theory proposed by Rokeach in terms of closed-mindedness and Dogmatism. We thought it important to obtain some kind of measure of authoritarian or dogmatic tendency in our subjects for two reasons. In the first place, there is the importance of this kind of concept in so many explanations of intergroup relations, and secondly there is the possibility of a connection between rigid, dogmatic and authoritarian thinking and orientations to mass media. Bailyn,[3] for instance, found a connection among children between heavy television viewing and liking for comic books together with liking for programmes that featured 'aggressive heroes', and a measure of stereotyped thinking. Stereotyped thinking was measured by a number of items closely resembling those to be found in the typical dogmatism, rigidity or authoritarianism scale, though she herself did not explicitly connect her concept of stereotyped thinking with the theory of the authoritarian personality. She also explained the correlation in terms of causation – exposure to stereotyped pictorial media may lead to stereotyped thinking – though on her own data an explanation in terms of the independent relation of these variables with social background factors would seem to be

[2] L. L. Thurstone, Comment (*Amer. J. Sociol.*, 52, 1946, pp. 39-50).
[3] L. Bailyn, 'Mass Media and Children. A Study of exposure habits and cognitive effects' (*Psychol. Monographs*, LXXI, 1959).

more appropriate. Lovibond[4] found a similar connection between heavy media exposure and a Children's F scale that he constructed, though he did not seek to explain the relationship in straightforward causal terms. His failure to control for class, however, renders his results suspect. We thought it appropriate, therefore, to test for ourselves the hypothesis of a connection between dogmatic and stereotyped thinking on the one hand and preference for stereotyped television on the other, particularly since the established relationship between dogmatism and hostility to minority groups raises the question of a connection between such hostility and preference for stereotyped television.

There are, however, theoretical and practical difficulties in the way of an attempt to assess dogmatism or authoritarianism in children. Theoretically, it is not certain that the authoritarian syndrome or 'closed-mindedness' as these have been described in adults, also exist in children. And if dogmatism or authoritarianism can be said to exist in children they do not necessarily have the same psychological or social significance as they do in adults. Furthermore, it is not clear that a measure of these characteristics in young people would necessarily resemble the type of measure commonly used for adults. What would be regarded as an excessive deference to authority and an obsessional concern with inflexible rules in an adult might be quite normal for young people at certain stages of development.

We are aware of only two attempts to measure this type of characteristic in children or young people – apart from Bailyn's[5] measure of stereotyped thinking – and these are the Children's F Scale used by Lovibond,[6] and a children's version of the dogmatism scale reported by Figert.[7] Neither of these was readily adaptable to our purposes. We therefore drew up a list of 28 items which, on the basis of the general theories underlying authoritarianism and dogmatism, previous scales and present purposes, seemed likely to tap this type of cognitive characteristic. The seven items loading most highly on a first principal component were selected to make up the scale shown as Item 10 of the written questionnaire. Four response categories were provided and items were scored from 1 to 4 with the more dogmatic responses getting the higher scores. Apart from the theoretical

[4] S. H. Lovibond, 'The Effect of Media stressing crime and violence on children's attitudes' (*Social Problems*, 15, 1967).
[5] Op. cit.
[6] Op. cit.
[7] R. L. Figert, 'An elementary school form of the dogmatism scale' (*Journal of Experimental Education*, 37, 2, Winter 1968).

considerations that we have referred to, this measure is not completely satisfactory on a number of grounds; the content of some items is not particularly convincing, and its reliability is only .55 (coefficient alpha).[8] Nevertheless, with large samples for making group comparisons or correlations, it is probably accurate enough for our purposes. We do not insist that this is measuring Authoritariansm as conceived by the original California researchers or their successors or, for that matter, dogmatism in Rokeach's sense (and it should be remembered that in practice measures of these two concepts are typically highly correlated, and as Howitt[9] has argued, are empirically very similar); more research would be needed to establish that. For present purposes it is sufficient to accept the scale at face value as measuring rigidity and intolerance of ambiguity, or 'stereotyped thinking'.

(b) The Adults' Measure

The parents' authoritarianism measure is shown as Item 50 (a-f) of the parents' questionnaire. The construction of this presented fewer problems, either theoretical or practical, than with the children's measure, for the use of such measures on adults is well-established. Items (b), (c) and (e) were those loading highly on a factor of 'parental authority' in an analysis by Lee and Warr[10] which they found also contributed to a broader factor of 'general authoritarianism'. Item (a) seemed intuitively appropriate to the present study and was among those loading highly on a mixed F and D factor in an analysis by Kerlinger and Rokeach[11] of F scale and D scale items. Items (d) and (f) were included to provide an overlap of content between the children's and parents' measures. This six-item scale, with five response categories for each item scored 1 to 5, had a reliability of .58 (coefficient alpha), and we are confident that it is a good *short* measure of major aspects of the authoritarian syndrome.

[8] L. J. Cronbach, 'Coefficient alpha and the internal structure of tests' (*Psychometrika,* 16, 297-334, 1951).

[9] Dennis Howitt, 'Dogmatism and Authoritarianism – Where the Difference Lies' (Centre for Mass Communication Research, University of Leicester, Mimeographed, 1972).

[10] R. E. Lee and P. B. Warr, 'The development and standardization of a balanced F Scale' (*J. General Psychol.,* 81, pp. 109-129, 1969).

[11] F. N. Kerlinger and M. Rokeach 'The factorial nature of the F and D scales' (*J. Pers. (Soc.) Psychol.,* 4, 391-399, 1966).

The Television Preference Scale

For the sake of relating the children's dogmatism measure to media use, we thought it preferable to obtain a direct measure of preference for stereotyped television rather than to infer this from our judgments of the type of programmes that they said they preferred. We therefore produced the television preference scale shown as Item 9 of the written questionnaire. The reliability of this was .41 (coefficient alpha), and factor analysis yielded a general principal component accounting for 26 percent of the variance. The existence of this general factor loading on all items shows that it is meaningful to add the items to obtain a total score. Items were scored 1 to 4 with higher scores for more 'stereotyped' responses. Rotation gave two varimax factors, the first loading most highly on items (a), (c), (e) and (f), the other on items (b) and (d).

The News Consumption Index

An index of total news consumption was calculated for the children from the number of television news broadcasts viewed per week, numbers of newspapers seen per week, and the documentary viewing index. (Questions 33-35, 37 and 38 of the interview, and Item 6 of the written questionnaire respectively.) The total news consumption was calculated by reducing each of these to a standard score (by subtracting it from the mean of the distribution for all children and dividing by the standard deviation) and adding them together; 10 was then added to obviate negative scores. On the basis of this, the sample was divided into four levels of exposure to news and documentary material. Radio news litsening (Q. 31 and 32) and viewing of the current affairs programme *24 hours* (Q. 36) were negligibly low among our youngsters and were therefore not included in this index.

The 'Contact' Indices

The replies to Questions 15, 18 and 20(a) on the amount of contact with coloured people were combined so as to divide the sample into four levels according to the amount of 'gross contact' they had with coloured people. In these questions the children were asked how many coloured children at their school they knew 'to talk to', how many not at their school they knew, and how many coloured adults they had spoken to recently. Their answers were recorded as 'none', 'one or two', 'three to ten', or 'more than ten' in each case. The lowest level of 'gross contact' based on these answers consisted of those who, to all three questions, answered that they knew no coloured people; the next of those who claimed to know one or two coloured people on at least one of the questions but who never answered '3-10'; the next level consisted of people answering '3-10' at least once but never 'more than 10'; and the highest level were those who answered 'more than 10' at least once. This measure is admittedly relatively crude but it did divide the sample broadly into those who had more and less contact with coloured people.

Questions 21(a), (b) and (c) were also combined to divide the sample into different levels of friendship contact. In these questions subjects were asked : 'Are there any coloured boys or girls that you would say are good friends of yours?' : 'Have you ever visited any of the coloured boys or girls that you know at their house?' and 'Have any coloured boys or girls ever visited you at your house?' The four levels on the friendship contact index consisted of those who said 'no' to all questions, those who said 'yes' to one, to two, and to three of them respectively.

Appendix V

RESPONSE CATEGORIES
FOR OPEN-ENDED QUESTIONS

(Children – Qs. 5, 6, 7 & 8; Adults – Qs. 8, 9, 10 & 11)

1. NO ANSWER – don't know, doesn't affect me, etc.

2. CULTURAL DIFFERENCES – religion, food, ways of living, live in communities, speak different languages. Simple description of cultural differences.

3. CULTURE CLASH – explicit or implicit negative evaluation of cultural differences. Smell of garlic, won't speak English, won't mix.

4. NUMBERS – references to large numbers entering or living in country or area, high birthrate, 'more blacks than whites', 'too many of them here', references to overpopulation.

5. TAKING OVER – clear indication that blacks do or will dominate the whites in terms of power, *eg*, taking over country, will be ruling us, (only when *respondent* holds this opinion).

6. TAKING JOBS – any clear statement or implication that employment opportunities of whites are reduced or threatened because of blacks, *e.g.* 'work for less money'.

7. TAKING HOUSES – clear indication that housing opportunities for whites are threatened by blacks.

8. RESENTMENT – indication that blacks are benefiting at expense of whites in other ways, *e.g.* live on National Assistance, retard whites' education, get more pay for same work, cause price rises, resentment at wealth of immigrants, 'taking our girls', or other resentments.

9. ANTI-IMMIGRATION – indication that *respondent* is opposed to immigration – 'should be stopped', 'sent home', 'too many *coming in*', etc. *Anti-immigrant* statements are 'unfavourable'. Statements of *others'* opposition to immigration is 'objects of prejudice'.

10. TROUBLE – riot, fighting – any association of immigrants with these either as cause or occasion, unless 'objects of hostility' is the dominant theme.

11. UNFAVOURABLE – generalized unfavourable statements that don't fit elsewhere, *e.g.* 'they smell', 'don't look after their houses', 'bring diseases' etc. Unfavourable attributes.

12. POOR HOUSING – overcrowding, 10 to a room, etc. Don't look after their houses' is 'unfavourable'.

13. OBJECTS OF PREJUDICE – discrimination or hostility, attributed to the intentions of some human agency.

14. DISADVANTAGED – not attributed to human agency, *e.g.* 'they are poor', 'they can't find jobs', 'have problems with the language'. Relates to position in *this country* only. Statements about disadvantage in home country is 'Other'.

15. ANTI-STEREOTYPE – 'Some are OK, some aren't, or equivalent statement.

16. FAVOURABLE – favourable attributes, *e.g.* hardworking.

17. PERSONAL DISLIKE – I dislike them, or equivalent statement. I wouldn't like to live/work near them.

18. EQUALITARIAN/TOLERANT – Same as us, same as everyone else type of statement. ' I don't mind them' statements of *tolerance.*

19. PERSONAL LIKING – I like them or equivalent.

20. OTHER – including simple descriptive statements such as reasons for migrating, conditions in home country, references to occupation etc. that don't fit elsewhere.

Appendix VI

TABLES

Table 4.1
CHILDREN'S SAMPLE BY AGE, SEX AND AREA

		HIGH AREAS	LOW AREAS	NO AREAS	TOTAL
11/12 year olds	*Boys*	58	51	41	150
	Girls	46	53	37	136
14/15 year olds	*Boys*	60	54	36	150
	Girls	43	50	34	127
Total	*Boys*	118	105	77	300
	Girls	89	103	71	263
Grand Total		207	208	148	563

Table 4.2
AGE DISTRIBUTION OF PARENTS

UNDER 30	30–39	40–49	50–59	OVER 60	UNKNOWN	TOTAL
1	95	148	62	5	6	317

Table 4.3
CLASS DISTRIBUTION OF PARENTS BY AREA

	UPPER MIDDLE	MIDDLE CLASS	LOWER MIDDLE	SKILLED WORKING	SEMI & UNSKILLED	LOWEST LEVEL OF SUB-SISTENCE	NO INFORMA-TION
Low Areas	0·6%	1·9%	12·3%	40·0%	38·1%	7·1%	0%
High Areas	0%	1·4%	9·5%	48·3%	38·8%	1·4%	0·7%
Total	0·3%	1·7%	10·9%	44·0%	38·4%	4·3%	0·3%

Table 4.4

CLASS DISTRIBUTION OF CHILDREN—
MAIN SAMPLE ONLY

(Children's classification)

UPPER MIDDLE	MIDDLE CLASS	LOWER MIDDLE	SKILLED WORKING	SEMI AND UNSKILLED	LOWEST LEVEL OF SUBSISTENCE	NO INFORMA- TION
0·5%	2·2%	8·9%	35·4%	39·0%	3·1%	10·8%

Table 4.5

CHILDREN'S NEWS AND DOCUMENTARY
EXPOSURE

Means (Standard Deviations are shown in brackets)

	NO AREAS	LOW AREAS	HIGH AREAS	LOW SCHOOLS	HIGH SCHOOLS	TOTAL
Weekly TV Viewing Hours	27·9 (9·48)	24·8 (9·38)	26·7 (9·61)	24·5 (8·84)	27·1 (10·04)	26·3 (9·58)
TV News broadcasts per week (weekdays only)	7·9 (3·52)	7·0 (3·72)	7·0 (3·49)	6·8 (3·46)	7·2 (3·75)	7·2 (3·61)
Documentary viewing index	4·3 (2·56)	3·8 (2·86)	3·7 (2·68)	3·8 (2·77)	3·8 (2·77)	3·9 (2·73)
Newspapers seen each week	6·3 (3·25)	9·2 (5·29)	7·9 (5·46)	8·1 (5·16)	9·0 (5·60)	8·0 (5·04)

Significant differences (t tests)

TV Viewing Hours
High schools > low schools
Younger > older
Boys > girls

Documentary viewing
No area > Rest

TV News
No area > Rest
Older > younger
Boys > girls
Class 4/5 > Class 2/3
Higher ability > lower ability

Newspaper reading
High and low areas > No area
Older > younger
Boys > girls
Higher ability > lower ability

Table 4.6
CHILDREN'S SOURCE REFERENCES FOR QUESTION 5

	NO AREAS N = 148	LOW AREAS N = 208	HIGH AREAS N = 207	LOW SCHOOLS N = 207	HIGH SCHOOLS N = 208	TOTAL N = 563
TV—Unspecified	50	32	17	27	22	99
TV News	37	26	22	26	22	85
TV Documentary	17	16	5	16	5	38
Newspaper	32	26	21	25	22	79
Radio & other media	3	3	3	5	1	9
Peers	4	22	17	20	19	43
Family	14	19	20	20	19	53
Other adults	10	15	8	17	6	33
Personal experience	53	153	196	147	202	402
"Own opinion"	18	32	29	39	22	79
Other source	9	8	1	7	2	18
Don't know	7	6	5	9	2	18
Mean media Reference	·94	·50	·33	·48	·35	·55
Score (SD in brackets)	(1·27)	(0·95)	(0·79)	(0·94)	(0·81)	(1·02)

Table 4.7
ADULTS' SOURCE REFERENCES FOR QUESTION 8

	LOW AREAS N = 155	HIGH AREAS 147	TOTAL 302
TV	29	8	37
Radio	1	1	2
Paper	42	17	59
Magazines	0	1	1
Children	8	3	11
Family	7	17	24
Friends	51	29	80
Pers. Exp.	245	206	451
Other source	1	2	3
Own opinion	39	38	77
Don't know	3	0	3
Mean Media Reference	·47	·18	·33
Score (SD in brackets)	(1·24)	(·55)	(·97)

Table 4.8

MEAN MEDIA SOURCE REFERENCES PER CHILD BY AMOUNT OF MEDIA EXPOSURE (Q. 5)

		LITTLE EXPOSURE	SOME EXPOSURE	MODERATE EXPOSURE	HIGH EXPOSURE	SIGNIFICANCE LEVEL
Documentaries		·36	·50	·59	·73	★
	N =	121	149	128	149	
TV News		·22	·48	·58	·79	★★
	N =	94	143	178	148	
Newspapers		·36	·61	·59	·64	NS
	N =	143	158	117	145	
Total news		·07	·38	·74	1·02	★★★
consumption★		(·38)	(·84)	(1·12)	(1·4)	
(SD in brackets)	N =	27	277	194	49	
Weekly TV		·46	·58	·43	·73	NS
viewing hours	N =	123	142	150	138	

★based on News Consumption Index

Table 4.9

MEAN "PERSONAL EXPERIENCE" SOURCE REFERENCES PER CHILD BY AMOUNT OF "GROSS" CONTACT (Q. 5)

GROSS CONTACT

		NIL	LOW	MODERATE	HIGH	SIGNIFICANCE LEVEL
No area	Mean	·15	·41	·71		★
	N =	61	59	28		
Low schools	Mean	·55	·58	·78	1·12	★
	N =	22	74	94	17	
High schools	Mean		·90	·95	1·04	NS
	N =		29	112	67	

Table 4.10

"PERSONAL EXPERIENCE" SOURCE REFERENCES PER CHILD BY AMOUNT OF FRIENDSHIP CONTACT (Q. 5)

FRIENDSHIP CONTACT

		NIL	LOW	MODERATE	HIGH	SIGNIFICANCE LEVEL
No area	*Mean*	·27		1·0		**
	N =	131		17		
Low schools	*Mean*	·63	·73	·93	·91	NS
	N =	120	49	15	23	
High schools	*Mean*	·88	·86	1·19	1·04	NS
	N =	68	65	27	48	

Table 4.11

MEAN "PERSONAL EXPERIENCE" REFERENCES PER ADULT BY CONTACT (Q. 8)

RESIDENTIAL PROXIMITY		LITTLE OR NONE	SOME	MODERATE	HIGH	F	SIGNIFICANCE LEVEL
	Mean	1·24	1·58	1·88	1·85		
	S	1·04	1·21	1·18	1·14	6·03	·001
	N =	153	59	42	48		

Number of coloured people spoken to recently		NONE	1–2	3–10	MORE	F	SIGNIFICANCE LEVEL
	Mean	1·14	1·65	1·59	2·02		
	S	1·13	1·11	1·12	0·96	8·74	·001
	N =	123	69	59	51		

Friendship		HAVING COLOURED FRIENDS	NO COLOURED FRIENDS	t	SIGNIFICANCE LEVEL
	Mean	1·77	1·39		
	S	1·02	1·17	2·60	·01
	N =	85	217		

Table 4.12
CHILDREN'S "GROSS" CONTACT

Aggregate number of coloured children in schools (% in brackets)		NO AREAS	LOW AREAS	HIGH AREAS	LOW SCHOOLS	HIGH SCHOOLS
		1	495	639	71	1063
		(0)	(9·0%)	(18·2%)	(1·6%)	(23·2%)
Coloured	None	131	53	26	71	8
children	1–2	16	35	67	77	25
known at	3–10	1	83	86	54	115
school	More	0	37	28	5	60
		†††		***		***
Also meet out of	No	145	125	117	143	99
school?	Yes	3	83	90	64	109
		†††		NS		***
Coloured	None	119	123	126	131	118
non-school	1–2	20	49	50	47	52
peers known	3–10	8	29	28	25	32
	More	1	7	3	4	6
		†††		NS		NS
Coloured	None	88	88	95	102	81
adults	1–2	39	47	56	42	61
spoken to	3–10	20	61	44	53	52
	More	1	12	12	10	14
		†††		NS		NS
Gross	None or					
Contact	Slight	61	13	11	22	2
Index	Little	59	43	58	74	27
	Moderate	26	108	98	94	112
	High	2	44	40	17	67
		†††		NS		***

Significance levels: (by Chi-square)	High vs. Low areas & schools	No area vs. Rest
5%	★	†
1%	★ ★	† †
·1%	★ ★ ★	† † †

Table 4.13
CHILDREN'S FRIENDSHIP CONTACT

		NO AREAS	LOW AREAS	HIGH AREAS	LOW SCHOOLS	HIGH SCHOOLS
Coloured friends		16	111	99	77	134
No coloured friends		132	96	108	130	74
		†††		NS	***	
Visited coloured friends		5	50	51	35	66
Not visited		143	158	156	172	142
		†††		NS	***	
Friends taken home		5	53	46	36	63
Not taken home		143	155	161	171	145
		†††		NS	**	
Friendship index	High	4	39	32	23	48
	Moderate	1	20	22	15	27
	Low	12	58	56	49	65
	Nil	131	91	97	120	68
		†††		NS	***	

Significance levels : *(by Chi-square)*	*High vs. Low areas & schools*	*No area vs. Rest*
5%	★	†
1%	★ ★	† †
·1%	★ ★ ★	† † †

Table 4.14
ADULTS' CONTACT BY AREA

RESIDENTIAL PROXIMITY	LITTLE OR NONE	SOME	MODERATE	HIGH	CHI-SQUARE	SIGNIFICANCE LEVEL
LOW AREAS	84	29	25	17		
HIGH AREAS	69	30	17	31	6·89	NS
TOTAL	153	59	42	48		

Number of coloured people spoken to recently	NONE	1–2	3–10	MORE		
LOW AREAS	64	38	33	20		
HIGH AREAS	59	31	26	31	3·91	NS
TOTAL	123	69	59	51		

Friendship	HAVING COLOURED FRIENDS	NO COLOURED FRIENDS		
LOW AREAS	40	115		
HIGH AREAS	45	102	0·64	NS
TOTAL	85	217		

Contact at work-place	CONTACT	NO CONTACT		
LOW AREAS	42	17		
HIGH AREAS	51	12	1·11	NS
TOTAL	93	29		

Table 5.1
H SCORES BY CLASS

		UPPER MIDDLE & MIDDLE CLASS	LOWER MIDDLE	SKILLED WORKING	SEMI AND UNSKILLED
Parents	Mean	24·78	21·04	22·75	23·94
	S				
	N =	6	33	133	129
Children	Mean	20·27	19·16	21·05	21·65
	S				
	N	11	37	147	175
Children by parents' classification	Mean =	15·67	19·61	21·32	21·79
	S				
	N =	6	33	133	129

Table 5.2

ADOLESCENTS' MEAN H SCORES BY AREA AND PROPORTION OF COLOURED CHILDREN IN SCHOOL

Proportion coloured children
in school

		HIGH (a)	LOW (b)	HIGH AREA TOTAL
HIGH AREAS	Mean	23·60	21·78	22·69
	S	6·066	5·742	5·976
	N =	104	103	207
		(c)	(d)	LOW AREA TOTAL
LOW AREAS	Mean	20·50	18·67	19·59
	S	5·979	5·700	5·912
	N =	104	104	208
		"HIGH" SCHOOLS TOTAL	"LOW" SCHOOLS TOTAL	MAIN SAMPLE TOTAL
	Mean	22·05	20·22	21·14
	S	6·219	5·929	6·144
	N =	208	207	415

NO AREA

Mean	19·25
S	5·799
N =	148

SIGNIFICANCE OF DIFFERENCES (2 TAILED T-TESTS)

	P		P
High vs Low Area	·001	"High" vs "Low" schools	·001
High vs No Area	·001	(a) vs (b)	·05
Low vs No Area	N.S.	(c) vs (d)	·05
No Area vs Rest	·01	(b) vs (c)	N.S.
(a) vs (c)	·001		
(b) vs (d)	·001		

Table 5.3
ADULTS' H SCORE BY AREA

	HIGH AREAS	LOW AREAS	TOTAL
Mean	24·51	21·75	23·09
S	6·827	6·925	7·014
N	147	155	302*

Significance of difference: $t = 3·49$, $P \angle ·001$
*In this and some other tables the total is less than the full sample size because complete data was not available for all subjects.

Table 5.4
ADOLESCENTS' H SCORE BY FRIENDSHIP

		HAVING COLOURED FRIENDS	NO COLOURED FRIENDS	TOTAL	t	P (ONE-TAILED)
	Mean	21·54	23·76	22·69		
High area	S	5·849	5·894	5·976	2·707	$\angle ·01$
Total	N	99	108	207		
	Mean	19·11	20·15	19·59		
Low area	S	5·205	6·599	5·912	1·263	NS
Total	N	112	96	208		
t (High vs Low)		3·178	4·109	5·302		
P (one-tailed)		$\angle ·01$	$\angle ·001$	$\angle ·001$		
	Mean	17·13	19·51	19·25		
"No" Area	S	4·400	5·894	5·799	1·556	NS
	N	16	132	148		
	Mean	20·026	21·06	20·64		
Total	S	5·626	6·385	6·112	1·968	$\angle ·05$
	N	227	336	563		

Table 5.5
ADULTS' H SCORE BY FRIENDSHIP

		HAVING COLOURED FRIENDS	NO COLOURED FRIENDS	TOTAL	t	P
High area	Mean	20·39	26·33	24·51	5·27	∠ ·001
	S	6·030	6·352	6·827		
	N	45	102	147		
Low area	Mean	18·03	23·04	21·75	4·13	∠ ·001
	S	6·018	6·749	6·925		
	N	40	115	155		
t (High vs Low)		1·78	3·67	3·48		
P (one-tailed)		∠ ·05	∠ ·001	∠ ·001		
Total	Mean	19·28	24·59	23·09	6·27	∠ ·001
	S	6·139	6·767	7·014		
	N	85	217	302		

Table 5.6
CORRELATIONS BETWEEN CHILDREN'S H SCALE SCORES, SELF RATINGS AND THEIR RATINGS OF OTHERS

	H SCALE	SELF RATING	PEER RATING	MOTHER RATING	FATHER RATING
Self rating	·55				
Peer rating	·28	·49			
Mother rating	·40	·48	·22		
Father rating	·39	·46	·24	·59	
Neighbour rating	·25	·36	·33	·34	·25

Table 5.8
MEAN H SCORES BY MEDIA EXPOSURE—CHILDREN
(Standard Deviations in Brackets)

	LITTLE EXPOSURE	SOME EXPOSURE	MODERATE EXPOSURE	HIGH EXPOSURE
Documentaries	21·39	21·07	20·17	19·93
	(6·576)	(5·784)	(5·498)	(6·337)
N =	110	135	116	134
TV News	20·69	20·48	21·03	20·09
	(5·859)	(6·094)	(5·984)	(6·223)
N =	88	127	162	133
Newspapers	21·07	20·30	20·82	20·27
	(5·453)	(6·307)	(6·535)	(5·916)
N =	126	146	105	133
Total News Media	20·20	21·12	20·43	18·87
	(6·112)	(6·108)	(5·960)	(6·049)
N =	25	249	175	46
Weekly TV viewing hours	20·60	19·95	20·65	21·18
	(5·755)	(6·016)	(6·094)	(6·292)
N =	112	130	138	121

Table 5.9
MEAN H SCORES OF CHILDREN BY ATTITUDES TO MEDIA TREATMENT OF COLOURED PEOPLE

Newspaper coverage of coloured people is:—

	TOO FAVOURABLE	FAIR	TOO UNFAVOURABLE	NO ANSWER
N	22	206	291	44
Mean	27·86	21·37	19·20	23·15
SD	4·948	6·429	5·462	5·132

Television coverage is:—

	TOO FAVOURABLE	FAIR	TOO UNFAVOURABLE	NO ANSWER
N	14	322	203	24
Mean	27·07	20·69	19·80	23·41
SD	6·840	6·038	5·826	5·892

Table 5.7

PERCENTAGES GIVING HOSTILE RESPONSES TO H SCALE ITEMS

	No Area		Low Area		High Area		Main Sample		Total	
	Children	Parents	Children	Parents	Children	Parents	Children	Parents	Children	Parents
1. Everyone in this country should be treated equally regardless of their colour	8·1	—	8·7	21·1	18·8	19·9	13·8	20·5	12·3	—
2. It is reasonable for people not to want to have coloured people as neighbours	42·6	—	55·3	70·2	65·2	71·8	60·3	71·0	55·6	—
3. Coloured people are naturally just as intelligent as white people	11·5	—	11·1	24·2	17·4	32·1	14·3	28·1	13·5	—
4. Coloured people are more often trouble-makers than white people	31·8	—	33·2	19·9	39·1	37·2	36·1	28·4	35·0	—
5. Coloured people in Britain should be encouraged to mix with white people as much as possible	18·2	—	17·8	24·8	29·5	30·1	23·6	27·4	22·2	—
6. Coloured people should not be put in positions of authority over white people	39·9	—	46·6	37·3	60·4	41·0	53·5	39·1	49·9	—
7. Coloured immigrants should be able to get council houses in the same way as English people do	19·6	—	14·4	31·1	27·5	41·0	21·0	36·0	20·6	—
8. This country would be better off if there were no coloured immigrants living here	41·2	—	41·8	46·0	59·9	55·1	50·9	50·5	48·3	—
9. Coloured immigrants should only be given jobs that the English don't want	23·0	—	22·6	26·1	29·5	18·6	26·0	22·4	25·2	—
10. Coloured people should be allowed to come and settle in Britain	27·0	—	32·2	39·8	43·0	62·2	37·6	50·5	34·8	—

Table 6.1

CHILDREN'S RESPONSES TO "CAN YOU TELL ME WHAT YOU KNOW ABOUT COLOURED PEOPLE LIVING IN BRITAIN TODAY?" (Q. 5)

RESPONSE CATEGORY	NO AREA N = 148	LOW AREA N = 208	HIGH AREA N = 207	HIGH & LOW N = 415	TOTAL N = 563
No answer	43	40	48	88	131
Cultural differences	19	32	33	65	84
Culture clash	2	4	24	28	30
Numbers	4	12	13	25	29
Taking over	1	4	3	7	8
Taking jobs	7	6	6	12	19
Taking houses	2	11	6	17	19
Resentment	4	23	9	32	36
Anti-immigration	2	7	5	12	14
Trouble	4	11	20	31	35
Unfavourable	4	20	32	52	56
Poor housing	15	9	18	27	42
Objects of prejudice	47	37	25	62	109
Disadvantaged	11	19	11	30	41
Anti-stereotype	6	23	28	51	57
Favourable	5	14	21	35	39
Personal dislike	1	1	6	7	8
Equalitarian	17	35	19	54	71
Personal liking	1	3	2	5	6
Other	28	26	11	37	65

Table 6.2

ADULTS' RESPONSES TO "CAN YOU TELL ME WHAT YOU KNOW ABOUT COLOURED PEOPLE LIVING IN BRITAIN TODAY?" (Q. 8)

RESPONSE CATEGORY	LOW AREA N = 161	HIGH AREA N = 156	TOTAL N = 317
No answer	14	14	28
Cultural differences	17	15	32
Culture clash	20	26	46
Numbers	28	7	35
Taking over	0	3	3
Taking jobs	3	6	9
Taking houses	3	6	9
Resentment	32	27	59
Anti-immigration	13	4	17
Trouble	7	3	10
Unfavourable	38	52	90
Poor housing	17	19	36
Objects of prejudice	15	4	19
Disadvantaged	6	2	8
Anti-stereotype	15	25	40
Favourable	55	30	85
Personal dislike	12	15	27
Equalitarian	37	25	62
Personal liking	1	1	2
Other	32	23	55

Table 6.3
RESPONSE-SOURCE LINKAGES: CHILDREN'S QUESTION 5
NO AREAS

Sources \ Response Category	No Answer	Cultural Differences	Culture Clash	Numbers	Taking Over	Taking Jobs	Taking Houses	Resentment	Anti-Immigration	Trouble	Unfavourable	Poor Housing	Objects of Prejudice	Disadvantaged	Anti-Stereotype	Favourable	Personal Dislike	Equalitarian	Personal Liking	Other	Total Linkages
Media		4 17%	1	4	0	6 60%	3	2	1	5	1	18 82%	55 76%	15 94%	2	2	0	4 19%	0	15	138
People		6 26%	0	1	0	2 20%	1	2	0	0	1	2 9%	11 15%	0	2	3	0	1 5%	0	5	37
Personal Experience		12 52%	1	2	0	2 20%	0	2	1	0	2	2 9%	5 7%	1 6%	2	1	0	6 29%	1	12	52
Own Opinion Don't Know etc.		1	0	0	1	0	0	1	1	0	1	0	1	0	2	0	1	10	0	6	25
Sum		23	2	7	1	10	4	7	3	5	5	22	72	16	8	6	1	21	1	38	252

Table 6.4

RESPONSE-SOURCE LINKAGES: CHILDREN'S QUESTION 5

LOW AREAS

Sources	No Answer	Cultural Differences	Culture Clash	Numbers	Taking Over	Taking Jobs	Taking Houses	Resentment	Anti-Immigration	Trouble	Unfavourable	Poor Housing	Objects of Prejudice	Disadvantaged	Anti-Stereotype	Favourable	Personal Dislike	Equalitarian	Personal Liking	Other	Total Linkages
Media		10 27%	0	10 56%	2	4	6 43%	6 21%	0	5 38%	3 14%	6 55%	24 44%	12 50%	0 —	0 —	0	4 11%	0	11	103
People		2 5%	0	2 11%	0	2	4 29%	8 28%	2	4 31%	3 14%	2 18%	20 36%	4 17%	2 8%	1 7%	0	1 3%	0	7	64
Personal Experience		24 65%	4	4 22%	2	2	3 21%	14 48%	1	3 23%	14 67%	2 18%	10 18%	6 25%	22 92%	13 87%	0	16 42%	1	12	153
Own Opinion Don't Know etc.		1 3%	0	2 11%	0	0	1	1	5	1	1	1	1	2	0	1	1	17 45%	2	1	38
Sum		37	4	18	4	8	14	29	8	13	21	11	55	24	24	15	1	38	3	31	358

Table 6.5

RESPONSE-SOURCE LINKAGES: CHILDREN'S QUESTION 5

HIGH AREAS

Sources	No Answer	Cultural Differences	Cultural Clash	Numbers	Taking Over	Taking Jobs	Taking Houses	Resentment	Anti-Immigration	Trouble	Unfavourable	Poor Housing	Objects of Prejudice	Disadvantaged	Anti-Stereotype	Favourable	Personal Dislike	Equalitarian	Personal Liking	Other	Total Linkages
Media		5 14%	2 8%	4 24%	1	3	3	2 18%	2	10 38%	0	2 11%	20 56%	8 44%	0	0	0	0	1	5	68
People		2 5%	3 12%	2 12%	0	4	2	3 27%	1	3 12%	5 14%	3 16%	5 14%	2 11%	3 10%	4 17%	0	1 5%	1	2	46
Personal Experience		30 81%	19 76%	10 59%	1	0	2	5 45%	1	12 46%	26 74%	12 63%	9 25%	6 33%	25 81%	19 83%	1	11 55%	1	6	196
Own Opinion Don't Know Etc.		0	1	1	1	0	0	1	1	1	4	2	2	2	3	0	5	8	0	2	34
Sum		37	25	17	3	7	7	11	5	26	35	19	36	18	31	23	6	20	3	15	344

Table 6.6

RESPONSE-SOURCE LINKAGES: ADULTS' QUESTION 8

LOW AREAS

Sources / Response Category	No Answer	Cultural Differences	Culture Clash	Numbers	Taking Over	Taking Jobs	Taking Houses	Resentment	Anti-Immigration	Trouble	Unfavourable	Poor Housing	Objects of Prejudice	Disadvantaged	Anti-Stereotype	Favourable	Personal Dislike	Equalitarian	Personal Liking	Other	Total Linkages
Media		1 6%	4 15%	17 43%	0	0	0	7 16%	10 56%	2	13 24%	3 14%	3 17%	0	2 11%	2	0	3 7%	0	2	69
People		1 6%	5 19%	2 5%	0	0	1	12 27%	1 6%	1	14 26%	6 27%	8 44%	2	2 11%	6 11%	0	1 2%	0	6	68
Personal Experience		16 89%	16 62%	20 50%	0	2	3	19 42%	2 11%	4	24 44%	12 55%	6 33%	4	14 78%	47 84%	5 38%	29 71%	1	26	250
Own Opinion Don't Know Etc.		0	1	1	1	1	0	7	5	2	3	1	1	1	0	1	8	8	0	5	45
Sum		18	26	40	0	3	4	45	18	9	54	22	18	7	18	56	13	41	1	39	432

267

Table 6.7
RESPONSE-SOURCE LINKAGES: ADULTS' QUESTION 8
HIGH AREAS

Sources	No Answer	Cultural Differences	Culture Clash	Numbers	Taking Over	Taking Jobs	Taking Houses	Resentment	Anti-Immigration	Trouble	Unfavourable	Poor Housing	Objects of Prejudice	Disadvantaged	Anti-Stereotype	Favourable	Personal Dislike	Equalitarian	Personal Liking	Other	Total Linkages
Media		3 17%	1 3%	0	1	1	0	4 11%	3	0	3 5%	1 5%	1	1	0	1 3%	1 6%	0	0	4	25
People		4 22%	3 10%	0	1	3	0	10 29%	1	2	13 20%	4 20%	2	0	2 8%	4 13%	1 6%	1 4%	0	1	52
Personal Experience		10 56%	23 77%	6	0	3	6	18 51%	0	0	43 67%	15 75%	1	1	20 77%	24 75%	9	17 63%	0	17	213
Own Opinion Don't Know Etc.		1	3	1	1	1	0	3	3	1	5	0	1	0	4	3	5	9	1	4	46
Sum		18	30	7	3	8	6	35	7	3	64	20	5	2	26	32	16	27	1	26	336

Table 6.8

CHILDREN'S RESPONSES TO "DO YOU THINK THAT THERE ARE ANY PROBLEMS CONNECTED WITH COLOURED PEOPLE LIVING IN THIS COUNTRY?" (Q. 6)

RESPONSE CATEGORY	NO AREA N = 148	LOW AREA N = 208	HIGH AREA N = 207	HIGH & LOW N = 415	TOTAL N = 563
No answer	54	57	64	121	175
Cultural differences	4	5	8	13	17
Culture clash	3	8	12	20	23
Numbers	18	20	22	42	60
Taking over	2	3	4	7	9
Taking jobs	15	11	11	22	37
Taking houses	7	8	14	22	29
Resentment	6	20	23	43	49
Anti-immigration	6	4	8	12	18
Trouble	17	25	18	43	60
Unfavourable	5	12	14	26	31
Poor housing	2	4	6	10	12
Objects of prejudice	53	57	53	110	163
Disadvantaged	4	12	19	31	35
Anti-stereotype	0	1	6	7	7
Favourable	0	4	1	5	5
Personal dislike	1	1	2	3	4
Equalitarian	12	16	6	22	34
Personal liking	0	0	1	1	1
Other	9	6	5	11	20

Table 6.9

ADULTS' RESPONSES TO "DO YOU THINK THERE ARE ANY PROBLEMS CONNECTED WITH COLOURED PEOPLE LIVING IN BRITAIN?" (Q. 10)

RESPONSE CATGEORY	LOW AREA N = 161	HIGH AREA N = 156	TOTAL N = 317
No answer	21	20	41
Cultural differences	13	1	14
Culture clash	23	29	52
Numbers	26	26	52
Taking over	3	0	3
Taking jobs	26	19	45
Taking houses	15	22	37
Resentment	47	54	101
Anti-immigration	10	2	12
Trouble	17	10	27
Unfavourable	22	31	53
Poor housing	16	25	41
Objects of prejudice	21	18	39
Disadvantaged	7	8	15
Anti-stereotype	0	2	2
Favourable	1	0	1
Personal dislike	6	5	11
Equalitarian	12	3	15
Personal liking	0	0	0
Other	23	20	43

Table 6.10

CHILDREN'S RESPONSES TO "HOW DOES THE FACT THAT COLOURED PEOPLE HAVE BEEN COMING TO LIVE IN BRITAIN AFFECT YOU NOW?" (Q. 7)

RESPONSE CATEGORY	NO AREA N = 148	LOW AREA N = 208	HIGH AREA N = 207	HIGH & LOW N = 415	TOTAL N = 563
No answer	125	154	121	275	400
Cultural differences	0	0	2	2	2
Culture clash	0	1	9	10	10
Numbers	4	7	13	20	24
Taking over	0	1	5	6	6
Taking jobs	1	6	8	14	15
Taking houses	0	3	5	8	8
Resentment	0	4	14	18	18
Anti-immigration	2	6	6	12	14
Trouble	3	0	2	2	5
Unfavourable	2	7	9	16	18
Poor housing	0	0	2	2	2
Objects of prejudice	2	3	8	11	13
Disadvantaged	1	0	1	1	2
Anti-stereotype	2	3	7	10	12
Favourable	1	3	1	4	5
Personal dislike	1	2	11	13	14
Equalitarian	8	12	15	27	35
Personal liking	1	2	1	3	4
Other	1	3	8	11	12

Table 6.11

CHILDREN'S RESPONSES TO "HOW DO YOU THINK THAT THE PRESENCE OF COLOURED PEOPLE IN THIS COUNTRY MIGHT AFFECT YOUR LIFE IN THE FUTURE?" (Q. 8)

RESPONSE CATEGORY	NO AREA N=148	LOW AREA N=208	HIGH AREA N=207	HIGH & LOW N=415	TOTAL N=563
No answer	80	106	92	198	278
Cultural differences	0	2	0	2	2
Culture clash	1	2	2	4	5
Numbers	17	28	40	68	85
Taking over	10	21	16	37	47
Taking jobs	24	34	49	83	107
Taking houses	4	5	16	21	25
Resentment	6	9	8	17	23
Anti-immigration	2	5	5	10	12
Trouble	10	13	7	20	30
Unfavourable	3	1	10	11	14
Poor housing	0	0	1	1	1
Objects of prejudice	2	5	6	11	13
Disadvantaged	0	1	1	2	2
Anti-stereotype	0	1	0	1	1
Favourable	1	4	4	8	9
Personal dislike	2	0	5	5	7
Equalitarian	9	8	4	12	21
Personal liking	0	1	1	2	2
Other	6	5	6	11	17

Table 7.1

AMOUNT OF RACE RELATED MATERIAL IN NATIONAL PRESS

(Mean items per day are shown in brackets)

	BRITISH	OVERSEAS	TOTAL	BRITISH AS % OF TOTAL
The Times	253 (1·3 p.d.)	403 (2·1 p.d.)	656 (3·4 p.d.)	38·6%
The Guardian	333 (1·7 p.d.)	417 (2·2 p.d.)	750 (3·9 p.d.)	44·4%
The Express	147 (0·8 p.d.)	169 (0·9 p.d.)	316 (1·6 p.d.)	46·5%
The Mirror	146 (0·8 p.d.)	138 (0·7 p.d.)	284 (1·5 p.d.)	51·4%
All papers	879 (4·6 p.d.)	1127 (5·8 p.d.)	2006 (10·4 p.d.)	43·8%

Table 7.2

NEWSPAPER MATERIAL RELATING TO BRITAIN BY TOPIC

Column inches. (Numbers of items are show in brackets)

	TIMES	GUARDIAN	EXPRESS	MIRROR	ALL PAPERS
Housing	74 (6)	82 (10)	29 (5)	54 (8)	239 (29)
Education	74 (9)	121 (15)	47 (5)	4 (1)	246 (30)
Health	108 (7)	18 (4)	0 (0)	19 (1)	145 (12)
Employment	75 (4)	80 (10)	24 (3)	27 (3)	206 (20)
Numbers	84 (10)	59 (5)	9 (3)	23 (4)	175 (22)
White Hostility	100 (8)	140 (14)	99 (7)	136 (9)	475 (38)
Black Hostility	50 (4)	63 (4)	46 (5)	71 (8)	230 (21)
Discrimination	86 (7)	345 (32)	33 (4)	106 (13)	570 (56)
Discrimination by coloureds	0 (0)	37 (2)	0 (0)	0 (0)	37 (2)
Police	72 (7)	83 (8)	34 (3)	52 (5)	241 (23)
Racial Harmony	0 (0)	17 (3)	72 (1)	8 (1)	97 (5)
Crime	213 (25)	125 (18)	358 (19)	218 (17)	914 (79)
Disturbance	16 (2)	116 (5)	32 (1)	0 (0)	164 (8)
Normal	150 (21)	107 (11)	275 (14)	258 (16)	790 (62)
Cultural differences	46 (5)	122 (10)	79 (5)	21 (3)	268 (23)
Celebrities	4 (1)	8 (1)	100 (6)	139 (7)	251 (15)
Immigration	691 (51)	754 (76)	382 (20)	228 (18)	2055 (165)
Legislation	284 (26)	213 (19)	76 (6)	11 (1)	584 (52)
Race Relations	493 (44)	738 (75)	327 (24)	189 (20)	1747 (163)
Sport	27 (2)	5 (1)	15 (1)	0 (0)	47 (4)
South Africa	39 (2)	0 (0)	2 (1)	0 (0)	41 (3)
Rhodesia	72 (1)	0 (0)	33 (2)	0 (0)	105 (3)
Other	82 (10)	92 (10)	157 (12)	220 (11)	551 (43)
TOTAL	2840 (252)	3325 (333)	2229 (147)	1784 (146)	10178 (878)

Name Index

Subject Index